WATERSHEDS OF THE WORLD:
ECOLOGICAL VALUE AND VULNERABILITY

CARMEN REVENGA
SIOBHAN MURRAY
JANET ABRAMOVITZ
ALLEN HAMMOND

W R I

World Resources Institute
Washington, D.C., U.S.A.

Worldwatch Institute
Washington, D.C., U.S.A.

CAROL ROSEN
PUBLICATIONS DIRECTOR

HYACINTH BILLINGS
PRODUCTION MANAGER

Each World Resources Institute Report represents a timely, scholarly treatment of a subject of public concern. WRI takes responsibility for choosing the study topics and guaranteeing its authors and researchers freedom of inquiry. It also solicits and responds to the guidance of advisory panels and expert reviewers. Unless otherwise stated, however, all the interpretation and findings set forth in WRI publications are those of the authors.

Copyright © 1998 World Resources Institute. All rights reserved.

ISBN 1-56973-254-X

Library of Congress Catalog Card No. 98-85401

Printed in the United States of America on recycled paper.

CONTENTS

Foreword iv

Acknowledgments v

Key Findings 1

Part 1: Overview and Global Analysis 1-3

    Introduction 1-3

    Watershed Degradation 1-5

    Global Analysis 1-8

    Conclusion 1-16

Part 2: Watershed Profiles 2-1

    Watershed Profiles for Africa 2-9

    Watershed Profiles for Europe 2-35

    Watershed Profiles for Asia and Oceania 2-69

    Watershed Profiles for North and Central America 2-107

    Watershed Profiles for South America 2-141

Appendix: Methodology and Technical Notes A-1

About the Authors A-6

FOREWORD

Wherever precipitation falls, the natural shape of the land gathers the runoff into streams and rivers. The resulting landscape constitutes a watershed that is linked together hydrologically. Watersheds are also linked economically, because rivers are arteries for transport and vital sources of water for hydropower, industrial processes, and agriculture, besides providing local communities with food and drinking water. Furthermore, as this report makes clear, watersheds are also linked ecologically. They are the habitat for 40 percent of the world's fish species, and they provide many ecosystems services, from water purification to flood control, nutrient recycling, and soil replenishment.

Yet, increasingly the scale and nature of human activities are threatening many of the watershed's key functions. Often when forests are cleared, the watershed loses some of its ability to store water and to protect against erosion and siltation—which can pose hydrological, economic, and ecological consequences downstream. Often when wetlands are drained or rivers are dammed or channelized, the aquatic ecosystem is altered—which can reduce fish catches, destroy habitats, increase the frequency and severity of flooding, or reduce the supply of soil nutrients to floodplains.

This report offers a unique portrait of the major watersheds of the world. It is the result of a collaboration between the Worldwatch Institute, which is studying the threats to freshwater ecosystems, and the World Resources Institute, which is developing a series of global, map-based analyses of the world's major ecosystems. These maps and data for the first time provide a global overview of watersheds as units and analyze the pattern of human activities that threaten to degrade watersheds and reduce the diversity of species that they harbor.

The report shows that watersheds with the highest biological value are also the most degraded. Thus, additional degradation will impose a high biological cost. Many of these species-rich watersheds also face serious additional threats from rising populations, urbanization, deforestation, withdrawal of water for irrigation, or construction of additional major dams. In arid areas, the watersheds' ability to provide fresh water to meet human and ecological needs is increasingly at risk, and thus the expansion of irrigation to feed rising human populations will be difficult. India, China, and Southeast Asia stand out as areas where pressures on watersheds are especially severe and where degradation is greatest. Watersheds that are relatively less degraded, such as the Amazon and the Congo, are nonetheless beginning to change rapidly.

If the growing stresses on watersheds are to be countered, we need to change the way we gather information and manage resources in these fragile areas. Now, we rarely consider watersheds as integral units. All too often, efforts to develop and use watersheds economically are not coordinated. Sometimes, plans may even directly conflict with efforts to manage watersheds sustainably and to protect the forests, wetlands, and other features that together provide a watershed's ecosystem services. We hope that this report will stimulate a more integrated, comprehensive approach to studying and managing watersheds worldwide.

JONATHAN LASH
President, World Resources Institute

iv

ACKNOWLEDGMENTS

The World Resources Institute would like to acknowledge the Swedish International Development Cooperation Agency, the U. S. Environmental Protection Agency, and the Netherlands' Ministry of Foreign Affairs for their encouragement and financial support.

The authors would like especially to thank the World Conservation Monitoring Centre for their effort in developing the database on fish species by watershed. We also wish to thank the following organizations and individuals for providing valuable data for our analysis: Robert Lozar, U.S. Army Corps of Engineers Construction Engineering Research Laboratories; Center for Remote Sensing and Spatial Analysis, Rutgers University; Tom Loveland, U.S. Geological Survey EROS Data Center; Alison Stattersfield, BirdLife International; and Chris Elvidge, National Oceanic and Atmospheric Administration.

The authors also wish to thank the following colleagues who provided valuable review comments and additional input on methodology throughout the project: Gumilla Björklund, Simon Blythe, David Butler, Brian Groombridge, Janina Jakubowska, Maurice Kottelat, David R. Maidment, Patrick McCully, Theirry Oberdorff, David Olson, Sandra L. Postel, Brian Richter, Ethan T. Smith, and Richard E. Sparks.

Many colleagues within WRI have helped us with this study. We thank Theresa Bradley, Jake Brunner, Nels Johnson, and Walt Reid for their comments and reviews. Special thanks are due to Dirk Bryant, Lauretta Burke, Manolo Clar, Sheila Ferguson, Norbert Henninger, Theresa Leland, Greg Mock, Eric Rodenburg, Dan Tunstall, and Robin White for their valuable support, guidance, and creative ideas throughout the project. We also thank Hyacinth Billings, Lori Han, and Carol Rosen for their valuable help in getting this report into print, and Julie Harlan and Patricia White for their assistance in distribution and outreach.

KEY FINDINGS

This report for the first time presents and analyzes a wide range of global data at the watershed level, assessing 145 watersheds around the world. The analysis focuses primarily on watersheds as ecological units and on the risks of degradation from human activities that may undermine their ability to provide ecological services and maintain intact the biodiversity found within them. The analysis is based on 15 global indicators that characterize watersheds in terms of their value, current condition, and vulnerability to potential degradation. These indicators, presented as maps, give a unique global perspective on the world's largest transboundary watersheds as well as many smaller basins.

The analysis shows that watersheds ranking highest in biological value are also generally the most degraded. Biological value was measured by the number of fish species and fish endemics, and the number of areas with endemic birds. Many of these species-rich watersheds also face serious additional threats. Many biologically rich watersheds, for example, have high population densities, high levels of modified and irrigated land, and high rates of deforestation, especially in tropical areas. Most of the additional major dams now planned are in biologically rich watersheds—11 more for the Yangtze basin in China, 6 more in the Ganges watershed of South Asia, and 4 more in the Paraná watershed of South America. Moreover, biologically rich watersheds often have very few protected areas: the Amazon, Paraná, Mississippi, Yangtze, Hwang He, and Indus watersheds, for example, all have high freshwater fish diversity but protect less than 5 percent of the watershed area. Many of these have also lost significant portions of their original forest cover. These findings illustrate the need for integrated, watershed-wide approaches to management and future development if further degradation is to be avoided.

The analysis also shows that many arid watersheds are likely to face pressures on water resources, perhaps severe enough to constrain economic development. Supplying water is perhaps the most basic ecosystem service that watersheds provide. But nearly a third of the watersheds analyzed in this report lie in arid regions—even though deserts and watersheds with non-permanent rivers and most of Australia and North Africa were excluded. These arid watersheds are home to more than 1 billion people and are primarily concentrated in the least developed areas of the world, particularly in the Sahel region and Southern Africa—where three-fourths of the watersheds studied were arid—and in India, Central Asia, and the Middle East. Watersheds in these regions—such as the Indus and the Tigris and Euphrates basins—depend heavily on agriculture, already have high population densities, and face relatively rapid population growth. Efforts to expand irrigation in such watersheds will be difficult and will require watershed-wide coordination, often across national boundaries.

The watersheds of the world face a wide variety of stresses that threaten to degrade their biological value and their ability to provide ecosystem and economic services. In some cases, these stresses are especially severe in watersheds already substantially modified or degraded. India, China, and Southeast Asia stand out as areas where most of the pressures on watersheds analyzed in this report—from expansion of irrigated cropland and deforestation to water scarcity and population growth—are not only affecting current conditions but are intensifying. Other major watersheds that are relatively less degraded, such as the Amazon and the Congo, are nonetheless beginning to experience rapid change, increasing deforestation, and growing populations. More attention to watersheds as ecological and economic units will be needed to counter these stresses.

PART 1
GLOBAL OVERVIEW AND ANALYSIS

INTRODUCTION

Often extending across one or more international boundaries, watersheds play a critical role in the natural functioning of the Earth. Hydrologically, watersheds integrate the surface water run-off of an entire drainage basin. Economically, they play a critical role as sources of water, food, hydropower, recreational amenities, and transportation routes. Ecologically, watersheds constitute a critical link between land and sea; they provide habitat—within wetlands, rivers, and lakes—for 40 percent of the world's fish species, some of which migrate between marine and freshwater systems. Watersheds also provide habitat—within the terrestrial ecosystems such as forests and grasslands—for most terrestrial plant and animal species; and they provide a host of other ecosystem services—from water purification and retention to flood control to nutrient recycling and restoration of soil fertility—vital to human civilizations.

The Watersheds Studied. In this report, a watershed or river basin is defined as the entire area drained by a major river system or by one of its main tributaries. Watersheds were modeled from elevation data using Geographic Information Systems (GIS) software. All large watersheds that crossed national boundaries were analyzed if data were available. Some smaller watersheds of regional significance were also studied if they had been analyzed in the UNEP publication *Water Quality of World River Basins*. Several island watersheds and several basins in Central America were added to provide more complete geographic coverage. Many small coastal watersheds, although ecologically important and often densely populated, were omitted because of data limitations; deserts and watersheds without permanent rivers were also omitted. In all, the watersheds analyzed represent 55 percent of the world's land area (excluding Antarctica).

The Risks of Degradation. Given the ecological importance of watersheds and the extent of human dependence on the services provided by them, watershed degradation has potentially enormous environmental and socio-economic costs. Yet efforts to develop and use the good and services provided by watersheds have not been well integrated with efforts to protect and manage watersheds sustainably. For example, vital economic resources, such as water, are usually managed with policies, institutions, and practices that are disconnected from, or even in direct conflict with, those designed to protect forests, wetlands, and other habitats from which the water comes. Moreover, watersheds face growing stress from rapid economic development, increasing human populations, and often wasteful use of natural resources. The result is to put watersheds at increasing risk of degradation and hence to jeopardize water supplies and other vital ecosystem services beneficial to human societies—services that can be extremely costly to replace.

The disconnect between economic development policies and sustainable management policies stems in part from the failure to consider watersheds as integral units. What happens upstream in a watershed, for example, can have a profound impact on conditions downstream. Removal of forests or other vegetation can sharply reduce water retention and increase erosion, resulting in reduced water availability in dry seasons and more siltation downstream. Dams are often a barrier to migratory fish and can degrade fisheries, disrupt aquatic ecosystems, and prevent the renewal of soil by flooding and siltation, reducing food supplies. Pollution from human activities can degrade water quality and even make water unusable for human needs, as well as threatening other species. Excessive withdrawal of water can damage or even destroy aquatic ecosystems and surrounding regions, as happened with the Aral Sea. Changes in river flow and sediment and pollutant loadings resulting from activities far inland can degrade downstream coastal ecosystems, such as mangroves and coral reefs. Sometimes downstream activities can even affect upstream conditions, as when alien species introduced into watersheds migrate upstream and threaten fisheries or economic activities. These linkages illustrate how watershed development can have unplanned and inadvertent effects—sometimes with devastating consequences—and underscore the importance of managing watersheds as integral units and planning development with the entire watershed in mind.

The Benefits of Integrated Management.

Watersheds have often been managed hydro-logically—although frequently in piecemeal fashion rather than as an integrated unit—to provide flood control and sources of water for irrigation or to improve navigation. Most major rivers of the world have been altered through channelization, dams, or drainage of wetlands, often with great benefit to human societies. However, watersheds have generally not been viewed, or managed, as units. Integrated management of both economic and ecological attributes of a watershed is admittedly difficult, because watersheds often span sectors of economic activity as well as international borders. Yet such cross-sectoral and regional approaches to management are likely to be essential, if the ability of watersheds to continue to provide ecological, hydrological, and economic services is to be sustained.

The Basis for Analysis.

To provide a quantitative basis for integrated management approaches, what is needed is to be able to characterize watersheds and gauge the nature and pattern of threats to them in quantitative terms. Yet data on the distribution of human populations, plant and animal species, the pattern of economic activities, and other relevant variables have only rarely been collected and analyzed by watershed units, making a global perspective on watersheds impossible to attain.

As an initial step toward correcting this situation, this report for the first time presents and analyzes global data at the watershed level, assessing 106 primary watersheds and a number of major tributaries or subbasins for a total of 145 watersheds around the world, including 91 that cross international borders. The global analysis is based on 15 indicators that characterize watersheds in terms of their ecological value, current condition, and vulnerability to potential degradation from human activities.

These indicators, and the underlying profiles of individual watersheds, should be regarded as preliminary. Neither the resolution nor the completeness of the underlying datasets are adequate to capture all aspects of the environmental status of watersheds or to assess all threats from human activities. Existing global datasets do not even have consistent watershed boundaries, which meant that this analysis required significant technical manipulation. The indicators provide insights into regional and global patterns, as well as revealing the status of individual watersheds.

This report is divided into two parts. The first highlights the ecological importance of watersheds and briefly describes major threats to them; then, based on a global analysis, it summarizes the state of major watersheds around the world with map-based indicators. The second section of the report provides profiles for 145 watersheds. Each profile contains a locator map and characterizes the watershed with a number of quantitative measures—demographically, ecologically, by the pattern of land use within a 5 kilometer buffer zone of major waterways, and in other ways. The appendix contains a detailed description of the data sets and methodology used.

WATERSHED DEGRADATION

There are many factors that act cumulatively and synergistically to contribute to put stress on watersheds. These factors include: physical alteration of inland water systems; habitat degradation through deforestation, mining, grazing, agriculture, soil erosion, industrialization and urbanization; excessive water withdrawal especially for agriculture; pollution; fisheries mismanagement; introduction of alien species; and the loss of freshwater biodiversity (1). Due to the lack of global data, not all of these stresses have been included in the watershed analysis.

Physical Modification. Around the world, the extent of physical changes to rivers and lakes has increased tremendously in this century. For example, the length of rivers altered for shipping increased from under 9,000 kilometers in 1900 to about 500,000 kilometers today (2). The construction of large dams—those at least 15 meters high—has skyrocketed in the past 50 years. Today, they number more than 40,000; almost half are in China (3). In addition to the large dams that constrict the world's rivers, there are many smaller ones. The United States, for example, has nearly 5,500 large dams and over 100,000 small ones (4).

Structural modifications, such as dams, flood control, and channelization, change the dynamics of aquatic ecosystems, fragment existing systems, and join previously unconnected ones. In many cases these structural modifications have made agriculture and transportation possible and therefore have played a key role in global food security. However, altering the structure of a river can also bring about costly changes, such as declines in fish catches, loss of freshwater biodiversity, increases in the frequency and severity of floods, loss of soil nutrients in the

flood plain, and increases in the incidence of diseases like schistosomiasis and malaria.

Dams are barriers to migrating fish and to the natural movement of sediments, nutrients, and water—all of which feed the surrounding floodplains and ultimately the sea. Egypt's Aswan High Dam, which impounds most of the Nile River's water and sediment flow, has caused the fertile Nile Delta to shrink and 30 out of 47 commercial fish species to become economically or biologically extinct. Reducing the flow of fresh water to the sea can also lead to the intrusion of salt water into previously fresh surface water and groundwater—rendering them undrinkable. (5)

The rising frequency and severity of floods occurring along large rivers such as the Mississippi River and its tributaries in recent years brought home the lesson that massive expenditures on flood control through engineering have actually increased the frequency and severity of floods while crippling the river's ability to support native fauna and flora. Records show that recent floods have been substantially higher than they would have been before flood control structures confined the river to a narrow channel (6). Such ecosystem mismanagement comes at great economic cost, as demonstrated by the decline of aquatic species, the subsidence of the Mississippi Delta, and the enormous financial toll of the 1993 flood (around US$16 billion) (7). In Europe, flooding of the Rhine River over the last few decades has also grown significantly more frequent and severe because of increased urbanization, river engineering, and walling the river off from its floodplain (8). The Rhine Action Plan launched in 1987 seeks to restore some of the river ecosystem in order to retrieve the benefits of its natural functions, such as providing safe drinking water, recharging groundwater supplies, and moderating floodwaters (9).

Despite recognition of the consequences of altering large watersheds, efforts are underway to modify intact systems. Plans to dam and divert the 4,200-kilometer Mekong River will affect fisheries, agriculture, and water supply along its length. Diversion of the natural flow of silt-laden waters will also cause the rich Mekong Delta to recede, yet 52 million people depend on the Mekong for their food and livelihood (10).

Habitat Degradation. Deforestation, mining, grazing, agriculture, industrialization, and urbanization all degrade rivers, lakes, wetlands, inland seas, and the watersheds they drain in ways that make them less able to support life and to provide valuable ecosystem services. Habitat degradation, from logging and extensive agriculture, for example, increases soil erosion and therefore siltation of rivers, lakes, and coastal waters. Excessive siltation affects downstream communities by increasing the frequency of floods, impairing hydropower and navigation operations, and choking streams and coastal habitat.

Habitat degradation also contributes to declines in catches from inland and coastal fisheries. For instance, deforestation, grazing, agricultural runoff, wetland conversion, water withdrawal for irrigation, and rapidly expanding human populations have all contributed to the loss of much of the salmon populations throughout the streams of the Pacific Northwest in the United States. Across the Canadian border, the effects of overfishing, logging, and mining on undammed major rivers such as the Fraser and the Skeena have cut salmon populations to less than 20 percent of previously recorded levels (11).

Water Use. Increasingly, aquatic ecosystems must compete with human beings for the very basis of their existence—water. Human societies use water for irrigation, domestic consumption, and urban and industrial uses, two-thirds of it for agriculture. The amount of fresh water withdrawn has risen 35-fold in the past 300 years; over half of that increase has occurred since 1950 (12). In many areas, groundwater is now withdrawn far faster than it can be recharged—mining what was once a renewable resource (13).

So much water is diverted from large rivers like the Colorado and the Ganges that little if any reaches the sea during the dry season, with harmful effects on inland and coastal habitats, fisheries, and peoples (14). China's Huang He (Yellow River) is so heavily used that the lower reaches were without water for two-thirds of 1997 (15). Lake Chad, in Africa's Sahel region, has shrunk by 75 percent in the last 30 years because of drought and diversion for agriculture, to the detriment of this important inland fishery (16).

Central Asia's Aral Sea is one of the most graphic examples of excess diversion of inland waters. Since 1960, this massive lake (once the fourth largest) has lost three-fourths of its volume. Today, 94 percent of the river flow that once fed the Aral Sea is diverted to irrigate thirsty crops such as cotton in this arid region. The sea's salinity levels have tripled and 20 of its 24 fish species have disappeared. The fish catch, which once measured 44,000 tons and supported 60,000 jobs, is now nonexistent. Over 36,000 square kilometers of former lake bottom are dry and bare. Severe dust storms carry toxic salts and dust thousands of kilometers and afflict three-quarters of the region's 3.5 million people with serious illnesses (17).

Often, water diversion projects fail to value fully other watershed services. For example, an intact Nigerian floodplain supports tens of thousands of people through fishing, agriculture, fuelwood and fodder production, livestock, and tourism, and recharges groundwater supplies. When the floodplain's current uses were compared with the alternative of a water diversion plan, the value of water maintained in the floodplain for those existing uses was worth US$45 per 1,000 cubic meters while the value of diverted water for increasing crop output was only US$0.04 (18).

Pollution. People have always relied on water systems to carry away their wastes, but the increased load of wastes, exacerbated by the loss of water withdrawn, has reduced the capacity of rivers to assimilate or flush pollutants from the system. The water that is finally returned to streams and rivers after irrigation is severely degraded by increased toxicity, excess nutrients, salinity, higher temperature, pathogen populations, sediments, and lower dissolved oxygen (19).

Fertilizer and pesticides from agriculture are major pollutants. Chemical pollutants are also released directly from industrial and municipal sites, and indirectly as runoff from farms, homes, roads, and cities. Toxic chemicals are also carried long distances by air currents, and many ultimately find their way into rivers and lakes.

The world's largest freshwater ecosystem, the Great Lakes of North America, has already felt the full range of anthropogenic stress. The region is now home to more than 38 million people (20)—and to significant portions of North America's industrial and agricultural activity. The health and composition of lake fish offer a good clue to the health of the whole system. In 1993, more than 1,275 fish consumption advisories were issued in the Great Lakes region—two-thirds of the U.S. total—mostly due to the presence of mercury, PCBs, chlordane, dioxins, and DDT (21).

According to the United Nations Commission on Sustainable Development, if current trends continue, by 2025 global industrial water use is expected to double and industrial pollution loads to increase four-fold. As developing nations industrialize, "leapfrogging" to less-polluting or zero emissions technologies will be essential to avoiding the problems faced in older indus-trialized nations. Around the world, reducing the pollutants that enter from non-point sources such as runoff from farms and homes remains a challenge (22).

Loss of Freshwater Biodiversity. As mentioned above, physical alteration, habitat degradation, water withdrawal, and pollution all contribute directly or indirectly to declines in freshwater species. In addition, the incursion of non-native, or alien, species and the mismanagement of inland fisheries are other factors contributing to the loss of freshwater organisms. Data on invasive species and fish catch data by watersheds are not available and have not been incorporated into the global analysis that follows. Nonetheless, the potential for degradation is significant.

Alien species may prey on native species, compete for food and breeding space, disrupt food webs, and even introduce new diseases. The spread of these species is a global phenomenon, one that is increasingly aided by the growth of aquaculture and by shipping and commerce. The list of alien introductions, both intentional and accidental, is long and includes vertebrates (e.g., fish and mammals), invertebrates (e.g., mussels), higher plants (e.g., water hyacinth), and microscopic plants and animals (e.g., spiny water flea, dinoflagellates). Most incursions are recent; for example, in the Northern Mediterranean, 60 percent of aliens have arrived in the last 40 years (23).

The introduction of the non-native Nile perch to Africa's Lake Victoria in 1954 combined with pollution loading and increased turbidity of the water have virtually eliminated the native fish population (24). Kenya, for example, reported only 0.5 percent of its commercial fish catch as the Nile perch in 1976; five years later the proportion reached 68 percent (25). Lake Victoria—the second largest lake in the world—has lost 200 taxa of endemic cichlids, species found nowhere else; the remaining 150 or more are endangered (26). Worldwide, two-thirds of the freshwater species introduced into the tropics have become established (27).

Transfers of alien species in ship's ballast water occur in every direction along all shipping routes, with serious economic and ecological consequences. About 10 years ago, an Atlantic Coast comb jelly was accidentally transferred to the Black and Azov seas, shutting down the once-productive Azov fisheries and virtually eliminating the Black Sea anchovy fisheries, at a loss of US$250 million per year (28). The minute zebra mussel, accidentally brought to the Great Lakes of North America in 1988 in ship ballast water, has already spread to most major rivers and lakes in the east. The cost to cities and industries of keeping this Caspian Sea native from clogging intake pipes and heat exchangers could reach US$5 billion by the year 2000 in the Great Lakes alone (29).

Overexploitation and mismanagement of fisheries, especially when combined with other stresses, can lead to the collapse of a region's fish fauna. The Food and Agriculture Organization of the United Nations (FAO) considers most inland fisheries to be exploited at or above sustainable levels. Yet fish are a critical food source, providing a significant proportion of animal protein for more than 1 billion people. In Africa, fish provide 21 percent of total animal protein, in Asia, 28 percent. In land-locked countries with no access to coastal and marine fisheries, inland fisheries are even more significant. International statistics do not reflect their full importance, because many of the fish that are caught never enter the formal economy (30).

In response to declining fisheries, much of the management effort has been expended on replacing natural production with hatcheries and

aquaculture rather than on maintaining natural systems more sustainably. These efforts often exacerbate degradation pressures. In the Pacific Northwest of North America, for example, hatchery-raised salmon have brought many remaining native stocks to the brink of extinction while hiding the decline of wild salmon and delaying real remedies. The rapid increase in the aquaculture production in recent decades hides the decline of natural fisheries and the role played by aquaculture itself in degrading inland and coastal systems through habitat conversion, pollution, and the accidental release of non-native species (31).

All watershed degradation stresses mentioned above occur all over the world, although the particular effects of these stresses vary from watershed to watershed. Understanding the wider implications requires examining how these stresses affect the combination of several features that together make the living watersheds. The following section of the report presents a global overview of the pattern of biological richness, existing land use practices, and vulnerability to future change caused by these stresses.

A GLOBAL ANALYSIS

This global analysis focuses on the ecological aspects of watersheds and the services that human societies derive from watersheds. It includes the world's largest transboundary watersheds and other smaller basins that are representative of a particular geographic area. Only permanent rivers are included. Altogether, the analysis covers 106 primary watersheds shown in Map 1. Some of the larger basins are further divided into subbasins and are analyzed as separate subbasins when data are available (Box 1), to give a total of 145 watersheds for which individual profiles are included. Omitted regions, shown in white on Map 1, are primarily smaller coastal drainage basins or regions with no permanent rivers.

The study is based on georeferenced data analyzed with GIS software. It incorporates 23 datasets that measure watershed characteristics and

---

Box 1. Subbasins of Large Watersheds Analyzed Separately

The Amazon, Congo, Mississippi, and Nile watersheds are divided into subbasins and analyzed separately in some of the Global Analysis Maps, when data are available.

Amazon subbasins: Ica-Putumayo, Japurá, Juruá, Madeira, Negro, Purus, Marañón, Tapajos, Ucayali, Xingu.
Congo subbasins: Kasai, Sangha, Lake Tanganyika, Ubangi.
Mississippi subbasins: Arkansas, Missouri, Ohio, Red.
Nile subbasin: Lake Victoria.

For the location of these basins within their major watersheds please refer to Part 2: Watershed Profiles.

human activities that potentially affect watersheds. The available georeferenced global datasets include such variables as land use, land cover, aridity, forest extent and loss, erosion, endemic bird species distributions, and population. Additional statistical datasets such as surface water run-off, fish species distributions, and location of major dams were included when they could be georeferenced or linked to major rivers or lakes. A complete list of the 15 indicators used in the global analysis are listed in Box 2.

Box 2. Global Analysis Indicators

Watershed Value
Fish species richness and endemism
Endemic Bird Areas
Aridity
Population density
Water scarcity

Watershed Condition
Modified landscape
Irrigated cropland
Existing major dams
Remaining original forest
Extent of original forest loss
Soil erosion from water

Future Vulnerability
Urban population growth
Tropical deforestation (1980–90)
Planned major dams
Level of protection

Data Limitations. Some additional information would have improved the analysis but was not available at the global scale for all watersheds studied. Examples of valuable but missing data include water quality and sediment loading, water withdrawal, global evapotranspiration, fish catch, prevalence of aquatic species other than fish, information on type and degree of watershed management practices, a more complete

georeferenced dataset on large and small dams, and other data on biological diversity or ecosystem complexity (vegetation, mammals, reptiles, etc.).

There are some limitations associated with the data used for the analysis. Watershed boundaries are coarse, and some small tributaries are not identified. Watersheds were modeled based on elevation data and therefore follow natural water drainages. Many rivers, particularly in developed regions, have been connected by canals and many of the flows reversed for water supply and transportation reasons. These changes in river flow are not reflected in our basins. Finally, some of the datasets used, particularly land cover data, are less reliable for characterizing smaller watersheds.

Watershed Value. Ecosystems can be evaluated according to their biological value and of the value that people derive from the ecosystem services—such as fresh water supply and erosion control—that watersheds provide or contain. The biological value of a watershed, considered first, is its biological uniqueness or importance in terms of the ecosystems, species, and genetic diversity or ecological complexity that it harbors. In absence of adequate measures of ecological complexity, this analysis uses as proxy indicators the number of fish species, the number of fish endemics (species that exist only in that particular area), and the number of endemic bird areas in each basin (as a measure of terrestrial biodiversity importance).

Which Are the Watersheds with the Highest Numbers of Fish Species and Endemic Fish? Some 27 watersheds have particularly high fish species richness or diversity. Of these, 56 percent are in the tropics, particularly Central Africa, mainland Southeast Asia, and South America (Map 2), even though only about a third of all watersheds analyzed are tropical. High fish diversity is also found in Central North America and in several basins in China and India.

Watersheds with the Highest Numbers of Fish Species

Size of Watershed	Watershed Name	No. of Fish Species
Large	Amazon	3,000
	Congo	700
	Mississippi	375
Medium	Rio Negro	600
	Mekong	400
	Madeira	398
Small	Lake Victoria	343
	Kapuas	320
	Lake Tanganyika	240

Watersheds with the Highest Numbers of Endemic Fish

Size of Watershed	Watershed Name	No. of Endemics
Large	Amazon	1,800
	Congo	500
	Mississippi	107
Medium	Xi Jiang (Pearl River)	120
	Orinoco	88
	Paraguay	85
Small	Lake Victoria	309
	Lake Tanganyika	216
	Salween	46

The pattern of unique species, or endemism, shows strong similarities to the pattern of species richness, particularly in Central Africa, South America, and Southeast Asia. In temperate regions, the Colorado, Rio Grande, and Alabama basins in North America stand out as having large numbers of endemic fish for their size.

Because there is a correlation between number of species and total area sampled, large watersheds tend to have more fish species than smaller ones (32). To help eliminate bias in size differences, we classified the basins into three categories, large (more than 1,500,000 square kilometers), medium (between 400,000 and 1,499,999 square kilometers) and small (less 400,000 square kilometers). Map 2 shows those basins that had the highest number of fish species within each size category: specifically, those large basins with more than 230 fish species, medium basins with more than 143 species, and small basins with more than 112 species. For endemic fish species, the cutoff points were basins with more than 166 species (large basins), 29 species (medium basins), and 15 species (small basins). Cutoff points for each category were determined by selecting the upper two-thirds within each range.

At least 20 percent of the world's more than 9,000 freshwater fish species have become extinct, threatened, or endangered in recent years (33). Threatened fish species data are not shown in the global maps but are included in the watershed profiles in Part 2 of this report. The highest numbers for known globally threatened fish species—reflected in the basin profiles—are found in Lake Victoria, the Danube, the Ohio, and the Alabama river basins. These basins have heavily modified landscapes, a large number of dams, and many introduced species, all of which threaten indigenous fish species. The available data for the status of threatened species are incomplete and therefore underestimate the current level of threat. One reason for this situation is that profile data on threatened fish species only reflect those species that are globally threatened, according to the *1996 IUCN Red List of Threatened Animals* (34). A second is that the Red List assessments for 1996 usually list species distribution by nation rather than by river or watershed and many of the fish species listed fall within watersheds not analyzed in this study. Finally, data are not comprehensive because we lack knowledge of species diversity in many freshwater systems. There are many nationally threatened species and subspecies that are not reflected in watershed profile figures; for example, many distinct populations of salmon in the Western United States are nationally endangered.

Which Watersheds Have High Numbers of Endemic Bird Areas? Birds can be good indicators of terrestrial biodiversity importance—particularly areas of high endemism. This is due, in part, to biological features such as specialized habitats and sensitivity to habitat degradation. Birds are also one of the most studied groups of animals and in addition to butterflies, one of the few taxa for which comprehensive global georeference data are available. For this analysis we used Endemic Bird Areas (EBA) developed by BirdLife International as an indicator of biological value. EBAs are those areas where species with restricted ranges tend to occur together. There are 218 EBAs that comprise 2,561 species, which represent close to 93 percent of all endemic or restricted range birds and over 25 percent of all bird species (35). The number of species found within each EBA varies between 2 and 80.

Watersheds with Highest Number of EBAs

No. of EBAs	Watersheds
24	Amazon
9	Orinoco, Magdalena
7	Mekong
6	Congo, Paraná, Yangtze
5	Balsas, Ganges, Jubba, Nile, Mangoky

Watersheds with very high numbers of EBAs largely parallel the pattern found in fish species richness. Watersheds in tropical areas, particularly in South America, mainland Southeast Asia, Central Africa, and China, have the highest numbers of EBAs (Map 3). The Amazon basin stands out as the watershed with the highest number of EBAs in the world—24 in total.

Which Watersheds Are Most Arid? And in Which Do People Face Widespread Potential Water Scarcity? Arid lands are those in which rainfall is very limited and in which average humidity is low. In such regions, perhaps the most valuable ecosystem service that watersheds provide is to gather together precipitation run-off into streams, rivers, and lakes that can be a source of fresh water for human use. Watersheds also recharge underground aquifers and reduce the impacts of floods. By their nature, arid lands are also relatively fragile and easily degraded through improper use.

Most Arid Watersheds	
Ural	Tigris & Euphrates
Yaqui	Colorado
Rio Grande	Syr Darya
Oued Draa	Lake Chad
Lake Balkhash	Senegal

This analysis excludes deserts and other regions with no permanent rivers, including most of North Africa, the Middle East, and Australia; it also excludes many small, but heavily populated coastal watersheds. Nonetheless, one-third of the watersheds analyzed in this study—47 in all—lie to a significant degree in an arid zone. Arid zones are defined as those with an aridity index (precipitation to evapotranspiration ratio) below 0.5. Map 4 shows those watersheds in which more than 30 percent of the watershed area is classified as arid. Over 1 billion people live within these arid or partially arid watersheds, especially in North America, Central Asia, and sub-Saharan Africa. In Africa alone, 60 percent of the watersheds analyzed fell within this arid category; these watersheds provide water to a rapidly growing population of more than 323 million people.

Aridity alone, however, does not necessarily mean that water for human use is in short supply. That depends not only on how many people the available supply must serve, as shown in the distribution of population density on Map 5, but also on how extensively water is used. It matters, for example, whether or not water is used for irrigation, or whether the water withdrawn from a river is returned and if it is of sufficient quality to be reused by others downstream. Nonetheless, the amount of water available for human use can indicate potential water scarcity. Water experts define an area as potentially *water stressed* if the available annual supply is less than 1,700 cubic meters per capita and as potentially *water scarce* if the supply is less than 1,000 cubic meters per capita (36) (37).

Watersheds with the Highest Population Density

Ganges	Po
Rhine-Meuse	Xi Jiang (Pearl River)
Krishna	Seine
Tapti	Wesser
Yangtze	Godavari

Map 6 applies these benchmarks to watershed units. Of the 65 basins for which data were available, we found 12 watersheds that were potentially *water stressed* and 8 that were potentially *water scarce*. These basins lie primarily in East and Southern Africa, South and Central Asia, Northern China, and the Western United States.

Data on per capita water availability are usually available by country and not by watershed. In calculating this indicator, water availability was based on the runoff—the amount of water that enters the rivers from rainfall—in each watershed. This indicator thus does not take into account the water that is recycled to the atmosphere through evapotranspiration in plants or how extensively water is used in human activities. For example, the Murray-Darling basin in Australia, which has

low population density, has more than 2,500 cubic meters per person based on runoff; however, irrigation usage in the basin is very high, with the result that the area is in fact under water stress (38).

Likely Condition of the Watershed. Human activities modify watersheds and, sometimes, degrade them. This section considers several measures of the extent to which watersheds have been modified from their original condition, as well as measures of degradation. Such indicators as the amount of land used for agriculture or urban settlements, the extent of irrigation, or the existence of major dams provide evidence of modification. Indicators such as extent of forest loss and extent of water erosion provide measures of watershed degradation.

Which Watersheds Have the Most Modified Land? Outside of the far north and regions in Africa, most of the world's watersheds have lost much of their natural vegetative cover. About a third (34 basins of those analyzed) have more than half their land area given over to agriculture or urban and industrial use (Map 7). In Europe 13 watersheds have more than 90 percent of their land area converted to agriculture or to urban and industrial use. Watersheds in India and China, such as the Ganges, the Yangtze, and the Xi Jiang (Pearl River) are also highly modified, due mostly to the extensive use of land for agriculture in these regions. These three watersheds alone have more than 2 million square kilometers of cropland.

Because irrigation both affects the land and withdraws water from rivers or underground aquifers, the extent of irrigated cropland is also a useful indicator of watershed modification. Those watersheds with the highest percentage of irrigated cropland are in Asia, particularly Central Asia, India, China, and Southeast Asia. Additional watersheds with a high percentage of irrigated cropland are found in the western part of North America and Mexico (Map 8). The data on which the indicator is based come from satellite imagery, in which such features as rice paddies are easily identified; irrigated rice and other major crop areas in North America and Asia are thus well represented. Other irrigated crops are not always as easily identified, so the extent of irrigation may be under-represented in such areas as Western and Central Europe and South America.

Watersheds with the Highest Percentage of Modified Land

Watershed	Modified Land
Loire	98%
Seine	98%
Wesser	97%
Oder	96%
Vistula	95%
Dnieper	95%
Elbe	94%
Dniester	92%
Don	92%
Garonne	91%

Watershed modification due to irrigation has increased substantially over the last half-century. From 1940 to 1990, for example, the amount of freshwater withdrawals from surface and ground water has increased by a factor of four (39). Most of this increase in demand has come from the agriculture sector, primarily from expansion of irrigation. Excessive water use can affect a watershed's ecological functioning, by withdrawing so much water that fish species suffer from low river flow or by altering floodplains and stream banks that are important spawning areas for many species. In addition, irrigation schemes can include the construction of channels that connect rivers previously unconnected, allowing species to migrate from one river to another and leading to local extinctions and alterations in species composition. Intensive agriculture of the type often associated

with irrigation can also lead to fertilizer and pesticide runoff, additional sediment loading of waterways from erosion, salinization, and waterlogging.

Which River Basins Have Been Altered Significantly by Major Dams? An additional indicator of watershed modification is the number of major dams in the basin. Such dams fundamentally alter the hydrological and ecological characteristics of a watershed. Most major rivers of the world have been heavily dammed—of the 106 primary watersheds considered in this study, 46 percent are modified by at least one major dam. *A major dam* is defined based on its height (greater than 150 meters), its volume (greater than 15 million cubic meters), its reservoir storage capacity (at least 25 cubic kilometers) or its generating capacity (greater than 1,000 megawatts) (40). There are 306 major dams in the world, most of them located in North America, Europe, and the Paraná river basin in South America (Map 9). The Paraná watershed alone has 14 major dams. There are two other basins in the world with 10 or more major dams, the Colorado and the Columbia, both in the United States.

Watersheds with More Than Five Major Dams

No. of Dams	Watersheds
14	Paraná
13	Columbia
12	Colorado
9	Mississippi
9	Volga
7	Tigris and Euphrates
7	Nelson
7	Danube
6	Yenisey

The freshwater species most affected by dams are migratory species such as the African shad and other species that migrate within the main stem of the river. The Columbia river basin, for example, has at least 11 species of diadromous fish (those that migrate between fresh and salt water), all of which have been affected by the large amount of dams in that basin. Other species, even though not migratory, require seasonal floods to fill the floodplains in order to breed. Dam construction not only decreases river flow, considerably decreasing flooding of these important breeding areas, but also causes changes in water temperature, depth, and oxygen concentration—all of which influence the composition and abundance of species.

Dams can have economic and social costs, as well. Fish catches of both commercially important fishes and subsistence fisheries have plummeted with the construction of large dams. This is particularly critical in inland basins in developing countries where fish are sometimes the principal source of animal protein for local communities.

Where Are Watersheds Most Degraded? Forests and other vegetation are crucial components of watersheds, they maintain water quality and moderate water flow—reducing runoff during high-water periods and maintaining flow during dry periods. In addition forests provide habitat for many terrestrial species, and in many floodplain areas, they also provide much of the food and breeding ground on which fish and other species depend. The extent of historical deforestation is thus a useful indicator of watershed degradation. As shown in Map 10, there are 42 watersheds that have lost more than 75 percent of their original forest cover—the closed forests that are believed to have existed 8,000 years ago, assuming current climate conditions. Fifteen of these have lost more than 95 percent of their original forest. Most of these basins, with the exception of the Tigris and Euphrates, are found in Africa, Central America, and Europe.

Map 10 also shows that large basins such as the Congo and the Amazon, which have extensive original forest cover, have lost a relatively small percentage of their original forest compared with smaller basins in Europe, India and Africa. However, the actual extent of forest lost is large; 9 basins have lost more than 500,000 square kilometers, including the Mekong, Ganges, Amazon, Paraná, Ob, Volga, and Mississippi river basins. The Yangtze and the Congo have lost more than 1 million square kilometers of original forest each (Map 11).

Watersheds with the Highest Percentage of Original Forest Loss	
Orange	Rio Colorado
Tigris and Euphrates	Limpopo
Lake Titicaca	Amu Darya
Lake Chad	Mania
Senegal	Mangoky

The extent of soil erosion from water provides another indicator of watershed degradation. The indicator is based on the Global Assessment of Soil Degradation (GLASOD) sponsored by the United Nations Environment Programme (UNEP) and developed by the International Soil Reference and Information Centre (ISRIC). This indicator shows those basins which have moderate to extreme levels of water-related soil erosion—loss of top soil and terrain deformation. The basins with the highest levels of water erosion are found mainly in China, Southeast Asia, India, and Madagascar. There are also individual basins, such as the Orange and Volta basins in Africa, the Danube, Dnieper, and the Guadalquivir in Europe, and the Balsas and Uruguay basins in Central and South America, respectively, where more than 15 percent of the land area has moderate to extreme water erosion (Map 12).

The different levels of soil erosion combined in this indicator are moderate, severe, and extreme. Moderate soil erosion refers to areas where the natural productivity of the land has been greatly reduced—the soil's biotic functions of processing nutrients has been partially destroyed. Severe soil erosion refers to areas where the soil's biotic functions are largely destroyed and restoration is only possible with major financial and technical inputs. Finally those areas with extreme soil erosion are areas beyond restoration, where all original biotic functions of the soil have been lost.

Vulnerability to Future Human Activities.

There are ongoing transformations that are likely to increase or intensify pressures on watersheds. This section focuses on watershed vulnerability to future changes by looking at such indicators as population growth rates, deforestation rates, planned or proposed construction of additional major dams, and the level of protection to the ecological functions of watersheds.

Where Are Future Pressures Highest? Rapidly growing populations place heavy demands on freshwater resources and intensify pressures on wildlands, for example, by increased conversion of forests into cropland. Because most population growth in coming decades will occur in urban areas, watersheds were ranked according to the population growth rate of major cities found within these basins. By this measure, 14 watersheds, most of which are in Africa and India, have urban growth rates exceeding 4 percent a year for the period 1995–2000 (Map 13). Of the basins analyzed that are facing very rapidly growing populations, those located in Africa are in arid areas, where water scarcity is already a problem.

An important limitation of this analysis, however, is the exclusion for data reasons of most small coastal basins, which are both biologically important and often the fastest growing in population. In addition, this indicator is limited to those cities for which projections of future population growth were available, so that growth rates for some basins may be underestimated.

Another indicator of vulnerability to future degradation is the rate of deforestation or conversion of forest land to other uses. Watershed-specific deforestation data are only available for 62 basins in tropical forest areas. Of these watersheds, the analysis shows that 14 basins lost more than 10 percent of their forest cover in the period between 1980 and 1990. Almost all these basins, except for Lake Tanganyika, are found in the Central and South America and in mainland Southeast Asia. For example minor basins in the Amazon and the Paraná in South America, and the Indus, Mekong, Irridawy, and Chao Phrya basins in Asia have the highest average deforestation rate, between 15 and 30 percent for the period 1980–90 (Map 14).

There are 56 additional major dams planned or under construction around the world (41). Just 5 watersheds account for a majority of these proposed dams—led by the Yangtze with 11, the Tigris and Euphrates with 7, the Ganges with 6, and the Hwang He and Paraná with 4 each. China leads all regions in planned additional dams, with South America also high (Map 9). Data for some countries in Europe and most in North America and Southeast Asia were not available.

Protection of vulnerable portions of watersheds could be a potential countervailing measure to the growing pressures on watersheds. But more than half—82 of the watersheds analyzed— have less than 5 percent of their land area protected. Only 18 basins meet the IUCN (The World Conservation Union) goal of 10 percent of the land area protected (Map 15). Moreover, the pattern of protection is such that most of the high value, species-rich watersheds are also the least protected. For example, the Paraná, much of the Amazon, the Congo, and almost all the basins in India, China, Southeast Asia and Papua New Guinea have less than 5 percent of their area protected. In the United Sates, the two most important basins with respect to fish species richness—the Mississippi and the Alabama—protect only 2 percent and less than 1 percent of their area, respectively.

Watersheds with the Highest Percentage of Land Area Protected

Watershed	Percent Protected
Yukon	29%
Orinoco	24%
Tarim	21%
Wesser	19%
Rhine-Meuse	18%
Thelon	18%
Lake Victoria	17%
Usumacinta	16%
Yaqui	16%
Rhone and Guadalquivir	14%

Protected areas included are those nationally protected areas that fall within one of the five IUCN management categories. These include completely protected areas and areas where sustainable use of resources is allowed.

CONCLUSION

Virtually every part of the globe has experienced extinction of freshwater aquatic species and degradation of freshwater ecosystems. Few watersheds have escaped the cascade of unintended and unanticipated economic and social disruptions that follow watershed degradation—from more frequent and devastating floods and droughts to the loss of clean and reliable water supplies, aquatic food resources, and livelihoods.

Efforts to sustain watersheds and the vital ecological services they provide to human societies will require a better understanding of their dynamic nature and a shift from today's piecemeal and short-sighted management of natural resources toward a more integrated approach that ensures their long-term viability.

Until now, watersheds have been exploited and controlled in fragmented ways partly because the view of ecosystems is fragmented. The tendency is to focus on only one element at a time—whether navigation, irrigation, power generation, fisheries, or even limited measures of water quality—without regard for the entire system and all its uses and services. Inland waters, along with their entire watershed and all their physical, chemical, and biological elements, need to be viewed as part of a complex, integrated system that includes human activities. Hence the importance of collecting and analyzing data for entire watershed units, as in this report, as a basis for watershed-wide management approaches.

Strategies to manage watersheds sustainably, so as to maintain the full range of ecosystem services they provide, can build on recent advances in resource economics, conservation biology, and institutional development. In some countries, full value pricing for natural resources such as timber has generated significant improvements in resource use efficiency, as well as revenues to reinvest in sustainable resource management. Conservation biologists now stress the importance of using regional approaches, such as bioregional management or ecosystem management, to maintain and restore biodiversity. Coordination and collaboration between a range of public and private organizations across political, disciplinary, and geographic boundaries, and more active public participation in planning and policy development, are critical to implementing more sustainable resource management strategies, including those that use economic incentives and bioregional approaches.

A top priority is to halt the further degradation of watersheds. In places where the landscape has already been highly altered, rehabilitation may be required. But it need not be highly disruptive to existing uses and users of the landscape. For example, restoring just half of the wetlands lost in the upper Mississippi River Basin would affect less than 3 percent of the region's agricultural, forest, or urban land, but could prevent a repeat of the 1993 flood that cost US$16 billion (42).

Ensuring the long-term viability of watersheds—with all their species and services—will require cooperation and concerted action from the local stream bank to international diplomatic halls. Watersheds do not begin and end at political boundaries. In fact, over 300 rivers cross national boundaries (as do many aquifers) (43). Mechanisms such as the Convention on Biological Diversity, the Climate Convention, and other global or regional agreements which encourage and support coordinated information sharing and action within and among countries, and efforts to more accurately assess the conditions and pressures on watersheds, provide valuable opportunities to chart a new course.

NOTES

1. Janet N. Abramovitz, "Imperiled Waters, Impoverished Future: The Decline of Freshwater Ecosystems," Worldwatch Paper #128 (Washington, D.C.: Worldwatch Institute, 1996).

2. Robert J. Naiman et al., eds., *The Freshwater Imperative: A Research Agenda* (Washington, D.C.: Island Press, 1995) as adapted from M.I. L'vovich and G.F. White, "Use and Transformation of Water Systems," in B.L. Turner II *et al.*, eds., *The Earth as Transformed by Human Action: Global and Regional Changes in the Biosphere over the Past 300 Years* (Cambridge: Cambridge University Press, 1990).

3. Patrick McCully, *Silenced Rivers: The Ecology and Politics of Large Dams* (New Jersey: Zed Books Ltd., 1996).

4. Robert S. Devine, "The Trouble With Dams," *Atlantic Monthly*, Aug 1995.

5. R.L. Welcomme, "Relationships Between Fisheries and the Integrity of River Systems," *Regulated Rivers: Research and Management*, 11:121–136, 1995; Peter B. Boyle and Robert A. Leidy, "Loss of Biodiversity in Aquatic Ecosystems: Evidence from Fish Faunas," in P.L. Fiedler and S.K. Jain, eds., *Conservation Biology: The Theory and Practice of Nature Conservation, Preservation, and Management* (New York: Chapman and Hall, 1992).

6. L.B. Leopold, "Flood Hydrology and the Floodplain," in Gilbert F. White and Mary Fran Myers, eds., *Water Resources Update: Coping with the Flood, the Next Phase* (Carbondale, IL: University Council on Water Resources, 1994); artificial channel length from Jeff Hecht, "The Incredible Shrinking Mississippi Delta," *New Scientist*, April 14, 1990.

7. Evolution of Mississippi River management and early estimates of 1993 flood costs from Mary Fran Myers and Gilbert F. White, "The Challenge of the Mississippi Flood," *Environment*, December 1993; flood heights from L.B. Leopold, "Flood Hydrology and the Floodplain," in White and Myers, eds., 1994, *Water Resources Update: Coping with the Flood, The Next Phase*, cited in Richard E. Sparks, "Need for Ecosystem Management of Large Rivers and Their Floodplains," *Bioscience*, March 1995; historic flood costs from William Stevens, "The High Costs of Denying Rivers Their Floodplains," *New York Times*, July 20, 1993; 1993 costs from Gerald E. Galloway, "The Mississippi Basin Flood of 1993," prepared for Workshop on Reducing the Vulnerability of River Basin Energy, Agriculture, and Transportation Systems to Floods, Foz do Iguaçu, Brazil, November 29, 1995.

8. 1995 flood data from Haig Simonian, "Flood of Tears on the Rhine," *Financial Times*, February 8, 1995; historic flood data from "Dyke Disaster," *Down to Earth*, March 15, 1995.

9. Antonin Lelek, "The Rhine River and Some of Its Tributaries Under Human Impact in the Last Two Centuries," in D.P. Dodge, ed., *Proceedings of the International Large River Symposium, Canadian Special Publication of Fisheries and Aquatic Sciences 106* (Ottawa: Department of Fisheries and Oceans, 1989); Fred Pearce, "Greenprint for Rescuing the Rhine," *New Scientist*, June 26, 1995.

10. *Op. cit. 1*.

11. T.G. Northcote and D.Y. Atagi, "Pacific Salmon Abundance Trends in the Fraser River Watershed Compared With Other British Columbia Systems," in Deanna J. Stouder, Peter A. Bisson, and Robert J. Naiman, eds., *Pacific Salmon and their Ecosystems: Status and Future Options* (New York: Chapman & Hall, in press).

12. National Research Council, *Upstream: Salmon and Society in the Pacific Northwest* (Washington, D.C.: National Academy Press, 1995); Igor A. Shiklomanov, "World Fresh Water Resources," in Peter H. Gleick, ed., *Water in Crisis: A Guide to the World's Fresh Water Resources* (New York: Oxford University Press, 1993).

13. Sandra Postel, "Dividing the Waters: Food Security, Ecosystem Health, and the New Politics of Scarcity," Worldwatch Paper #132 (Washington D.C.: Worldwatch Institute, 1996).

14. *Ibid*.

15. "Yellow River Resumes Water Flow in Lower Reaches," Xinhua News Agency, January 2, 1998.

16. Moyle and Leidy, "Loss of Biodiversity in Aquatic Ecosystems: Evidence from Fish Faunas," in Fiedler and Jain, eds., 1992, *Conservation Biology: The Theory and Practice of Nature Conservation, Preservation, and Management*.

17. Sandra Postel, "Rivers Drying Up," *World Watch*, May/June 1995; "UN to Assess Aral Sea Shrinkage," *Financial Times*, September 19, 1995; Judith Perera, "A Sea Turns to Dust," *New Scientist*, October 23, 1993.

18. David H.L. Thomas, "Artisenal Fishing and Environmental Change in a Nigerian Floodplain Wetland," *Environmental Conservation*, Summer 1995; economic estimates in David Pearce and Dominic Moran, *The Economic Value of Biodiversity* (London:

Earthscan, 1994).

19. Shiklomanov, "World Fresh Water Resources," in Gleick, ed., 1993, *Water Crisis: A Guide to the World's Fresh Water Resources.*

20. James L. Tyson, "Delicate Ecosystem, Great Lakes Weighs the Economic Demands of Heavy Industry Manufacturing With the Environment's Needs," *Christian Science Monitor,* March 14, 1994.

21. With more comprehensive data, as it is, the picture would likely be much worse; only 1 percent of the 30,000 different chemicals entering the lakes are reliably monitored. Fish consumption advisories from United States Environmental Protection Agency (U.S. EPA), *The Quality of Our Nation's Water: 1992* (Washington, D.C.: U.S. EPA, 1994) (for a complete listing, see U.S. EPA, Office of Water, National Listing of Fish Consumption Advisories Database); estimates of chemicals entering the system from Tyson, "Delicate Ecosystem, Great Lakes Weighs the Economic Demands of Heavy Industry Manufacturing with the Environment's Needs," *Christian Science Monitor,* March 14, 1994; number of chemicals monitored from George R. Francis and Henry A. Reiger, "Barriers and Bridges to the Restoration of the Great Lakes Basin Ecosystem," in Lance H. Gunderson *et al.,* eds., *Barriers & Bridges to the Renewal of Ecosystems and Institutions* (New York: Columbia University Press, 1995).

22. United Nations Commission on Sustainable Development, *Comprehensive Assessment of the Freshwater Resources of the World,* Report of the Secretary-General to the Fifth Session of the Commission on Sustainable Development, New York, April 5–25, 1997.

23. Melanie Stiassney, "An Overview of Freshwater Biodiversity: With Some Lessons From African Fishes," *Fisheries,* in press.

24. Ole Seehausen, Jacques J.M. van Alphen, and Frans Witte, "Cichlid Fish Diversity Threatened by Eutrophication That Curbs Sexual Selection," *Science* 277, September 19, 1997, Vol. 277, pp. 1808–1811.

25. "Fishing Industry Devours Itself," *Panoscope,* July 1994.

26. Les Kaufman, "Catastrophic Change in Species-Rich Freshwater Ecosystems: The Lessons of Lake Victoria," *Bioscience,* December 1992; Rosemary Lowe-McConnell, "Fish Faunas of the African Great Lakes: Origins, Diversity and Vulnerability," *Conservation Biology,* September 1993.

27. Malcolm C. Beveridge, Lindsay G. Ross, and Liam A. Kelly, "Aquaculture and Biodiversity," *Ambio,* December 1994.

28. Alliance for the Chesapeake Bay, "Species Invasions Around the World That Have Brought Havoc," *Bay Journal,* April 1995.

29. Great Lakes Commission, *Great Lakes Panel on Aquatic Nuisance Species: Annual Report* (Ann Arbor, MI: Great Lakes Commission, March 1995); Michael L. Ludyanskiy *et al.,* "Impact of the Zebra Mussel, a Bivalve Invader," *Bioscience,* September 1993.

30. Food and Agriculture Organization of the United Nations (FAO), *State of World Fisheries and Aquaculture* (Rome: FAO, 1995); International Center for Living Aquatic Resources Management (ICLARM) and Consultative Group on International Agricultural Research (CGIAR), *From Hunting to Farming Fish* (Washington, D.C. :The World Bank, 1995).

31. National Research Council, 1995, *Upstream: Salmon and Society in the Pacific Northwest;* Willa Nehlsen, Jack E. Williams, and James A. Lichatowich, "Pacific Salmon at the Crossroads: Stocks at Risk From California, Oregon, Idaho and Washington," *Fisheries,* March–April 1991; The Conservation Fund and National Fish and Wildlife Foundation, *Report of the National Fish Hatchery Review Panel,* Washington, D.C., December 30, 1994; Pacific Rivers Council, *Coastal Salmon and Communities at Risk: The Principles of Coastal Salmon Recovery* (Eugene, OR, July 1995); Jack K. Sterne, Jr., "Supplementation of Wild Salmon Stocks: A Cure for the Hatchery Problem or More Problem Hatcheries," *Coastal Management,* 23:123–152, 1995.

32. Thierry Oberdorff, Jean-Françoise Guégan, and Bernard Hugueny, "Global Scale Patterns of Fish Species Richness in Rivers," *Ecography,* 18:345–352, 1995.

33. *Op. cit.* 16.

34. IUCN (TheWorld Conservation Union) *1996 IUCN Red List of Threatened Animals* (Switzerland, Gland, 1996).

35. BirdLife International, *Endemic Bird Areas of the World: Priorities for Biodiversity Conservation* (Cambridge, UK, 1998).

36. Peter H. Gleick, ed., *Water in Crisis: A Guide to the World's Freshwater Resources* (New York: Oxford University Press, 1993).

37. Malin Falkenmark and Carl Widstrand, "Population and Water Resources: A Delicate Balance," *Population Bulletin,* (Washington D.C.: Population Reference Bureau, 1992), p. 19.

38. *Op. cit.* 13.

39. *Op. cit.* 36.

40. *Op. cit.* 3.

41. "Dams (>15 m) under construction," *International Water Power and Dam Construction Handbook,* 1995, pp. 98–108.

42. Donald Hey and Nancy Phillipi, "Flood Reduction Through Wetland Restoration: The Upper Mississippi River Basin as a Case History," *Restoration Ecology,* March 1995.

43. *Op. cit.* 22.

Map 1: Primary Watersheds

Africa	*Europe*	35 Po	51 Ganges	69 Sepik	85 Mississippi	101 Parnaiba
1 Congo	18 Dalalven	36 Rhine & Meuse	52 Godavari	70 Syr Darya	86 Nelson	102 Rio Colorado
2 Lake Chad	19 Danube	37 Rhone	53 Hong (Red River)	71 Tapti	87 Rio Grande	103 São Francisco
3 Jubba	20 Daugava	38 Seine	54 Hwang He	72 Tarim	88 Rio Grande de Santiago	104 Lake Titicaca
4 Limpopo	21 Dnieper	39 Tagus	55 Indigirka	73 Xi Jiang	89 Sacramento	105 Tocantins
5 Mangoky	22 Dniester	40 Tigris & Euphrates	56 Indus	74 Yalu Jiang	90 St. Lawrence	106 Uruguay
6 Mania	23 Don	41 Ural	57 Irrawaddy	75 Yangtze	91 Susquehanna	
7 Niger	24 Ebro	42 Vistula	58 Kapuas	76 Yenisey	92 Thelon	
8 Nile	25 Elbe	43 Volga	59 Kolyma		93 Usumacinta	
9 Ogooue	26 Garonne	44 Weser	60 Krishna	*North & Central America*	94 Yaqui	
10 Okavango Swamp	27 Glama		61 Lena	77 Alabama & Tombigbee	95 Yukon	
11 Orange	28 Guadalquivir	*Asia & Oceania*	62 Mahakam	78 Balsas		
12 Oued Draa	29 Kemijoki	45 Amu Darya	63 Mahanadi	79 Brazos	*South America*	
13 Senegal	30 Kura-Araks	46 Amur	64 Mekong	80 Colorado	96 Amazon	
14 Shaballe	31 Loire	47 Lake Balkhash	65 Murray-Darling	81 Columbia	97 Chubut	
15 Turkana	32 Neva	48 Brahmaputra	66 Narmada	82 Fraser	98 Magdalena	
16 Volta	33 North Dvina	49 Chao Phrya	67 Ob	83 Hudson	99 Orinoco	
17 Zambezi	34 Oder	50 Fly	68 Salween	84 Mackenzie	100 Paraná	

© 1998 World Resources Institute

Map 2: Freshwater Fish Species Richness and Endemism

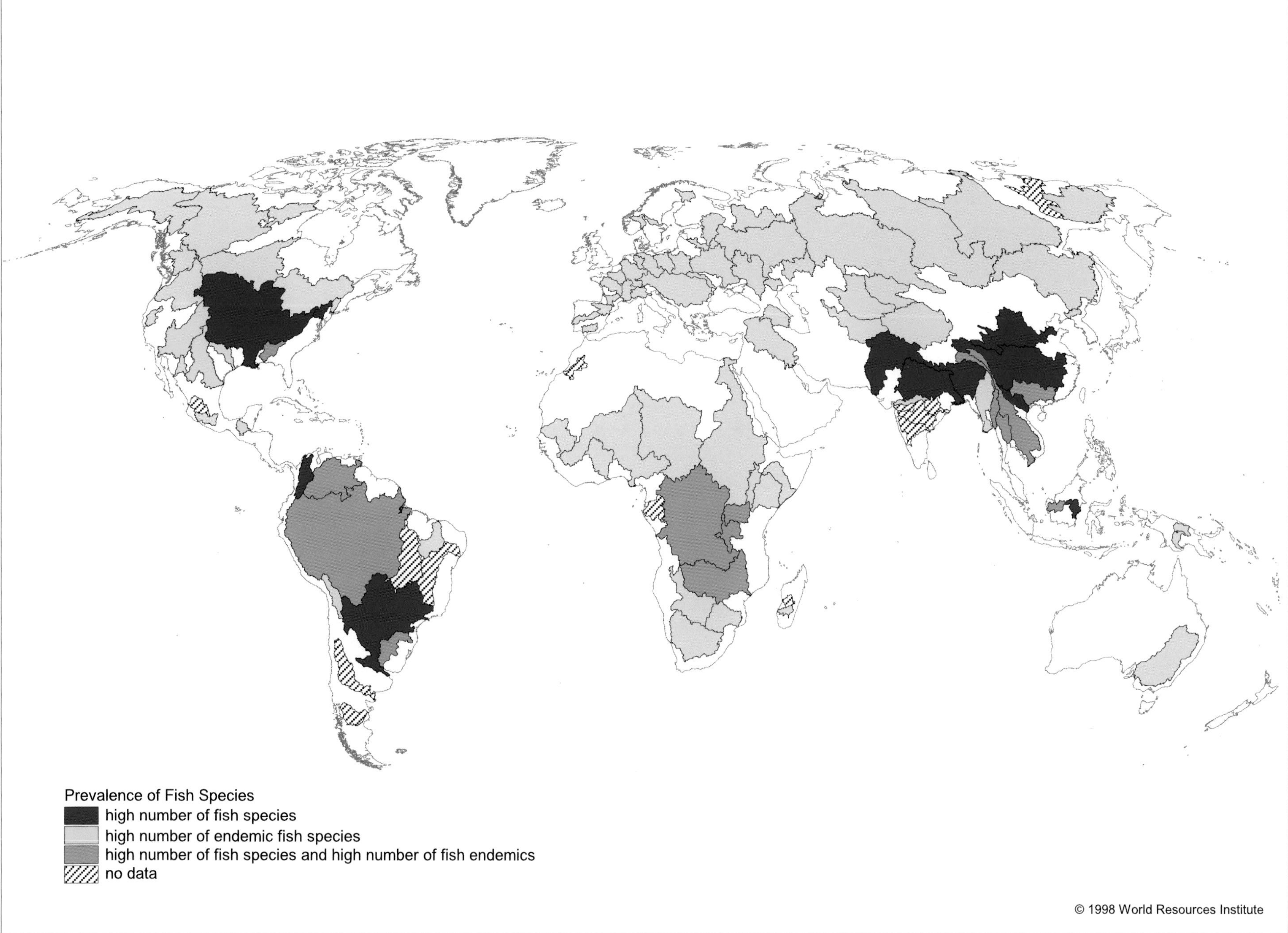

© 1998 World Resources Institute

Prevalence of Fish Species

- high number of fish species
- high number of endemic fish species
- high number of fish species and high number of fish endemics
- no data

Map 3: Endemic Bird Areas

© 1998 World Resources Institute

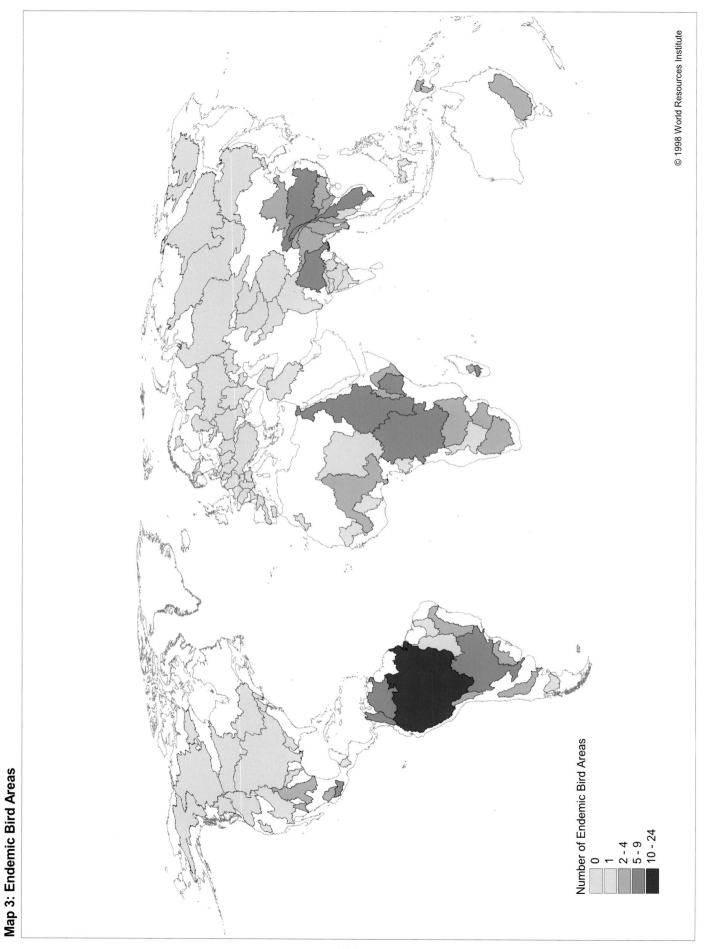

Number of Endemic Bird Areas

0
1
2 - 4
5 - 9
10 - 24

1-21

Map 4: Aridity

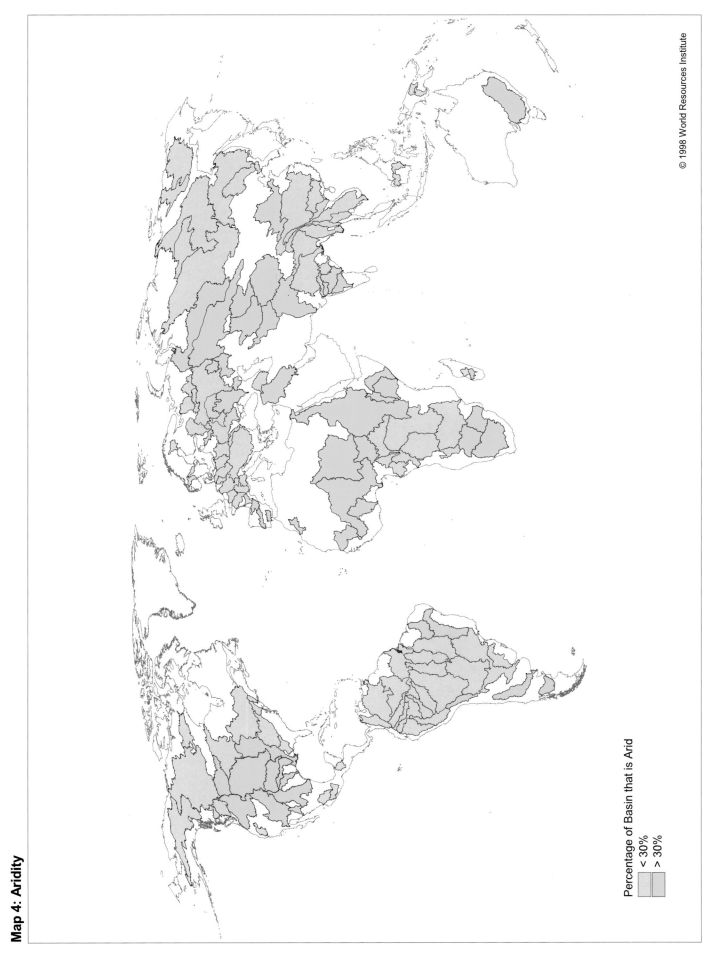

Percentage of Basin that is Arid

< 30%

> 30%

© 1998 World Resources Institute

Map 5: Population Density

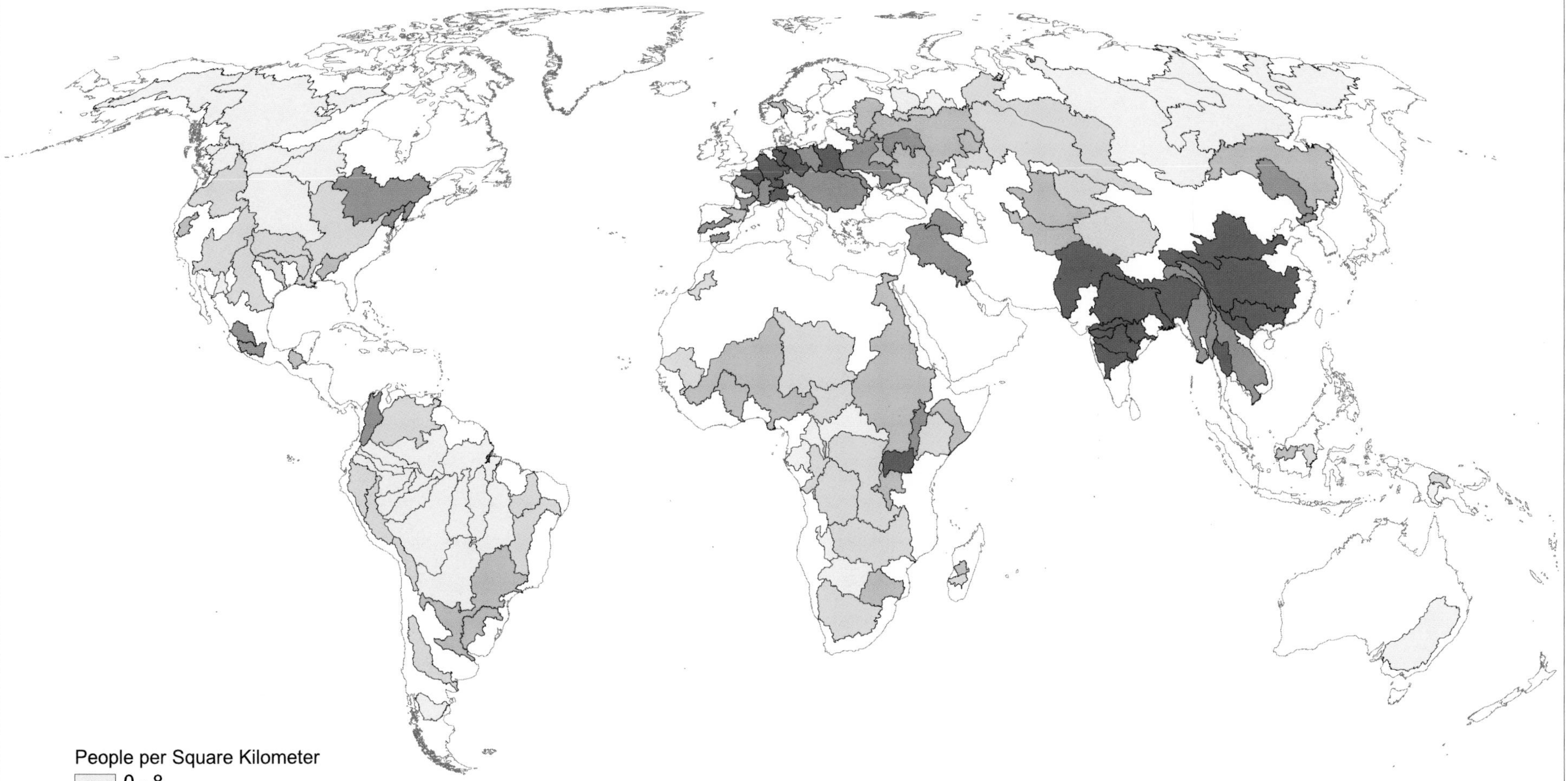

© 1998 World Resources Institute

People per Square Kilometer

0 - 8
9 - 21
22 - 49
54 - 117
118 - 1114

Map 6: Water Availability

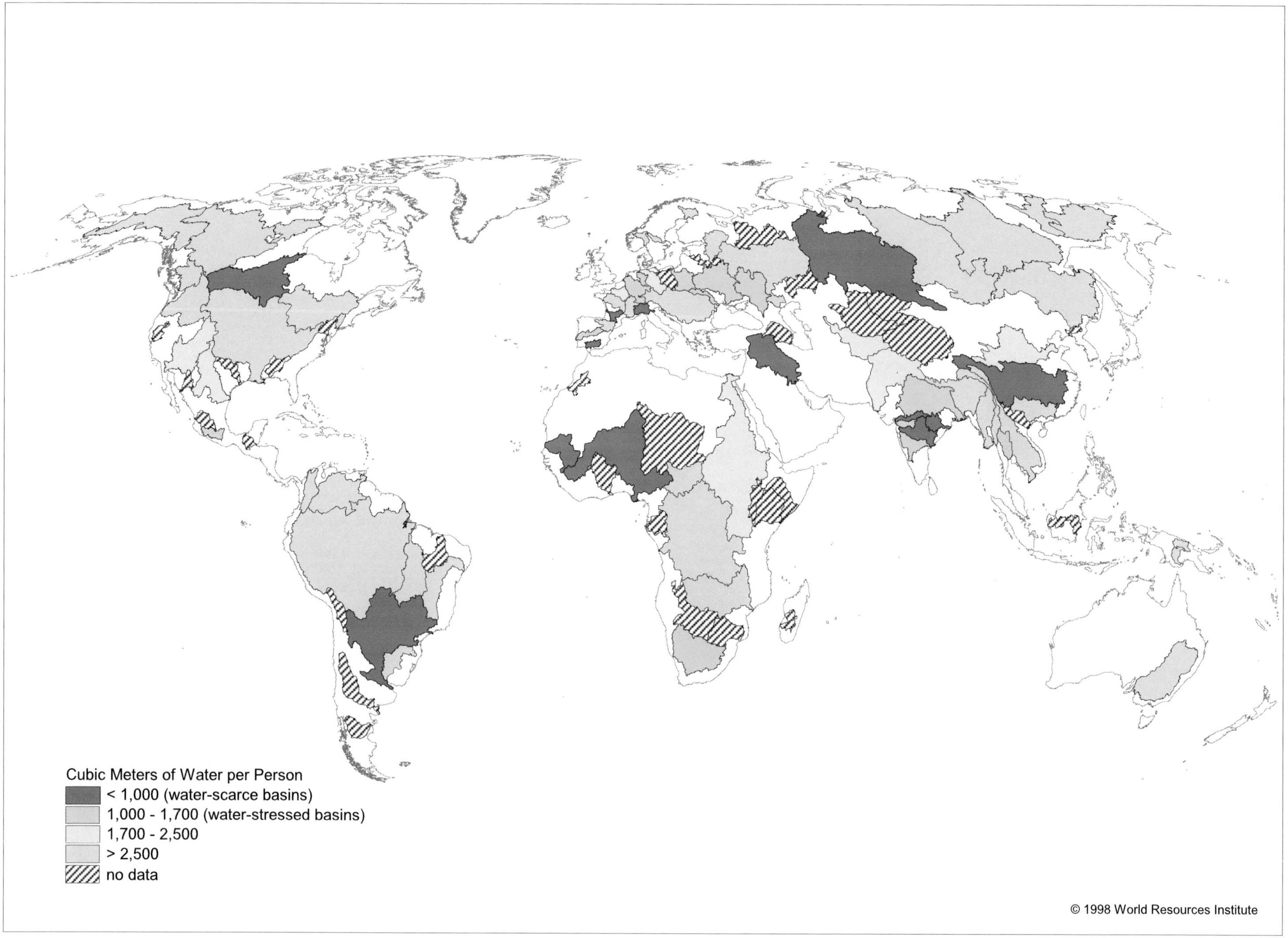

© 1998 World Resources Institute

Cubic Meters of Water per Person

▨	< 1,000 (water-scarce basins)
▨	1,000 - 1,700 (water-stressed basins)
▨	1,700 - 2,500
▨	> 2,500
▧	no data

Map 7: Modified Landscape (Cropland and Developed Areas)

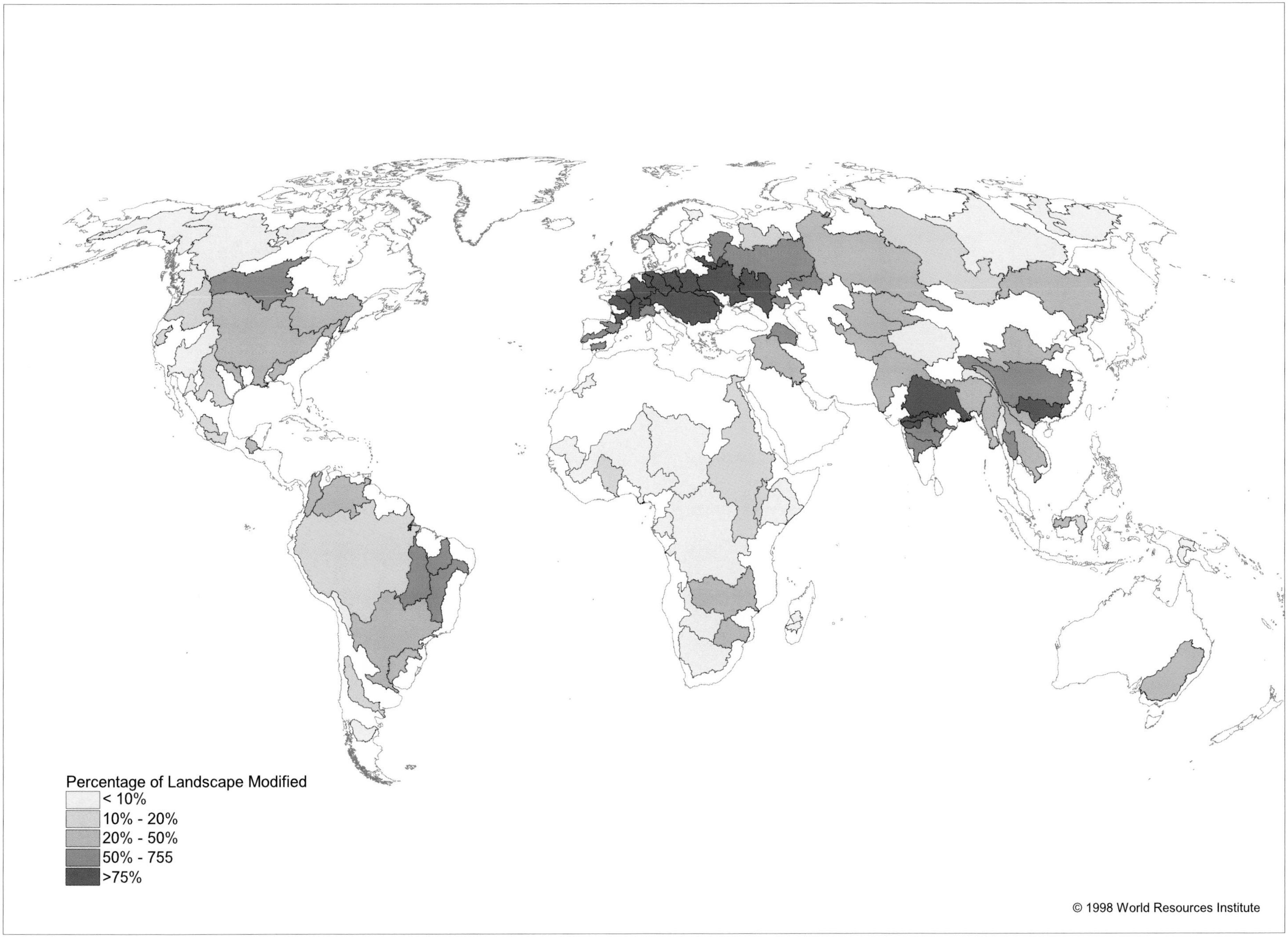

© 1998 World Resources Institute

Percentage of Landscape Modified
< 10%
10% - 20%
20% - 50%
50% - 755
>75%

Map 8: Cropland Irrigation

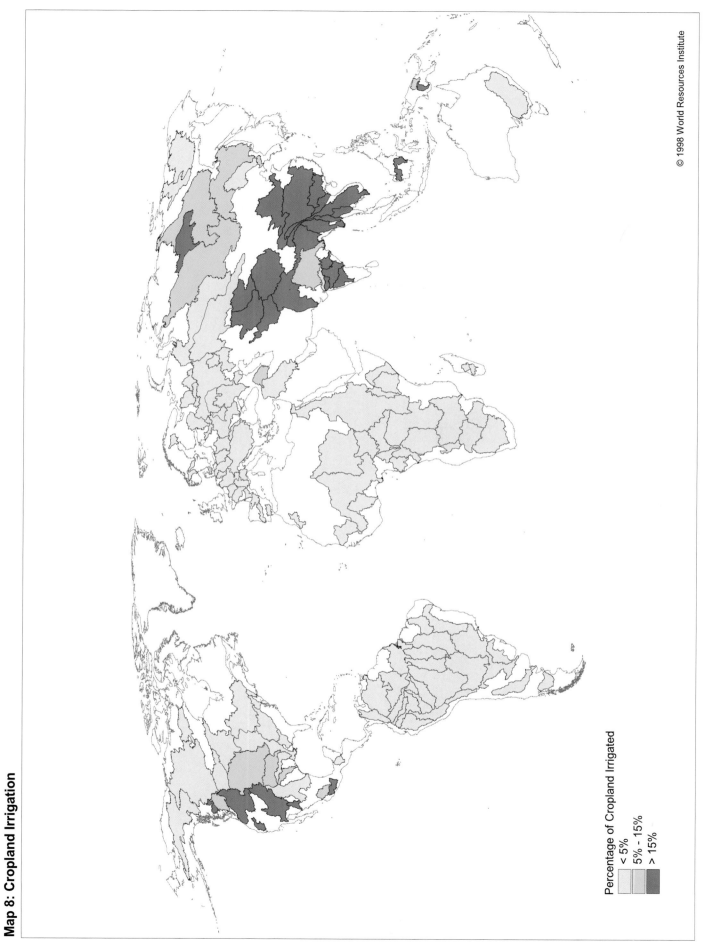

Percentage of Cropland Irrigated

< 5%

5% - 15%

> 15%

© 1998 World Resources Institute

Map 9: Existing and Proposed Major Dams

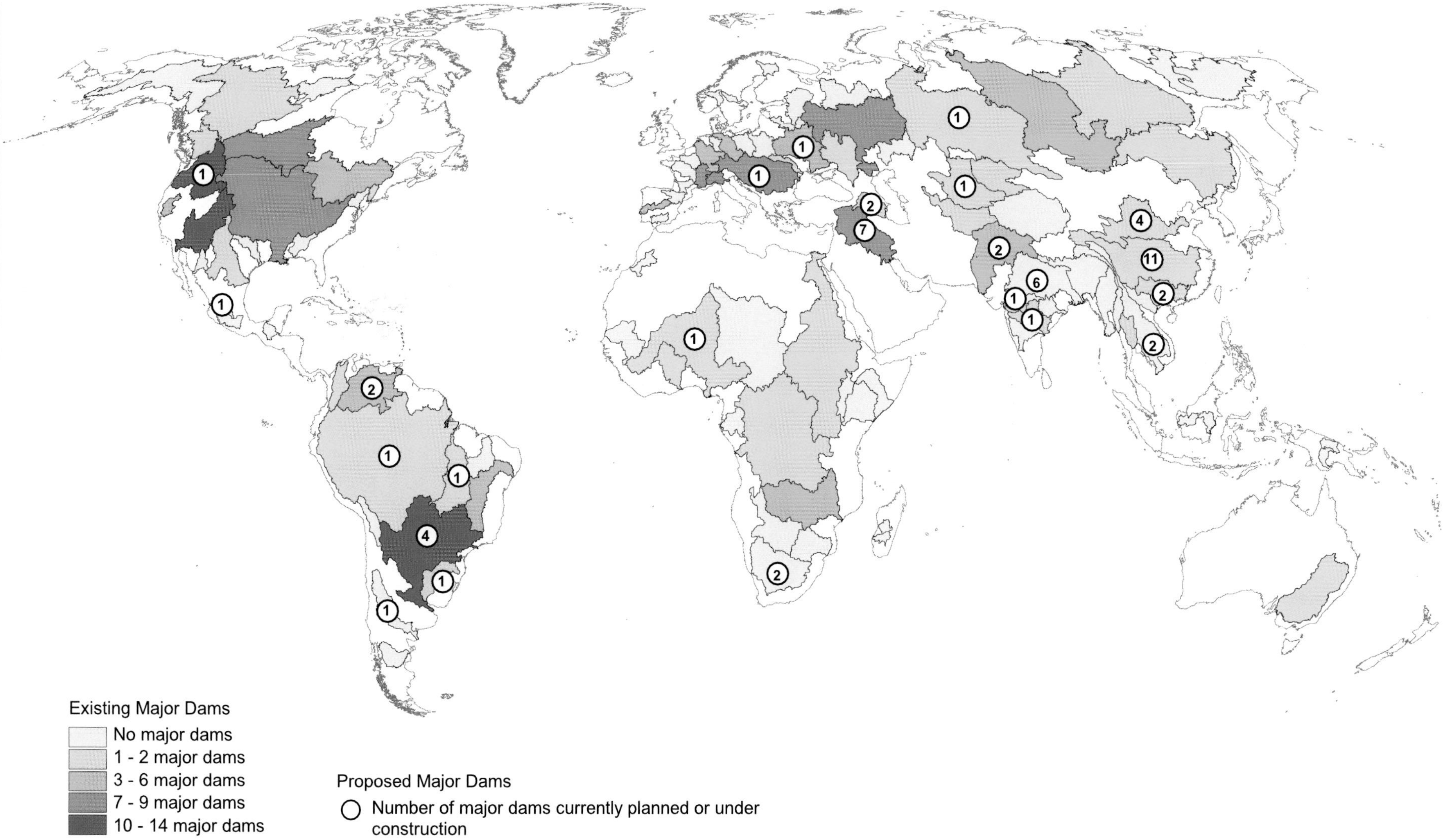

© 1998 World Resources Institute

Existing Major Dams
- No major dams
- 1 - 2 major dams
- 3 - 6 major dams
- 7 - 9 major dams
- 10 - 14 major dams

Proposed Major Dams
○ Number of major dams currently planned or under construction

Map 10: Remaining Original Forest Cover

© 1998 World Resources Institute

Percentage of Original Forest Remaining

< 25%
25%- 50%
50% - 75%
>75%

Map 11: Extent of Original Forest Cover Lost

© 1998 World Resources Institute

Area Deforested

< 100,000 km²

500,000 km² - 1,000,000 km²

> 1,000,000 km²

Map 12: Area Affected by Water Erosion

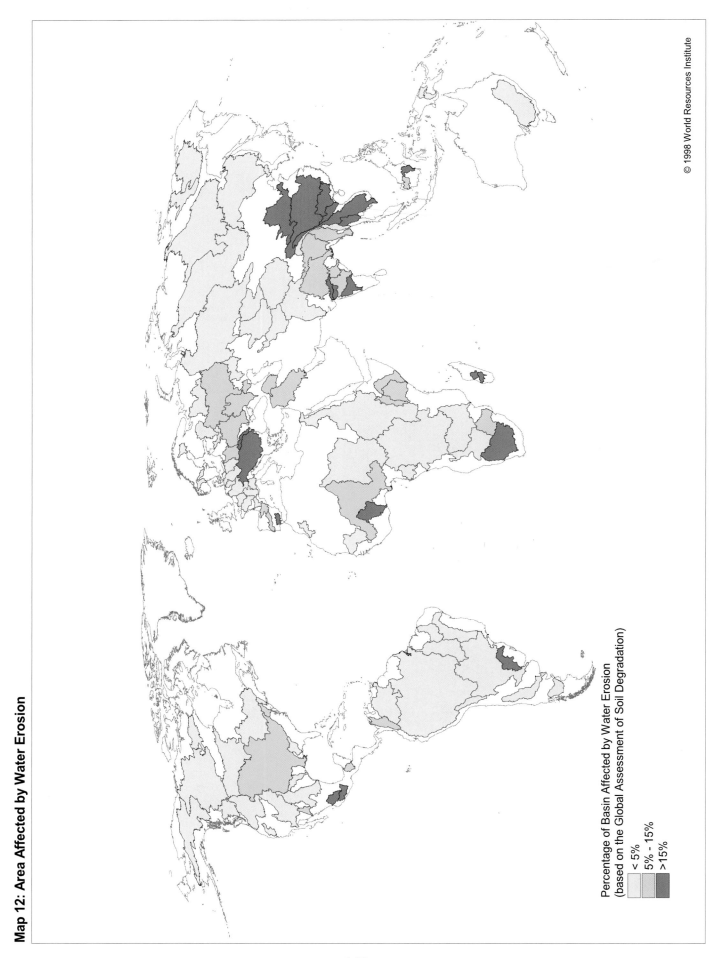

© 1998 World Resources Institute

Percentage of Basin Affected by Water Erosion
(based on the Global Assessment of Soil Degradation)

< 5%
5% - 15%
>15%

1-30

Map 13: Urban Population Growth (1995 - 2000)

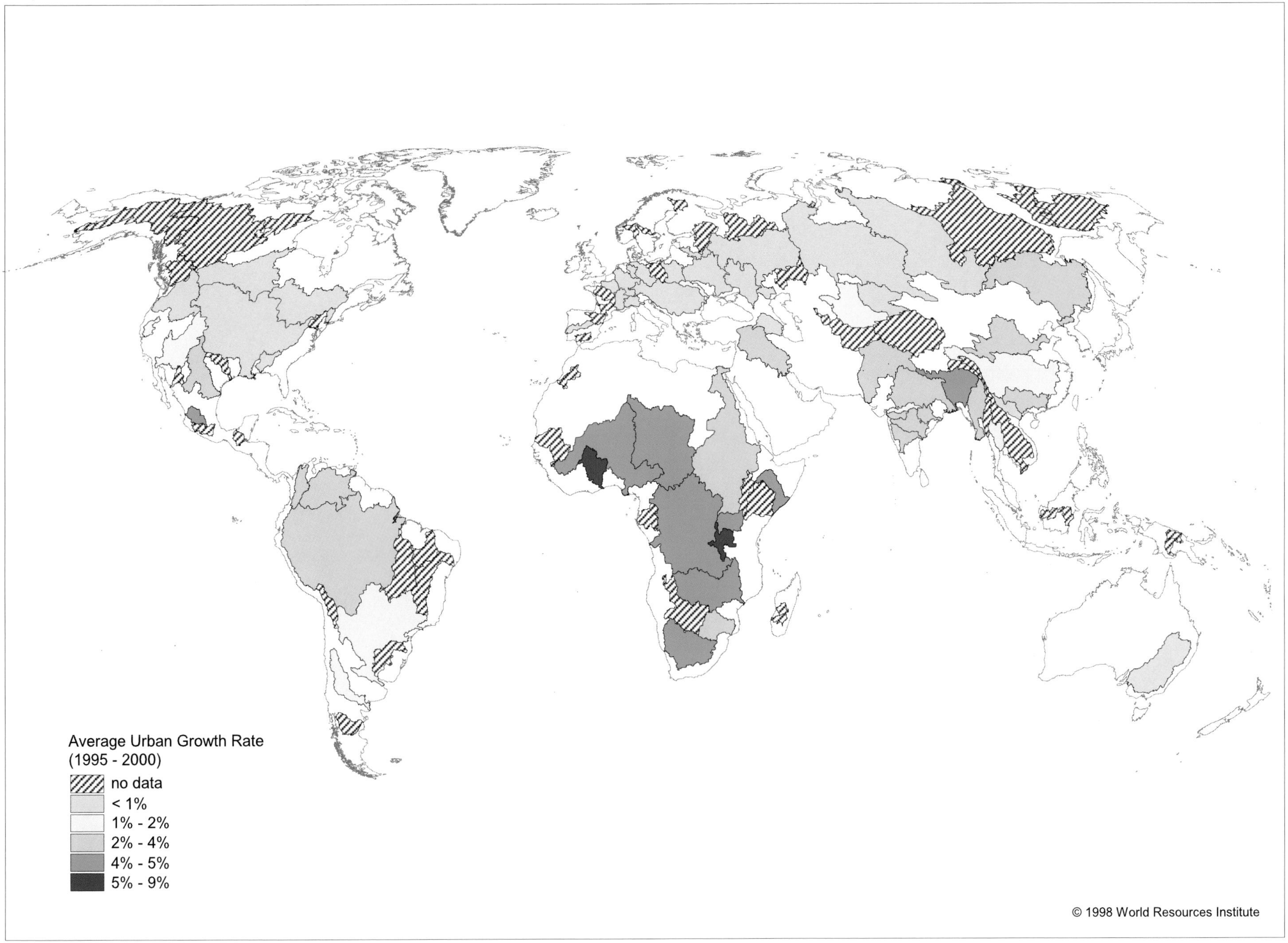

© 1998 World Resources Institute

Average Urban Growth Rate
(1995 - 2000)

no data
< 1%
1% - 2%
2% - 4%
4% - 5%
5% - 9%

Map 14: Tropical Deforestation (1980 - 1990)

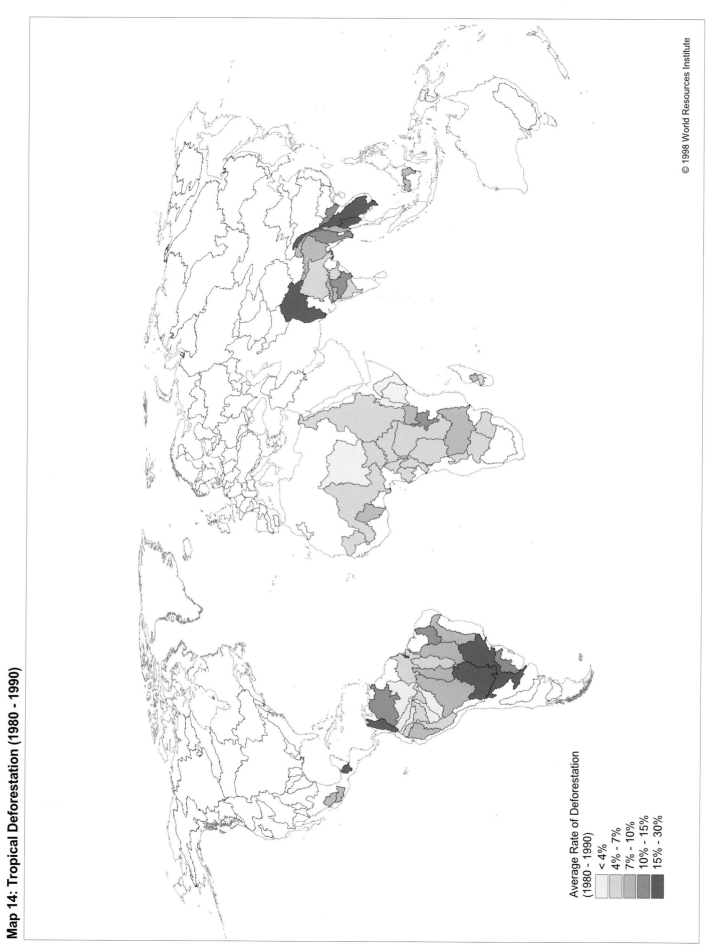

© 1998 World Resources Institute

Average Rate of Deforestation
(1980 - 1990)

	< 4%
	4% - 7%
	7% - 10%
	10% - 15%
	15% - 30%

Map 15: Protected Area

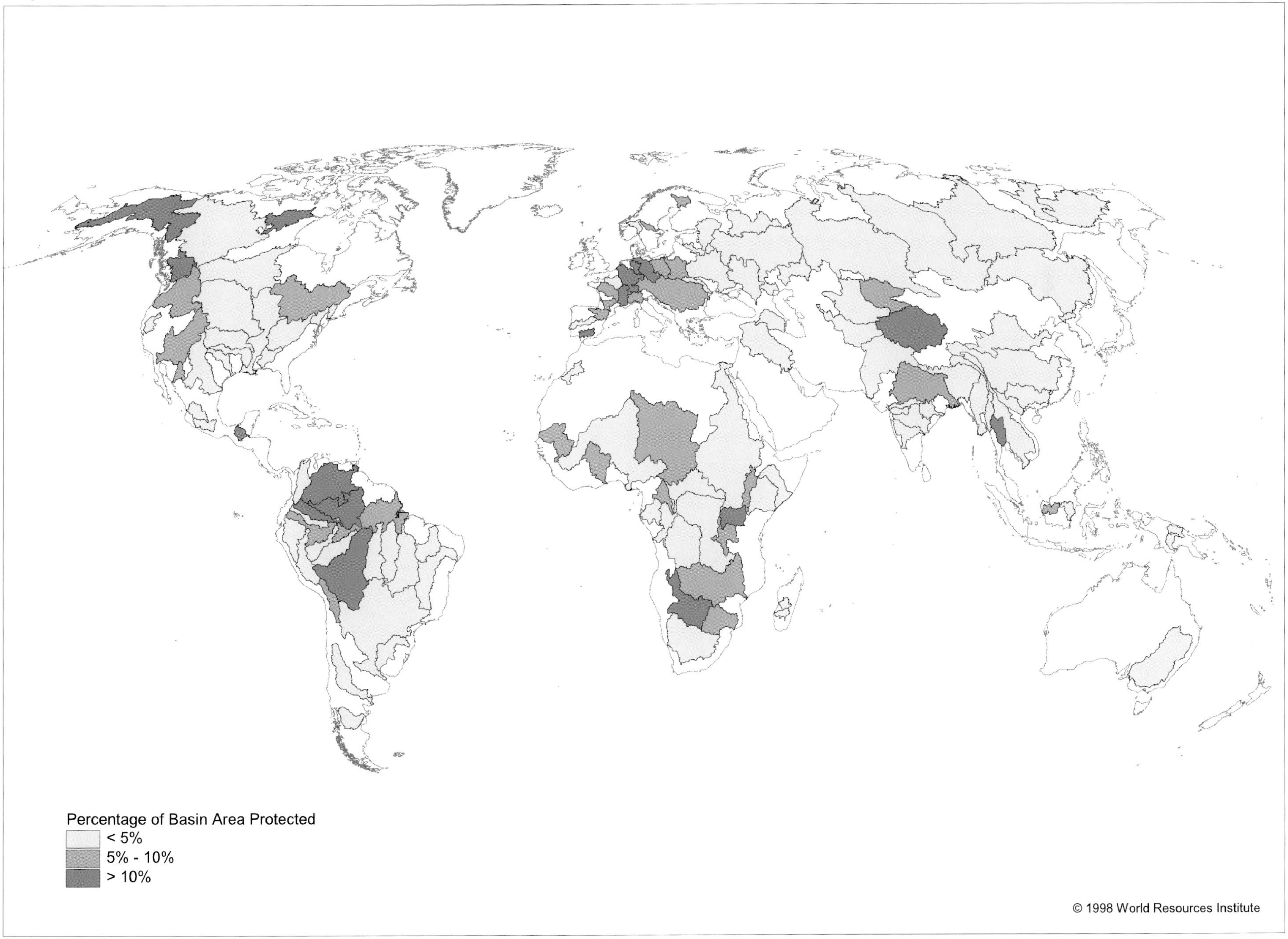

© 1998 World Resources Institute

Percentage of Basin Area Protected

< 5%

5% - 10%

> 10%

PART 2
WATERSHED PROFILES

There are 145 basin profiles, each one with a locator map, a bar chart of land cover and use within a five kilometer buffer from major rivers, and 24 indicators that characterize each basin. There are 106 primary basins, some of which are further divided into subbasins. Profiles are organized in alphabetical order by geographic region. Subbasins are included after the primary basin within which they fall. The locator map, indicators and bar chart are described below.

WATERSHED PROFILES FOR AFRICA

Congo 2-11
  Subbasins
  Kasai 2-12
  Sangha 2-13
  Lake Tanganyika 2-14
  Ubangi 2-15
Lake Chad 2-16
  Subbasin
  Chari 2-17
Jubba 2-18
Limpopo 2-19
Mangoky 2-20
Mania 2-21
Niger 2-22
Nile 2-23
  Subbasin
  Lake Victoria 2-24
Ogooue 2-25
Okavango Swamp 2-26
  Subbasin
  Cubango 2-27
Orange 2-28
Oued Draa 2-29
Senegal 2-30
Shaballe 2-31
Lake Turkana 2-32
Volta 2-33
Zambezi 2-34

WATERSHED PROFILES FOR EUROPE

Dalalven 2-37
Danube 2-38
Daugava 2-39
Dnieper 2-40
   Subbasin
   Desna 2-41
Dniester 2-42
Don 2-43
Ebro 2-44
Elbe 2-45
Garonne 2-46
Glama 2-47
Guadalquivir 2-48
Kemijoki 2-49
Kura-Araks 2-50
Loire 2-51
Neva 2-52
North Dvina 2-53
   Subbasins
   Sukhona 2-54
   Vychegda 2-55
Oder 2-56
Po 2-57
Rhine & Meuse 2-58
Rhone 2-59
Seine 2-60
Tagus 2-61
Tigris & Euphrates 2-62
Ural 2-63
Vistula 2-64
Volga 2-65
   Subbasins
   Kama 2-66
   Oka 2-67
Weser 2-68

WATERSHED PROFILES FOR ASIA AND OCEANIA

Amu Darya 2-71
Amur 2-72
   Subbasin
   Songhua Yiang 2-73
Lake Balkhash 2-74
Brahmaputra 2-75
Chao Phrya 2-76
Fly 2-77
Ganges 2-78
Godavari 2-79

Hong (Red River) 2-80
Hwang He 2-81
Indigirka 2-82
Indus 2-83
Irrawaddy 2-84
Kapuas 2-85
Kolyma 2-86
Krishna 2-87
Lena 2-88
    Subbasin
    Viljuj 2-89
Mahakam 2-90
Mahanadi 2-91
Mekong 2-92
Murray-Darling 2-93
Narmada 2-94
Ob 2-95
    Subbasin
    Irtysh 2-96
Salween 2-97
Sepik 2-98
Syr Darya 2-99
Tapti 2-100
Tarim 2-101
Xi Jiang (Pearl River) 2-102
Yalu Jiang 2-103
Yangtze 2-104
Yenisey 2-105
    Subbasin
    Lake Baikal 2-106

WATERSHED PROFILES FOR NORTH AND CENTRAL AMERICA
Alabama & Tombigbee 2-109
Balsas 2-110
Brazos 2-111
Colorado 2-112
Columbia 2-113
Fraser 2-114
    Subbasin
    Nechako 2-115
Hudson 2-116
Mackenzie 2-117
    Subbasins
    Great Bear Lake 2-118
    Great Slave Lake 2-119
Mississippi 2-120
    Subbasins
    Arkansas 2-121

Missouri 2-122
Ohio 2-123
Red 2-124
Nelson 2-125
Subbasin
Saskatchewan 2-126
Rio Grande 2-127
Rio Grande de Santiago 2-128
Sacramento 2-129
Saint Lawrence 2-130
Subbasins
Lakes Huron & Erie 2-131
Lake Michigan 2-132
Lake Ontario 2-133
Lake Superior 2-134
Susquehanna 2-135
Thelon 2-136
Usumacinta 2-137
Yaqui 2-138
Yukon 2-139

WATERSHED PROFILES FOR SOUTH AMERICA
Amazon 2-143
Subbasins
Ica-Putumayo 2-144
Japurá 2-145
Juruá 2-146
Madeira 2-147
Negro 2-148
Purus 2-149
Marañón 2-150
Tapajos 2-151
Ucayali 2-152
Xingu 2-153
Chubut 2-154
Magdalena 2-155
Orinoco 2-156
Paraná 2-157
Subbasin
Paraguay 2-158
Parnaiba 2-159
Rio Colorado 2-160
São Francisco 2-161
Lakes Titicaca & Salar de Uyuni 2-162
Tocantins 2-163
Uruguay 2-164

LOCATOR MAP

Each locator map presents the area occupied by the basin, the number of cities with a population over 100,000, the number of Ramsar sites—sites of wetlands of international importance—and the extent of the modified landscape within the basin. Modified landscape refers to cropland and developed area (urban centers, roads, etc.). For regions below the equator in Asia and above 54°N in North America data on developed area were not available; thus in these watersheds the modified landscape is under-estimated. This is particularly true for the Murray-Darling basin in Australia. For reference, the subbasins locator maps contain part of the main river.

WATERSHED CHARACTERISTICS

Each basin profile contains 24 descriptive indicators. Some data were not available for all basins, as indicated by "–" in the profiles. Land cover percentages, such as forests or grasslands, may not add up to 100 percent due to rounding and to the exclusion of areas covered by ice. Please refer to the Appendix for detailed information on data sources and methodology used.

Basin area: area occupied by the entire watershed in square kilometers.

Population density: number of people per square kilometer in each basin. This was calculated by dividing total population living in the basin by the area.

Urban growth rate: average urban growth rate for cities within the basin. Growth rates were available from the United Nations Urban Agglomerations dataset for only 432 cities around the world, therefore, this indicator should be interpreted with caution. Of these 432 cities, 213 fell within one of the selected watersheds. The urban growth rates for these 213 cities ranged from 0 percent in cities such as London and Milan, to 8.77 percent in Tabara, Tanzania. The

urban population in these cities varied between 750,000 and 16,533,000.

Large cities: number of cities with population of over 100,000. The number of large cities per basin varied between 0 and 73.

Total fish species: total number of known fish species in the basin. Number of introduced [intr.] and diadromous [diad.] fish are included where data are available. Introduced fish species are those that are not native to that freshwater system but have adapted and survived in it after its accidental or intentional introduction. Diadromous fish are those that migrate between fresh and salt water. For some basins, number of fish species was only available for the major river in the basin, for example, the number of fish species in the St. Lawrence basin refers only to those species found in the St. Lawrence River, and not in the basin as a whole.

Fish endemics: number of known endemic fish species in the basin. Endemic species are those that exist only in that particular area.

Threatened fish species: number of fish species refers to the number of species that fall within the IUCN (The World Conservation Union) categories of critically endangered, endangered or vulnerable to extinction. These figures refer exclusively to known globally threatened species, and do not include subspecies or distinct populations.

Endemic bird areas: number of areas where species of birds with restricted ranges tend to occur together. There are 218 Endemic Bird Areas (EBAs) in the world that comprise 2,561 species. The number of bird species per EBA varies between 2 and 80. Many EBAs are divided into non-contiguous subunits that may expand across watersheds; therefore, the number of EBAs in the profile refers to both, entire EBAs and partial or EBA-subunits that fall within that particular watershed.

Ramsar sites: refers to the number of wetlands of international importance under the Convention on Wetlands of International Importance Especially as Waterfowl Habitat signed in Ramsar, Iran in 1971. Those countries that agree to respect a site's integrity and establish wetland reserves can designate "wetlands of international importance."

Protected areas: percent of the basin area designated as protected area under one of the five IUCN (The World Conservation Union) management categories. IUCN management categories include a) totally protected areas that are maintained in a natural state and closed to extractive uses and b) partially protected areas that may be managed for specific uses, such as recreation, and where some extractive use is allowed.

Wetlands: percentage of the basin area that is occupied by wetlands. Wetlands include bogs, marshes, lakes, freshwater and tidal wetlands, permanent and seasonal wetlands, mangroves, and lagoons. In North America the area occupied by the Great Lakes, the Great Bear Lake, the Great Slave Lake, and Lake Winnipeg are not included in the calculation of wetland area.

Arid: percentage of the basin that is within the arid, semiarid, or hyperarid categories under the United Nations Environment Program's *World Atlas of Desertification*. These areas have an *aridity index*, calculated as the ratio between precipitation and evapotranspiration, between 0.05–0.50.

Forest: percentage of the basin that is forested. Forest types included are evergreen (broadleaf and needleleaf), deciduous (needleleaf and broadleaf), and mixed forests.

Cropland: percentage of the basin area occupied by crops or a mixture of crops and natural vegetation.

Cropland irrigated: percentage of cropland within the basin that is irrigated. Irrigated cropland is fairly well-defined for North America and Asia, but is less accurate for the rest of the world, therefore these data should be interpreted with caution. This inconsistency in the data is related to the lack of reference data on irrigated agriculture for some regions, and to the coarse resolution of the raw data in relation to smaller irrigated areas in many parts of the world.

Developed: percentage of the land area within each basin with stable lights (cities, roads, etc.), including frequently observed light sources such as gas flares at oil drilling sites. This figure is a good indicator of the spatial distribution of settlements and infrastructure but should not be interpreted as a measure of population density. (The mean settlement size required to produce enough light to be detected is much greater in developing countries than in industrialized countries because of differences in energy consumption.) The *Nighttime Lights of the World* data in which this indicator is based, are more highly correlated with measures of economic activity and energy consumption and are therefore considered a measure of relative development within the watershed. Data were not available for regions in Asia below the equator or for regions above 54°N in North America.

Shrub: percentage of the basin that is occupied by closed and open shrublands.

Grassland: percentage of the basin area occupied by woody savannas, savannas, and grasslands.

Barren: percentage of the basin area with barren or sparsely vegetated land.

Loss of original forest: percentage of original forest lost within a basin. Original forest refers to closed forests estimated to cover the planet 8,000 years ago, assuming current climate conditions, before large-scale disturbance by humans begun.

Deforestation rate: rate of forest loss for the period 1980–90. Deforestation data were only available for tropical regions of the world.

Eroded area: percentage of the basin that has moderate to extreme soil erosion from water—loss of topsoil and terrain deformation based on the Global Assessment of Soil Degradation (GLASOD).

Large dams: number of large (at least 15 meters high) and major dams in the basin. Major dams are those with a height over 150 meters, volume of 15 million cubic meters, storage capacity of at least 25 cubic kilometers, and/or a generating capacity of 1,000 megawatts. All major dams are included; however, a comprehensive database of large dams was only available for the United States, therefore the number of large dams in some basins, particularly those in China and Russia may be underestimated.

Planned major dams: number of major dams planned or under construction included in the list of "Dams (>15m) under construction" in the International Water Power and Dam Construction Handbook, 1995. Data on dams planned or under construction were not available for all countries, therefore these numbers underestimate the number of major dams planned or under construction in the world.

BAR GRAPH

The bar graph represents the different types of land cover and use within a 5 kilometer buffer around the major rivers in each basin. Land use is shown as a percentage of the total area in the buffer. Land cover and use within 5 kilometers of a major river may vary greatly from the land cover and use present in the watersheds as a whole.

WATERSHED PROFILES

FOR

AFRICA

Congo Watershed

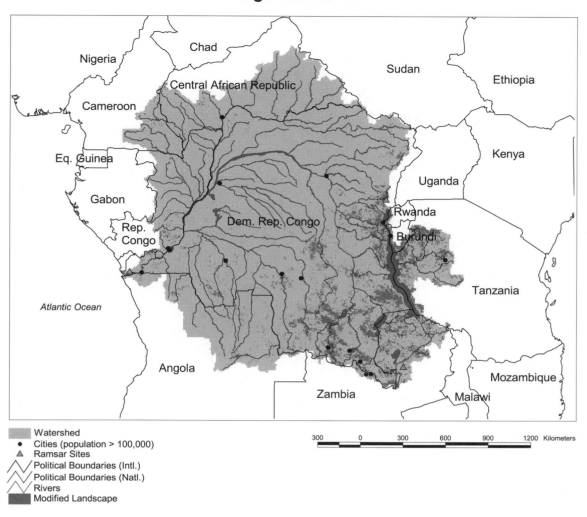

Watershed
● Cities (population > 100,000)
△ Ramsar Sites
Political Boundaries (Intl.)
Political Boundaries (Natl.)
Rivers
Modified Landscape

Basin area:	3,730,474 km²
Population density:	15 people per km²
Urban growth rate:	5.0%
Large cities:	18
Total fish species:	700
Fish endemics:	500
Threatened fish species:	0
Endemic bird areas:	6
Ramsar sites:	3
Protected areas:	5%
Wetlands:	9%
Arid:	0%

Forest:	44%
Cropland:	7%
Cropland irrigated:	0%
Developed:	< 1%
Shrub:	0%
Grassland:	46%
Barren:	1%
Loss of original forest:	46%
Deforestation rate:	7%
Eroded area:	1%
Large dams:	3
Planned major dams:	-

Land Cover Within 5 km of Major Rivers

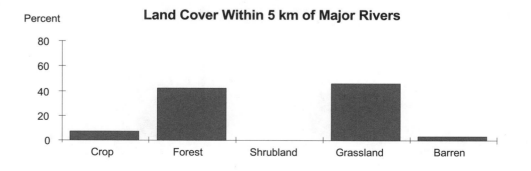

Percent

Crop   Forest   Shrubland   Grassland   Barren

2 - 11

© 1998 World Resources Institute

Congo Watershed: Kasai Subbasin

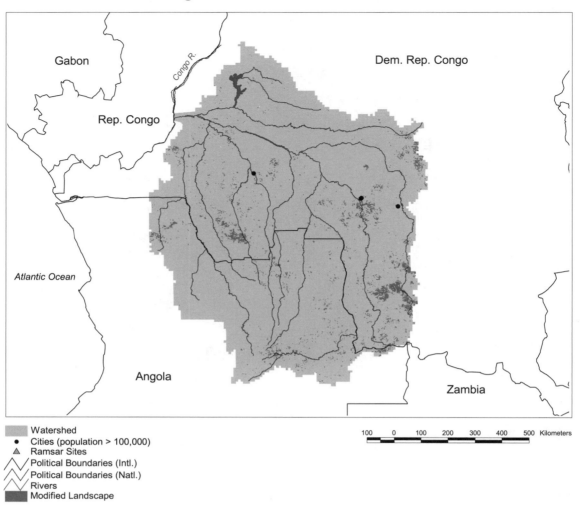

Watershed
● Cities (population > 100,000)
▲ Ramsar Sites
/\/ Political Boundaries (Intl.)
/\/ Political Boundaries (Natl.)
/\/ Rivers
■ Modified Landscape

Basin area:	925,172 km²	Forest:	40%
Population density:	14 people per km²	Cropland:	3%
Urban growth rate:	-	Cropland irrigated:	0%
Large cities:	4	Developed:	< 1%
Total fish species:	129	Shrub:	0%
Fish endemics:	-	Grassland:	56%
Threatened fish species:	0	Barren:	0%
Endemic bird areas:	0	Loss of original forest:	66%
Ramsar sites:	0	Deforestation rate:	6%
Protected areas:	2%	Eroded area:	1%
Wetlands:	3%	Large dams:	0
Arid:	0%	Planned major dams:	-

Land Cover Within 5 km of Major Rivers

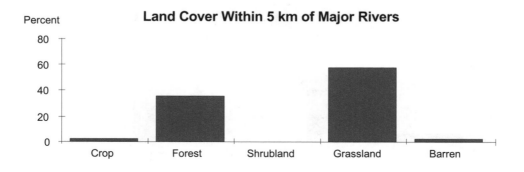

© 1998 World Resources Institute

Congo Watershed: Sangha Subbasin

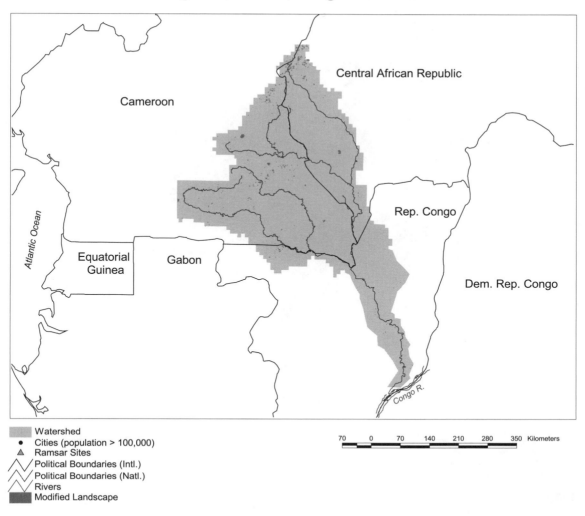

Watershed
- Cities (population > 100,000)
▲ Ramsar Sites
/\/\ Political Boundaries (Intl.)
/\/\ Political Boundaries (Natl.)
/\/\ Rivers
■ Modified Landscape

70   0   70   140   210   280   350 Kilometers

Basin area:	180,418 km²	Forest:	64%
Population density:	5 people per km²	Cropland:	1%
Urban growth rate:	-	Cropland irrigated:	0%
Large cities:	0	Developed:	< 1%
Total fish species:	-	Shrub:	0%
Fish endemics:	-	Grassland:	34%
Threatened fish species:	0	Barren:	0%
Endemic bird areas:	1	Loss of original forest:	30%
Ramsar sites:	0	Deforestation rate:	4%
Protected areas:	6%	Eroded area:	4%
Wetlands:	11%	Large dams:	0
Arid:	0%	Planned major dams:	-

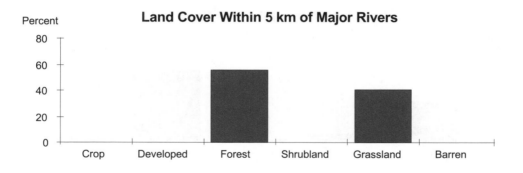

Land Cover Within 5 km of Major Rivers

Percent

2 - 13

© 1998 World Resources Institute

Congo Watershed: Lake Tanganyika Subbasin

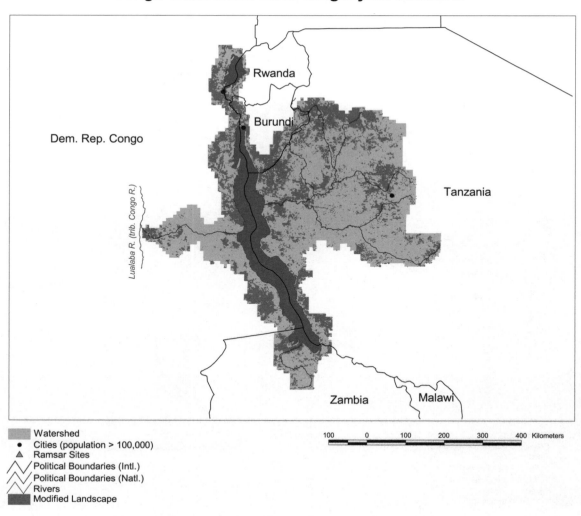

Watershed
● Cities (population > 100,000)
▲ Ramsar Sites
Political Boundaries (Intl.)
Political Boundaries (Natl.)
Rivers
Modified Landscape

100 0 100 200 300 400 Kilometers

Basin area:	273,156 km²	Forest:	12%
Population density:	33 people per km²	Cropland:	31%
Urban growth rate:	8.8%	Cropland irrigated:	0%
Large cities:	3	Developed:	< 1%
Total fish species:	240 (intr: 0)	Shrub:	2%
Fish endemics:	216	Grassland:	53%
Threatened fish species:	0	Barren:	1%
Endemic bird areas:	4	Loss of original forest:	54%
Ramsar sites:	0	Deforestation rate:	13%
Protected areas:	9%	Eroded area:	3%
Wetlands:	18%	Large dams:	0
Arid:	0%	Planned major dams:	-

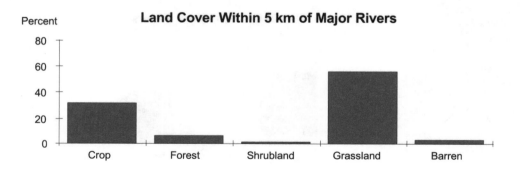

Land Cover Within 5 km of Major Rivers

Percent

© 1998 World Resources Institute

Congo Watershed: Ubangi Subbasin

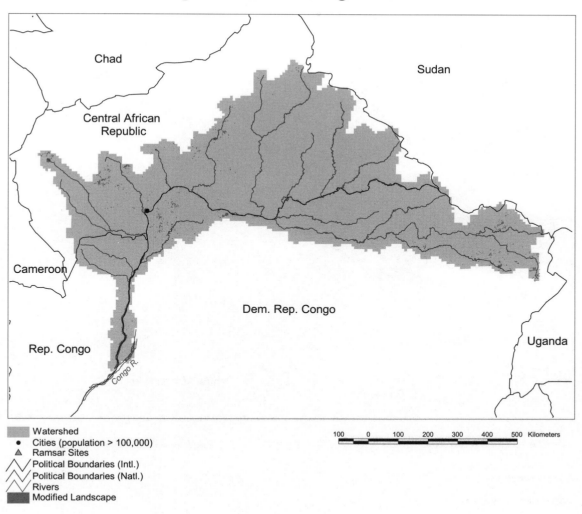

Watershed
● Cities (population > 100,000)
▲ Ramsar Sites
Political Boundaries (Intl.)
Political Boundaries (Natl.)
Rivers
Modified Landscape

100   0   100   200   300   400   500   Kilometers

Basin area:	613,202 km²	Forest:	26%
Population density:	11 people per km²	Cropland:	1%
Urban growth rate:	-	Cropland irrigated:	0%
Large cities:	1	Developed:	< 1%
Total fish species:	263	Shrub:	0%
Fish endemics:	-	Grassland:	71%
Threatened fish species:	0	Barren:	0%
Endemic bird areas:	2	Loss of original forest:	72%
Ramsar sites:	0	Deforestation rate:	4%
Protected areas:	5%	Eroded area:	-
Wetlands:	5%	Large dams:	0
Arid:	0%	Planned major dams:	-

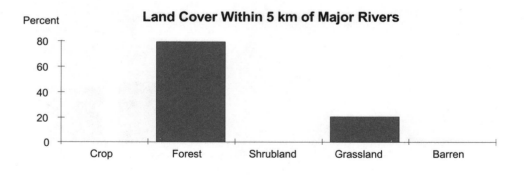

Land Cover Within 5 km of Major Rivers

© 1998 World Resources Institute

Lake Chad Watershed

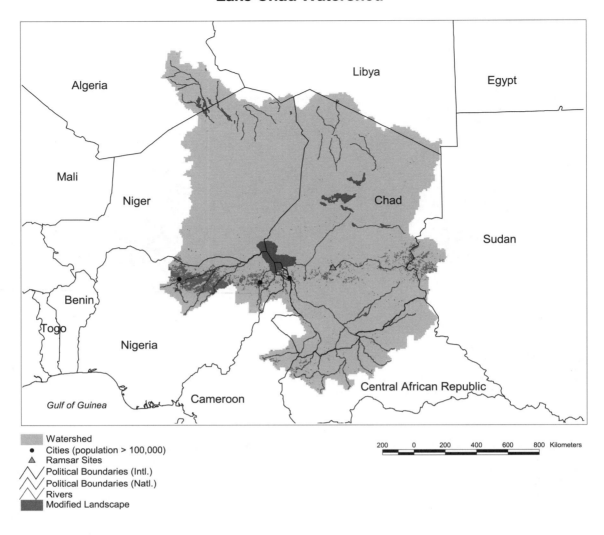

Legend:
- Watershed
- ● Cities (population > 100,000)
- △ Ramsar Sites
- Political Boundaries (Intl.)
- Political Boundaries (Natl.)
- Rivers
- Modified Landscape

200 0 200 400 600 800 Kilometers

Basin area:	2,497,918 km²	Forest:	0%
Population density:	11 people per km²	Cropland:	3%
Urban growth rate:	4.7%	Cropland irrigated:	0%
Large cities:	3	Developed:	< 1%
Total fish species:	93 (Lake Chad only)	Shrub:	4%
Fish endemics:	9 (Lake Chad only)	Grassland:	42%
Threatened fish species:	0 (Lake Chad only)	Barren:	52%
Endemic bird areas:	0	Loss of original forest:	100%
Ramsar sites:	1	Deforestation rate:	2%
Protected areas:	10%	Eroded area:	2%
Wetlands:	8%	Large dams:	0
Arid:	83%	Planned major dams:	-

Land Cover Within 5 km of Major Rivers

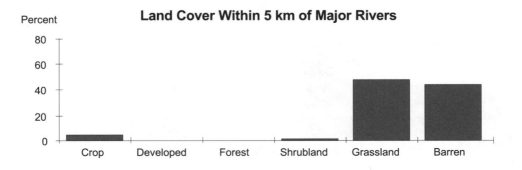

Percent

© 1998 World Resources Institute

Lake Chad Watershed: Chari Subbasin

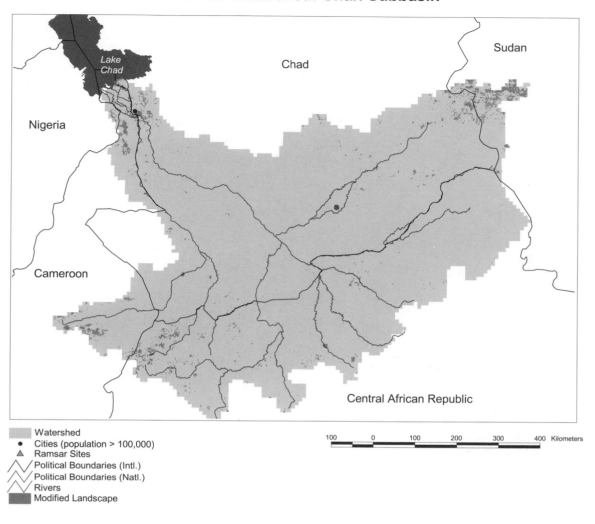

Watershed
● Cities (population > 100,000)
▲ Ramsar Sites
Political Boundaries (Intl.)
Political Boundaries (Natl.)
Rivers
Modified Landscape

100 0 100 200 300 400 Kilometers

Basin area:	548,747 km²	Forest:	1%
Population density:	11 people per km²	Cropland:	2%
Urban growth rate:	4.7%	Cropland irrigated:	0%
Large cities:	1	Developed:	< 1%
Total fish species:	130	Shrub:	0%
Fish endemics:	1	Grassland:	97%
Threatened fish species:	0	Barren:	0%
Endemic bird areas:	0	Loss of original forest:	100%
Ramsar sites:	0	Deforestation rate:	5%
Protected areas:	13%	Eroded area:	3%
Wetlands:	23%	Large dams:	0
Arid:	34%	Planned major dams:	-

Land Cover Within 5 km of Major Rivers

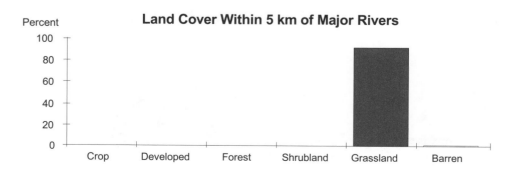

© 1998 World Resources Institute

Jubba Watershed

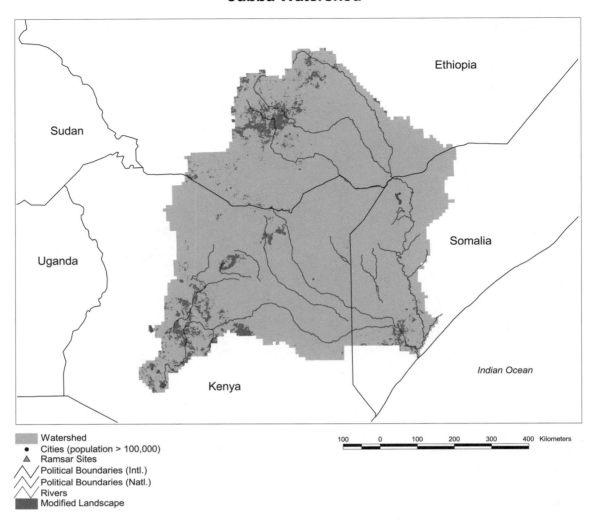

Watershed
● Cities (population > 100,000)
▲ Ramsar Sites
Political Boundaries (Intl.)
Political Boundaries (Natl.)
Rivers
Modified Landscape

Basin area:	497,655 km²	Forest:	3%
Population density:	12 people per km²	Cropland:	5%
Urban growth rate:	-	Cropland irrigated:	0%
Large cities:	0	Developed:	< 1%
Total fish species:	34	Shrub:	55%
Fish endemics:	3	Grassland:	35%
Threatened fish species:	0	Barren:	3%
Endemic bird areas:	5	Loss of original forest:	70%
Ramsar sites:	2	Deforestation rate:	2%
Protected areas:	2%	Eroded area:	6%
Wetlands:	4%	Large dams:	0
Arid:	72%	Planned major dams:	-

Land Cover Within 5 km of Major Rivers

© 1998 World Resources Institute

Limpopo Watershed

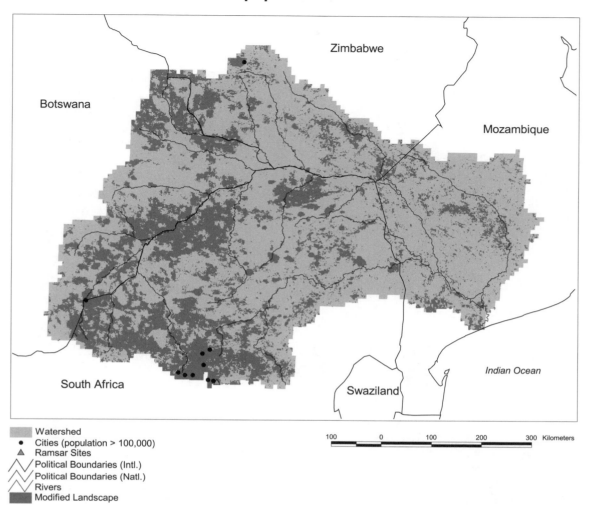

- Watershed
- • Cities (population > 100,000)
- ▲ Ramsar Sites
- Political Boundaries (Intl.)
- Political Boundaries (Natl.)
- Rivers
- Modified Landscape

Basin area:	421,168 km²	Forest:	1%
Population density:	35 people per km²	Cropland:	28%
Urban growth rate:	3.2%	Cropland irrigated:	0%
Large cities:	10	Developed:	4%
Total fish species:	57 (intr: 10)	Shrub:	1%
Fish endemics:	2	Grassland:	70%
Threatened fish species:	0	Barren:	0%
Endemic bird areas:	3	Loss of original forest:	99%
Ramsar sites:	1	Deforestation rate:	5%
Protected areas:	8%	Eroded area:	10%
Wetlands:	3%	Large dams:	1
Arid:	47%	Planned major dams:	-

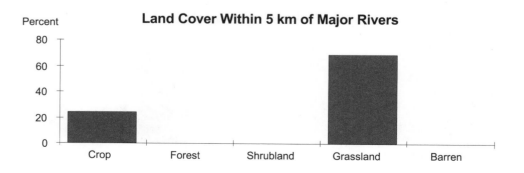

Land Cover Within 5 km of Major Rivers

© 1998 World Resources Institute

Mangoky Watershed

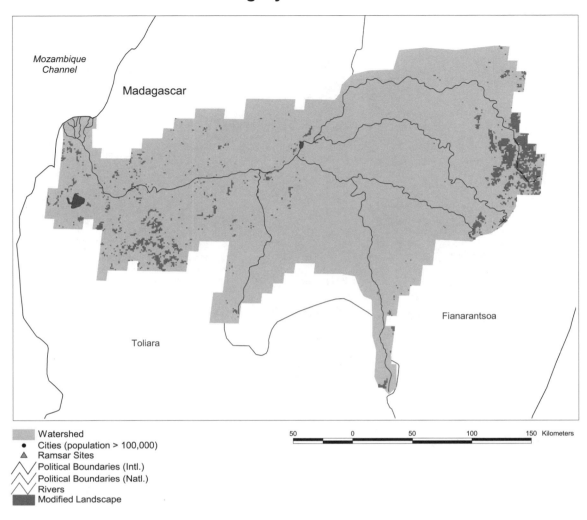

Watershed		Political Boundaries (Intl.)	
● Cities (population > 100,000)		Political Boundaries (Natl.)	
▲ Ramsar Sites		Rivers	
		Modified Landscape	

Basin area:	58,845 km²	Forest:	3%
Population density:	16 people per km²	Cropland:	5%
Urban growth rate:	-	Cropland irrigated:	0%
Large cities:	0	Developed:	< 1%
Total fish species:	8 (intr: 5)	Shrub:	0%
Fish endemics:	0	Grassland:	91%
Threatened fish species:	2	Barren:	0%
Endemic bird areas:	5	Loss of original forest:	97%
Ramsar sites:	0	Deforestation rate:	7%
Protected areas:	1%	Eroded area:	25%
Wetlands:	0%	Large dams:	0
Arid:	39%	Planned major dams:	-

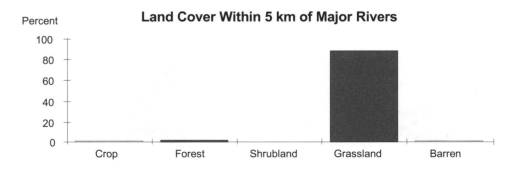

Land Cover Within 5 km of Major Rivers

Percent

2 - 20

© 1998 World Resources Institute

Mania Watershed

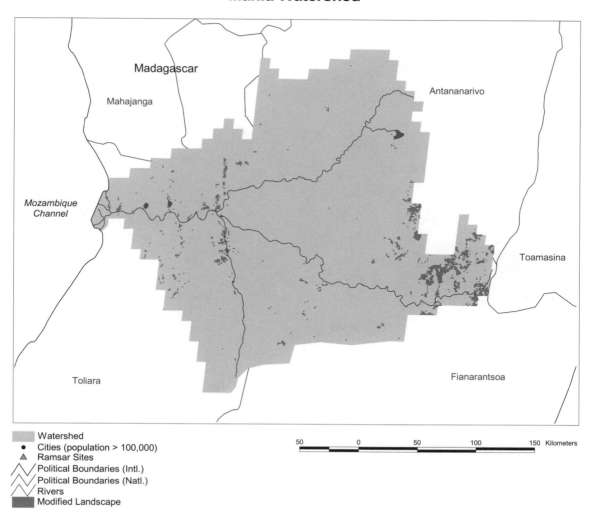

Watershed	
•	Cities (population > 100,000)
▲	Ramsar Sites
	Political Boundaries (Intl.)
	Political Boundaries (Natl.)
	Rivers
	Modified Landscape

50   0   50   100   150 Kilometers

Basin area:	56,116 km²	Forest:	6%
Population density:	26 people per km²	Cropland:	3%
Urban growth rate:	-	Cropland irrigated:	0%
Large cities:	0	Developed:	< 1%
Total fish species:	-	Shrub:	0%
Fish endemics:	-	Grassland:	90%
Threatened fish species:	-	Barren:	0%
Endemic bird areas:	4	Loss of original forest:	98%
Ramsar sites:	0	Deforestation rate:	8%
Protected areas:	0%	Eroded area:	17%
Wetlands:	1%	Large dams:	0
Arid:	0%	Planned major dams:	-

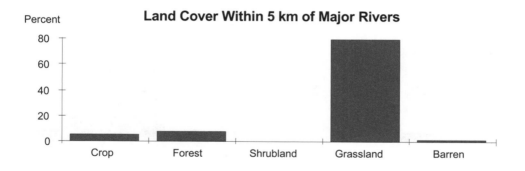

Land Cover Within 5 km of Major Rivers

Percent

80
60
40
20
0

Crop   Forest   Shrubland   Grassland   Barren

© 1998 World Resources Institute

Niger Watershed

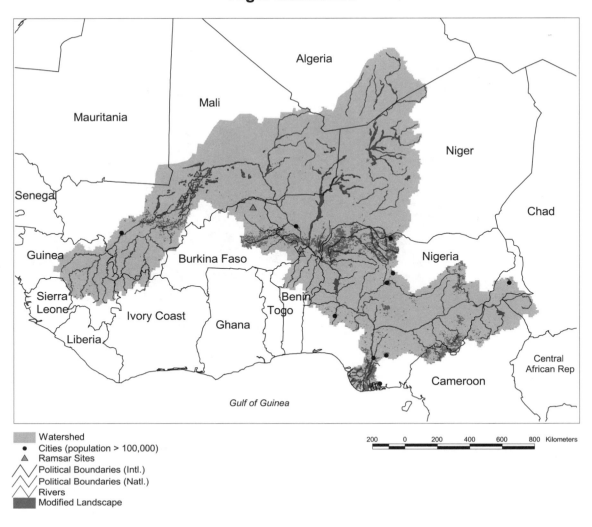

Watershed	
•	Cities (population > 100,000)
▲	Ramsar Sites
	Political Boundaries (Intl.)
	Political Boundaries (Natl.)
	Rivers
	Modified Landscape

Basin area:	2,261,763 km²	Forest:	0%
Population density:	31 people per km²	Cropland:	5%
Urban growth rate:	4.7%	Cropland irrigated:	3%
Large cities:	10	Developed:	1%
Total fish species:	164	Shrub:	11%
Fish endemics:	13	Grassland:	57%
Threatened fish species:	0	Barren:	25%
Endemic bird areas:	3	Loss of original forest:	96%
Ramsar sites:	6	Deforestation rate:	6%
Protected areas:	5%	Eroded area:	10%
Wetlands:	4%	Large dams:	6
Arid:	65%	Planned major dams:	1

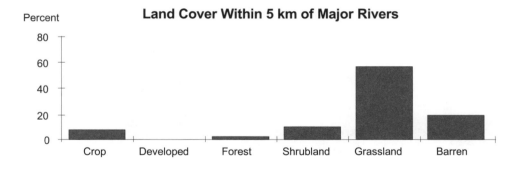

Land Cover Within 5 km of Major Rivers

2 - 22

© 1998 World Resources Institute

Nile Watershed

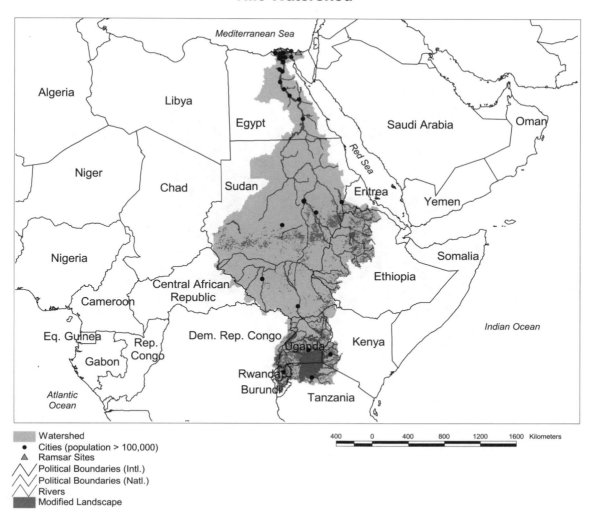

Watershed	
•	Cities (population > 100,000)
▲	Ramsar Sites
	Political Boundaries (Intl.)
	Political Boundaries (Natl.)
	Rivers
	Modified Landscape

Basin area:	3,254,555 km²	Forest:	2%
Population density:	44 people per km²	Cropland:	10%
Urban growth rate:	4.0%	Cropland irrigated:	5%
Large cities:	30	Developed:	1%
Total fish species:	129 (Nile River only)	Shrub:	4%
Fish endemics:	26 (Nile River only)	Grassland:	52%
Threatened fish species:	0 (Nile River only)	Barren:	30%
Endemic bird areas:	5	Loss of original forest:	91%
Ramsar sites:	2	Deforestation rate:	6%
Protected areas:	5%	Eroded area:	5%
Wetlands:	6%	Large dams:	7
Arid:	67%	Planned major dams:	-

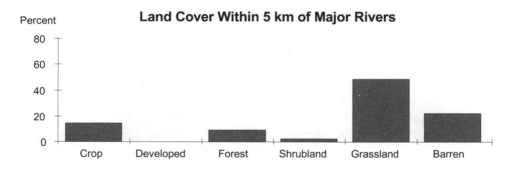

Land Cover Within 5 km of Major Rivers

© 1998 World Resources Institute

Nile Watershed: Lake Victoria Subbasin

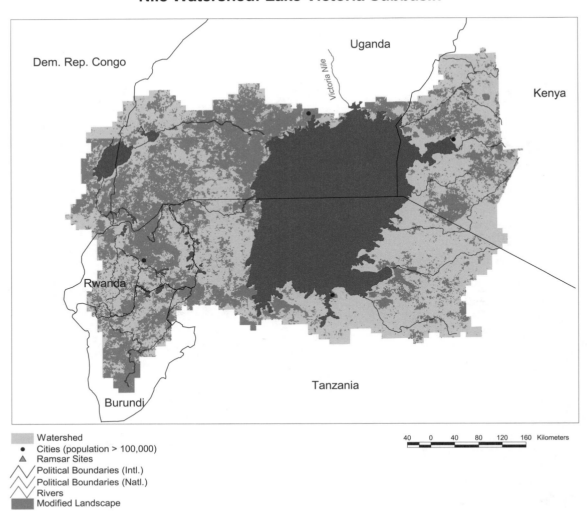

Dem. Rep. Congo

Uganda

Victoria Nile

Kenya

Rwanda

Tanzania

Burundi

- ░░ Watershed
- • Cities (population > 100,000)
- ▲ Ramsar Sites
- ∿ Political Boundaries (Intl.)
- ∿ Political Boundaries (Natl.)
- ∿ Rivers
- ▓ Modified Landscape

40 0 40 80 120 160 Kilometers

Basin area:	283,168 km²	Forest:	9%
Population density:	160 people per km²	Cropland:	40%
Urban growth rate:	4.7%	Cropland irrigated:	0%
Large cities:	4	Developed:	1%
Total fish species:	343 (intr: 5)	Shrub:	10%
Fish endemics:	309	Grassland:	37%
Threatened fish species:	26	Barren:	2%
Endemic bird areas:	4	Loss of original forest:	89%
Ramsar sites:	1	Deforestation rate:	7%
Protected areas:	17%	Eroded area:	8%
Wetlands:	31%	Large dams:	1
Arid:	26%	Planned major dams:	0

Land Cover Within 5 km of Major Rivers

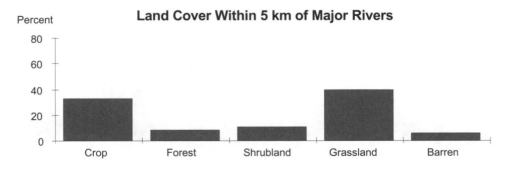

Percent

80

60

40

20

0

Crop   Forest   Shrubland   Grassland   Barren

2 - 24

© 1998 World Resources Institute

Ogooue Watershed

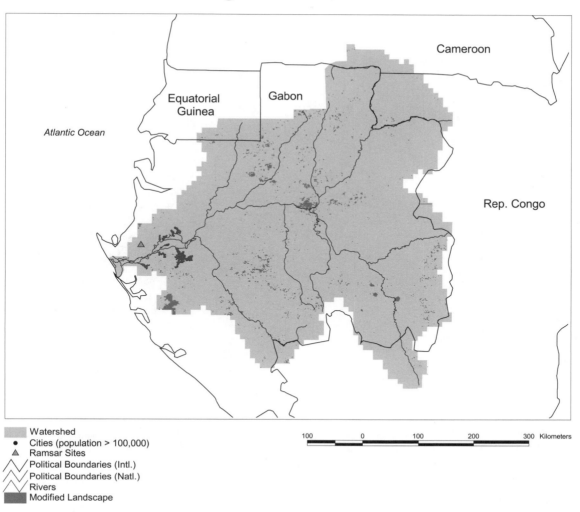

Watershed	
●	Cities (population > 100,000)
△	Ramsar Sites
	Political Boundaries (Intl.)
	Political Boundaries (Natl.)
	Rivers
	Modified Landscape

100   0   100   200   300 Kilometers

Basin area:	223,856 km²	Forest:	75%
Population density:	4 people per km²	Cropland:	2%
Urban growth rate:	-	Cropland irrigated:	0%
Large cities:	0	Developed:	< 1%
Total fish species:	-	Shrub:	0%
Fish endemics:	-	Grassland:	22%
Threatened fish species:	0	Barren:	0%
Endemic bird areas:	1	Loss of original forest:	9%
Ramsar sites:	1	Deforestation rate:	5%
Protected areas:	4%	Eroded area:	0%
Wetlands:	6%	Large dams:	0
Arid:	0%	Planned major dams:	-

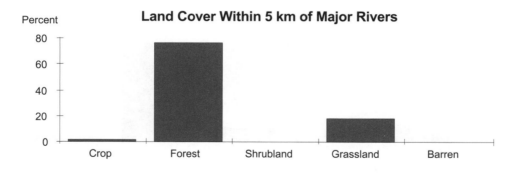

Land Cover Within 5 km of Major Rivers

2 - 25

© 1998 World Resources Institute

Okavango Swamp Watershed

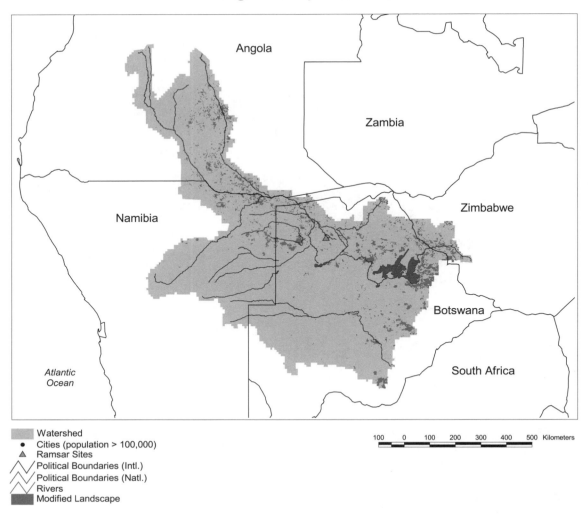

Watershed
● Cities (population > 100,000)
▲ Ramsar Sites
⋀ Political Boundaries (Intl.)
⋀ Political Boundaries (Natl.)
⋀ Rivers
■ Modified Landscape

Basin area:	721,277 km²	Forest:	2%
Population density:	3 people per km²	Cropland:	6%
Urban growth rate:	-	Cropland irrigated:	0%
Large cities:	0	Developed:	< 1%
Total fish species:	80 (intr: 1)	Shrub:	11%
Fish endemics:	0	Grassland:	80%
Threatened fish species:	0	Barren:	1%
Endemic bird areas:	1	Loss of original forest:	0%
Ramsar sites:	1	Deforestation rate:	5%
Protected areas:	12%	Eroded area:	3%
Wetlands:	4%	Large dams:	1
Arid:	76%	Planned major dams:	-

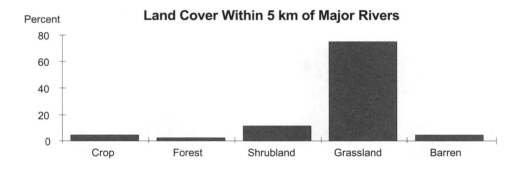

Land Cover Within 5 km of Major Rivers

© 1998 World Resources Institute

Okavango Swamp Watershed: Cubango Subbasin

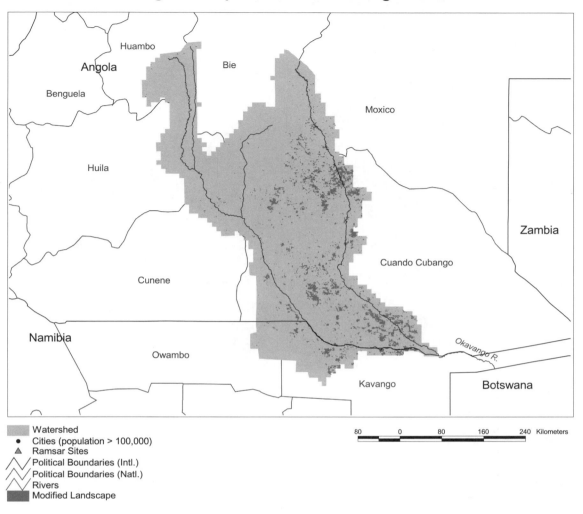

Huambo

Angola

Bie

Benguela

Moxico

Huila

Zambia

Cunene

Cuando Cubango

Namibia

Okavango R.

Owambo

Kavango

Botswana

Watershed
● Cities (population > 100,000)
▲ Ramsar Sites
Political Boundaries (Intl.)
Political Boundaries (Natl.)
Rivers
Modified Landscape

80   0   80   160   240 Kilometers

Basin area:	158,650 km²	Forest:	7%
Population density:	6 people per km²	Cropland:	6%
Urban growth rate:	-	Cropland irrigated:	0%
Large cities:	0	Developed:	< 1%
Total fish species:	63	Shrub:	0%
Fish endemics:	1	Grassland:	87%
Threatened fish species:	0	Barren:	0%
Endemic bird areas:	1	Loss of original forest:	0%
Ramsar sites:	0	Deforestation rate:	7%
Protected areas:	0%	Eroded area:	5%
Wetlands:	3%	Large dams:	1
Arid:	14%	Planned major dams:	-

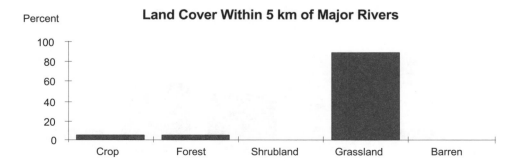

Percent

Land Cover Within 5 km of Major Rivers

100
80
60
40
20
0

Crop   Forest   Shrubland   Grassland   Barren

© 1998 World Resources Institute

Orange Watershed

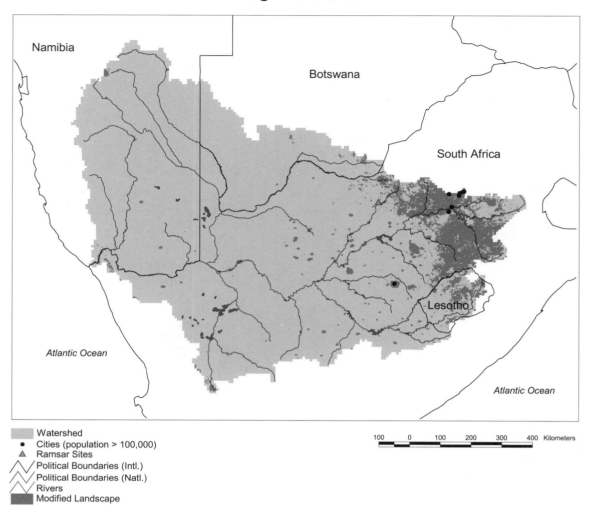

Watershed
● Cities (population > 100,000)
▲ Ramsar Sites
Political Boundaries (Intl.)
Political Boundaries (Natl.)
Rivers
Modified Landscape

100   0   100   200   300   400   Kilometers

Basin area:	941,421 km²	Forest:	0%
Population density:	12 people per km²	Cropland:	7%
Urban growth rate:	4.6%	Cropland irrigated:	0%
Large cities:	9	Developed:	2%
Total fish species:	24	Shrub:	43%
Fish endemics:	7	Grassland:	44%
Threatened fish species:	2	Barren:	6%
Endemic bird areas:	2	Loss of original forest:	100%
Ramsar sites:	1	Deforestation rate:	-
Protected areas:	5%	Eroded area:	21%
Wetlands:	1%	Large dams:	4
Arid:	77%	Planned major dams:	2

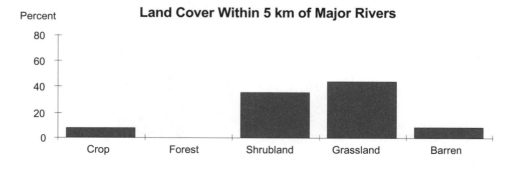

Land Cover Within 5 km of Major Rivers

Percent

© 1998 World Resources Institute

Oued Draa Watershed

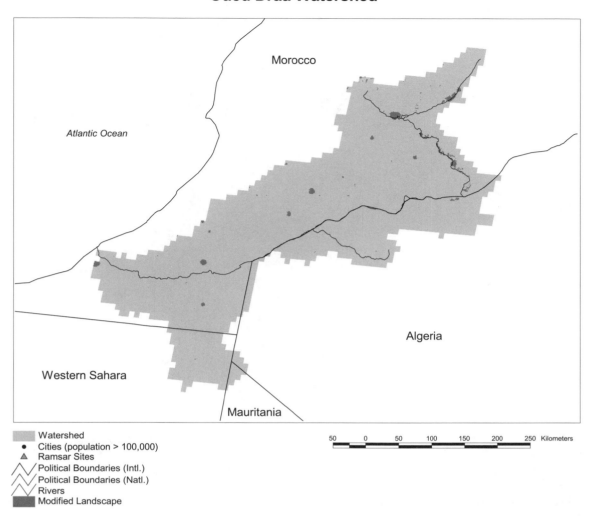

Morocco

Atlantic Ocean

Algeria

Western Sahara

Mauritania

	Watershed
●	Cities (population > 100,000)
▲	Ramsar Sites
/\/	Political Boundaries (Intl.)
/\/	Political Boundaries (Natl.)
/\/	Rivers
	Modified Landscape

50 0 50 100 150 200 250 Kilometers

Basin area:	114,569 km²	Forest:	0%
Population density:	11 people per km²	Cropland:	0%
Urban growth rate:	-	Cropland irrigated:	0%
Large cities:	0	Developed:	1%
Total fish species:	-	Shrub:	9%
Fish endemics:	-	Grassland:	3%
Threatened fish species:	0	Barren:	87%
Endemic bird areas:	0	Loss of original forest:	84%
Ramsar sites:	0	Deforestation rate:	-
Protected areas:	0%	Eroded area:	4%
Wetlands:	0%	Large dams:	0
Arid:	95%	Planned major dams:	-

Land Cover Within 5 km of Major Rivers

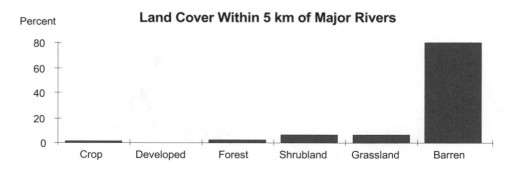

Percent

2 - 29

© 1998 World Resources Institute

Senegal Watershed

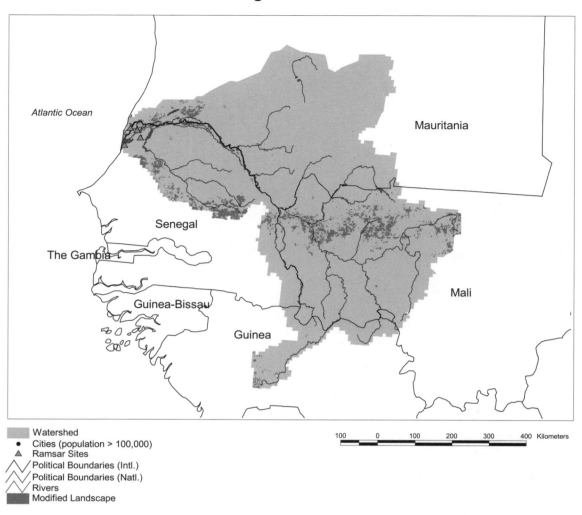

Watershed	
●	Cities (population > 100,000)
▲	Ramsar Sites
	Political Boundaries (Intl.)
	Political Boundaries (Natl.)
	Rivers
	Modified Landscape

100 0 100 200 300 400 Kilometers

Basin area:	419,659 km²	Forest:	0%
Population density:	12 people per km²	Cropland:	5%
Urban growth rate:	-	Cropland irrigated:	0%
Large cities:	0	Developed:	< 1%
Total fish species:	115	Shrub:	10%
Fish endemics:	26	Grassland:	59%
Threatened fish species:	0	Barren:	25%
Endemic bird areas:	0	Loss of original forest:	100%
Ramsar sites:	4	Deforestation rate:	5%
Protected areas:	6%	Eroded area:	1%
Wetlands:	4%	Large dams:	1
Arid:	82%	Planned major dams:	-

Land Cover Within 5 km of Major Rivers

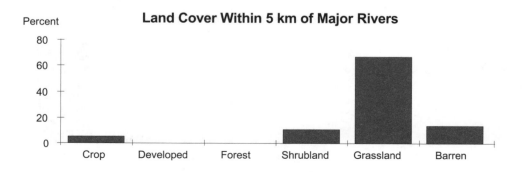

© 1998 World Resources Institute

Shaballe Watershed

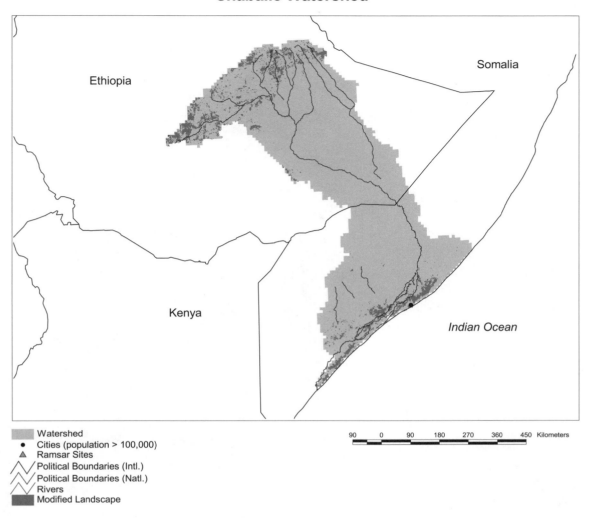

90	0	90	180	270	360	450 Kilometers

Legend:
- Watershed
- ● Cities (population > 100,000)
- ▲ Ramsar Sites
- Political Boundaries (Intl.)
- Political Boundaries (Natl.)
- Rivers
- Modified Landscape

Basin area:	336,627 km²	Forest:	1%
Population density:	28 people per km²	Cropland:	6%
Urban growth rate:	5.0%	Cropland irrigated:	0%
Large cities:	1	Developed:	< 1%
Total fish species:	27	Shrub:	73%
Fish endemics:	0	Grassland:	16%
Threatened fish species:	0	Barren:	4%
Endemic bird areas:	3	Loss of original forest:	88%
Ramsar sites:	0	Deforestation rate:	1%
Protected areas:	1%	Eroded area:	9%
Wetlands:	2%	Large dams:	0
Arid:	81%	Planned major dams:	-

Land Cover Within 5 km of Major Rivers

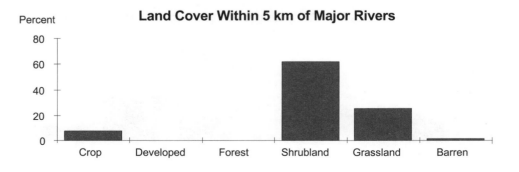

© 1998 World Resources Institute

Lake Turkana Watershed

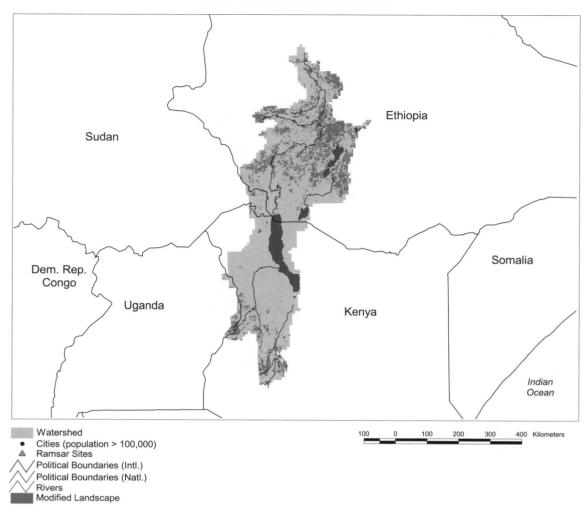

Watershed
• Cities (population > 100,000)
▲ Ramsar Sites
〜 Political Boundaries (Intl.)
〜 Political Boundaries (Natl.)
〜 Rivers
■ Modified Landscape

100 0 100 200 300 400 Kilometers

Basin area:	209,157 km²	Forest:	12%
Population density:	59 people per km²	Cropland:	20%
Urban growth rate:	-	Cropland irrigated:	0%
Large cities:	0	Developed:	< 1%
Total fish species:	47 (intr: 0)	Shrub:	26%
Fish endemics:	17	Grassland:	28%
Threatened fish species:	0	Barren:	13%
Endemic bird areas:	3	Loss of original forest:	60%
Ramsar sites:	0	Deforestation rate:	3%
Protected areas:	9%	Eroded area:	11%
Wetlands:	6%	Large dams:	1
Arid:	33%	Planned major dams:	-

Percent

Land Cover Within 5 km of Major Rivers

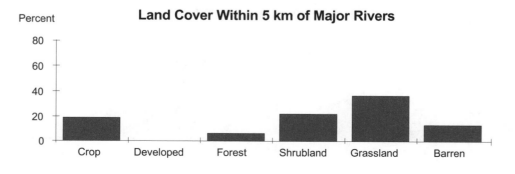

© 1998 World Resources Institute

Volta Watershed

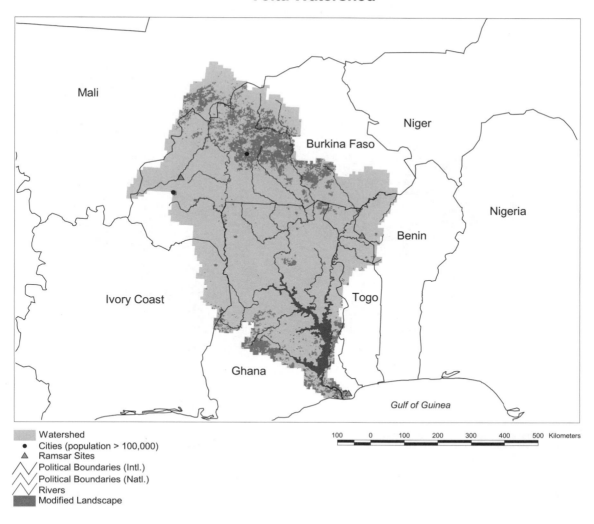

Watershed
- Cities (population > 100,000)
▲ Ramsar Sites
Political Boundaries (Intl.)
Political Boundaries (Natl.)
Rivers
Modified Landscape

Basin area:	407,097 km²	Forest:	0%
Population density:	42 people per km²	Cropland:	11%
Urban growth rate:	6.3%	Cropland irrigated:	0%
Large cities:	2	Developed:	1%
Total fish species:	141	Shrub:	0%
Fish endemics:	8	Grassland:	85%
Threatened fish species:	0	Barren:	1%
Endemic bird areas:	1	Loss of original forest:	97%
Ramsar sites:	3	Deforestation rate:	10%
Protected areas:	8%	Eroded area:	19%
Wetlands:	5%	Large dams:	2
Arid:	60%	Planned major dams:	-

Land Cover Within 5 km of Major Rivers

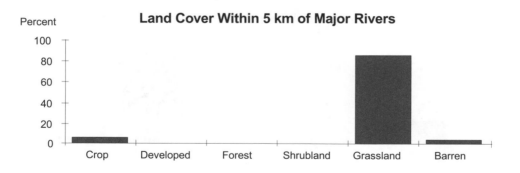

2 - 33

© 1998 World Resources Institute

Zambezi Watershed

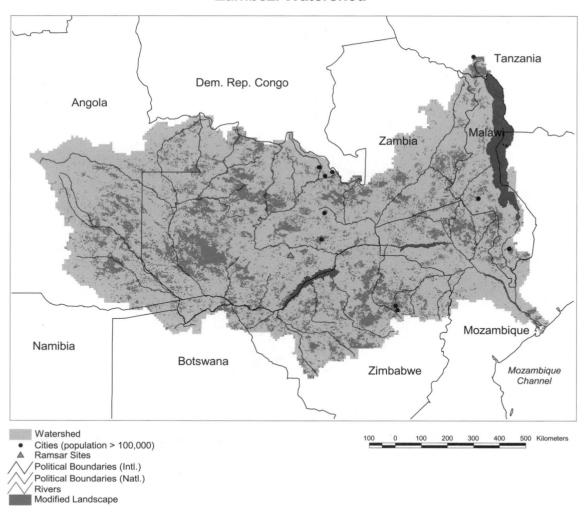

Watershed
● Cities (population > 100,000)
▲ Ramsar Sites
〰 Political Boundaries (Intl.)
〰 Political Boundaries (Natl.)
〰 Rivers
▨ Modified Landscape

100   0   100   200   300   400   500 Kilometers

Basin area:	1,332,574 km²		Forest:	4%
Population density:	18 people per km²		Cropland:	20%
Urban growth rate:	5.0%		Cropland irrigated:	0%
Large cities:	10		Developed:	1%
Total fish species:	122 (intr: 7)		Shrub:	0%
Fish endemics:	25		Grassland:	74%
Threatened fish species:	1		Barren:	1%
Endemic bird areas:	3		Loss of original forest:	43%
Ramsar sites:	1		Deforestation rate:	9%
Protected areas:	8%		Eroded area:	2%
Wetlands:	8%		Large dams:	6
Arid:	9%		Planned major dams:	-

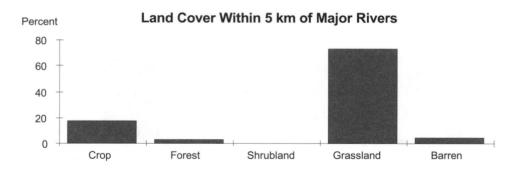

Land Cover Within 5 km of Major Rivers

Percent

© 1998 World Resources Institute

WATERSHED PROFILES

FOR

EUROPE

Dalalven Watershed

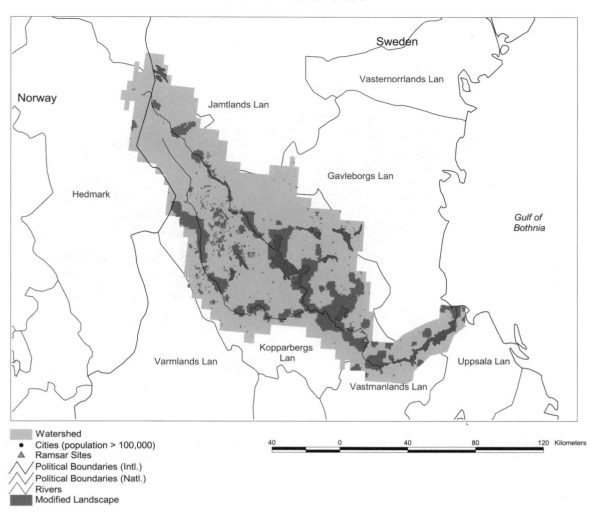

Watershed
● Cities (population > 100,000)
▲ Ramsar Sites
Political Boundaries (Intl.)
Political Boundaries (Natl.)
Rivers
Modified Landscape

Basin area:	28,106 km²	Forest:	70%
Population density:	8 people per km²	Cropland:	3%
Urban growth rate:	-	Cropland irrigated:	0%
Large cities:	0	Developed:	18%
Total fish species:	41 (intr: 3 diad: 9)	Shrub:	1%
Fish endemics:	0	Grassland:	1%
Threatened fish species:	0	Barren:	0%
Endemic bird areas:	0	Loss of original forest:	4%
Ramsar sites:	1	Deforestation rate:	-
Protected areas:	8%	Eroded area:	0%
Wetlands:	20%	Large dams:	0
Arid:	0%	Planned major dams:	-

Land Cover Within 5 km of Major Rivers

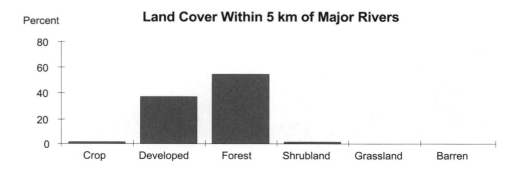

© 1998 World Resources Institute

Danube Watershed

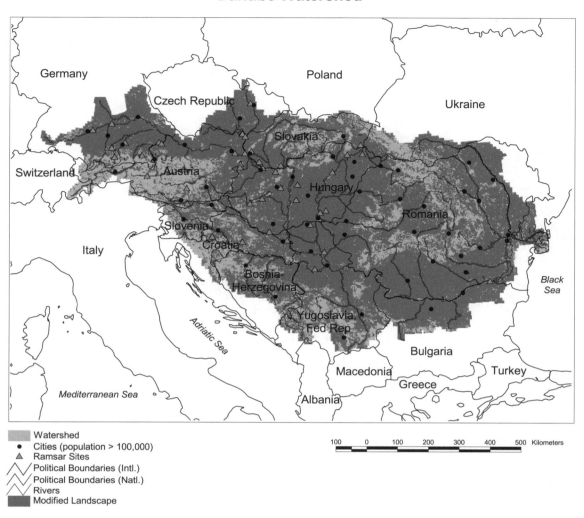

Watershed
• Cities (population > 100,000)
▲ Ramsar Sites
Political Boundaries (Intl.)
Political Boundaries (Natl.)
Rivers
Modified Landscape

Basin area:	795,686 km²	Forest:	20%
Population density:	103 people per km²	Cropland:	67%
Urban growth rate:	0.5%	Cropland irrigated:	0%
Large cities:	60	Developed:	11%
Total fish species:	103 (intr: 13 diad: 9)	Shrub:	0%
Fish endemics:	7	Grassland:	1%
Threatened fish species:	18	Barren:	0%
Endemic bird areas:	0	Loss of original forest:	63%
Ramsar sites:	47	Deforestation rate:	-
Protected areas:	7%	Eroded area:	18%
Wetlands:	1%	Large dams:	11
Arid:	3%	Planned major dams:	1

Land Cover Within 5 km of Major Rivers

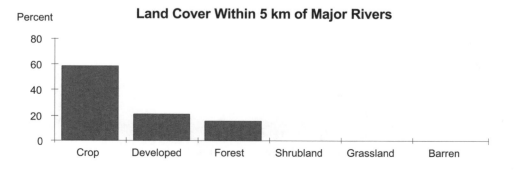

© 1998 World Resources Institute

Daugava Watershed

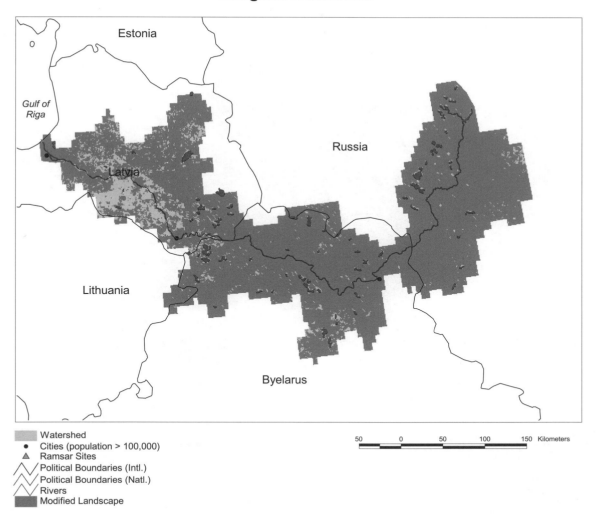

Watershed
● Cities (population > 100,000)
▲ Ramsar Sites
〰 Political Boundaries (Intl.)
〰 Political Boundaries (Natl.)
〰 Rivers
▓ Modified Landscape

Basin area:	79,406 km²	
Population density:	33 people per km²	
Urban growth rate:	0.0%	
Large cities:	3	
Total fish species:	50 (intr: 6 diad: 8)	
Fish endemics:	0	
Threatened fish species:	1	
Endemic bird areas:	0	
Ramsar sites:	0	
Protected areas:	5%	
Wetlands:	3%	
Arid:	0%	

Forest:	7%
Cropland:	84%
Cropland irrigated:	0%
Developed:	7%
Shrub:	0%
Grassland:	0%
Barren:	0%
Loss of original forest:	78%
Deforestation rate:	-
Eroded area:	4%
Large dams:	0
Planned major dams:	-

Land Cover Within 5 km of Major Rivers

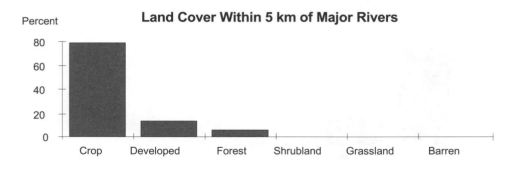

Percent

2 - 39

© 1998 World Resources Institute

Dnieper Watershed

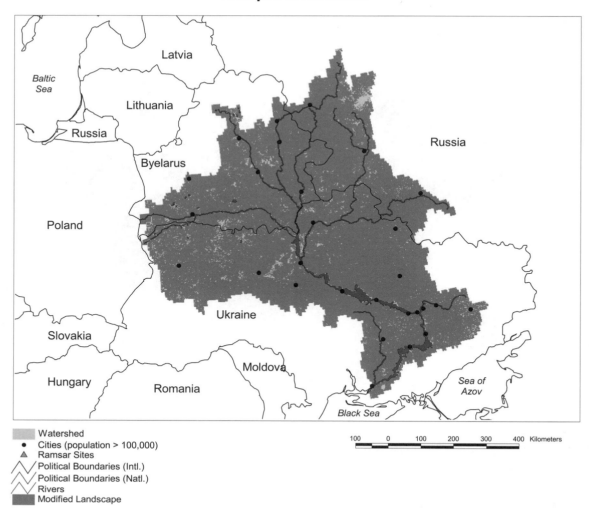

Watershed	
●	Cities (population > 100,000)
▲	Ramsar Sites
⋀⋁	Political Boundaries (Intl.)
⋀⋁	Political Boundaries (Natl.)
⋀⋁	Rivers
	Modified Landscape

100   0   100   200   300   400 Kilometers

Basin area:	531,817 km²	Forest:	3%
Population density:	67 people per km²	Cropland:	85%
Urban growth rate:	0.4%	Cropland irrigated:	0%
Large cities:	28	Developed:	10%
Total fish species:	50 (intr: 3 diad: 5)	Shrub:	0%
Fish endemics:	1	Grassland:	0%
Threatened fish species:	7	Barren:	0%
Endemic bird areas:	0	Loss of original forest:	78%
Ramsar sites:	0	Deforestation rate:	-
Protected areas:	2%	Eroded area:	8%
Wetlands:	6%	Large dams:	6
Arid:	3%	Planned major dams:	1

Land Cover Within 5 km of Major Rivers

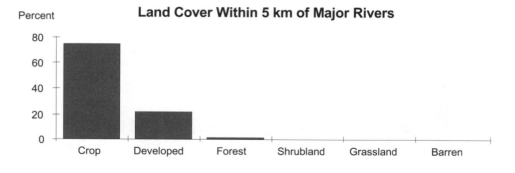

© 1998 World Resources Institute

Dnieper Watershed: Desna Subbasin

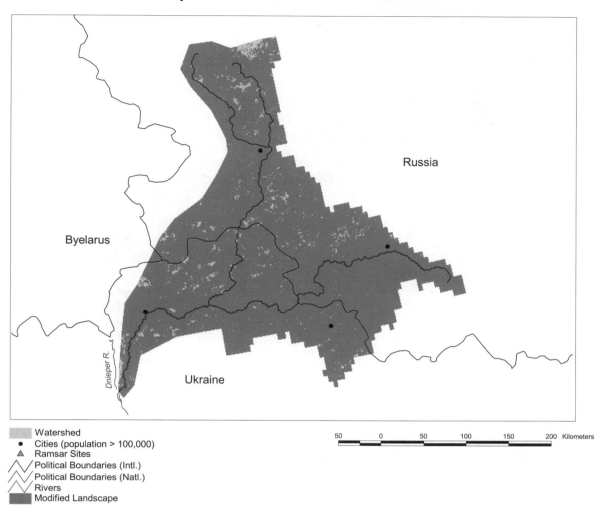

Russia

Byelarus

Dnieper R.

Ukraine

▨	Watershed
●	Cities (population > 100,000)
▲	Ramsar Sites
◇	Political Boundaries (Intl.)
◇	Political Boundaries (Natl.)
◇	Rivers
▨	Modified Landscape

50   0   50   100   150   200   Kilometers

Basin area: 97,293 km²

Basin area:	97,293 km²	Forest:	3%
Population density:	48 people per km²	Cropland:	88%
Urban growth rate:	-	Cropland irrigated:	0%
Large cities:	4	Developed:	9%
Total fish species:	40 (intr: 3 diad: 0)	Shrub:	0%
Fish endemics:	0	Grassland:	0%
Threatened fish species:	0	Barren:	0%
Endemic bird areas:	0	Loss of original forest:	87%
Ramsar sites:	0	Deforestation rate:	-
Protected areas:	1%	Eroded area:	14%
Wetlands:	6%	Large dams:	0
Arid:	0%	Planned major dams:	-

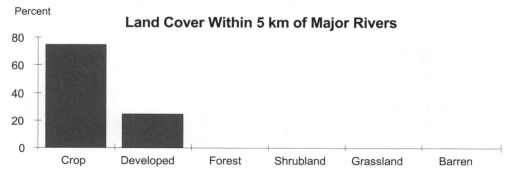

Land Cover Within 5 km of Major Rivers

Percent

Crop   Developed   Forest   Shrubland   Grassland   Barren

© 1998 World Resources Institute

Dniester Watershed

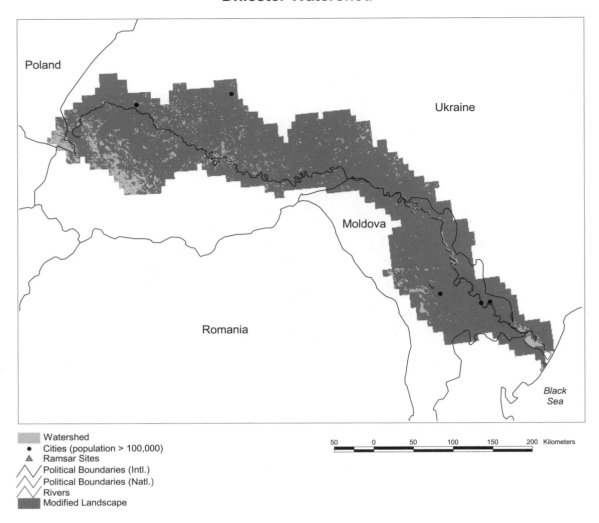

Basin area:	68,634 km²	Forest:	7%
Population density:	105 people per km²	Cropland:	82%
Urban growth rate:	1.6%	Cropland irrigated:	0%
Large cities:	5	Developed:	10%
Total fish species:	57 (intr: 5 diad: 6)	Shrub:	0%
Fish endemics:	0	Grassland:	0%
Threatened fish species:	9	Barren:	0%
Endemic bird areas:	0	Loss of original forest:	85%
Ramsar sites:	0	Deforestation rate:	-
Protected areas:	1%	Eroded area:	29%
Wetlands:	1%	Large dams:	1
Arid:	6%	Planned major dams:	-

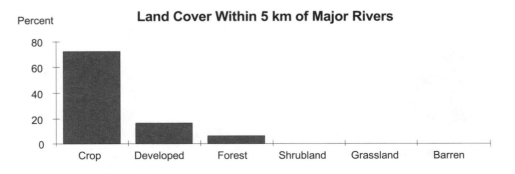

Land Cover Within 5 km of Major Rivers

© 1998 World Resources Institute

Don Watershed

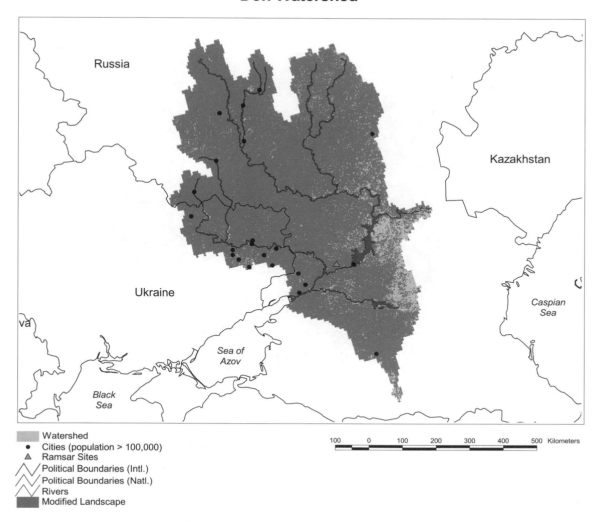

Watershed
● Cities (population > 100,000)
▲ Ramsar Sites
⋀⋁ Political Boundaries (Intl.)
⋀⋁ Political Boundaries (Natl.)
⋁ Rivers
▬ Modified Landscape

Basin area:	458,703 km²	Forest:	2%
Population density:	48 people per km²	Cropland:	83%
Urban growth rate:	0.1%	Cropland irrigated:	0%
Large cities:	22	Developed:	9%
Total fish species:	49 (intr: 2 diad: 5)	Shrub:	0%
Fish endemics:	0	Grassland:	5%
Threatened fish species:	1	Barren:	0%
Endemic bird areas:	1	Loss of original forest:	76%
Ramsar sites:	1	Deforestation rate:	-
Protected areas:	0%	Eroded area:	8%
Wetlands:	1%	Large dams:	2
Arid:	33%	Planned major dams:	-

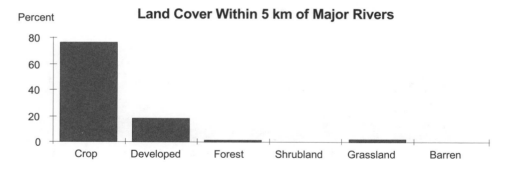

Land Cover Within 5 km of Major Rivers

© 1998 World Resources Institute

Ebro Watershed

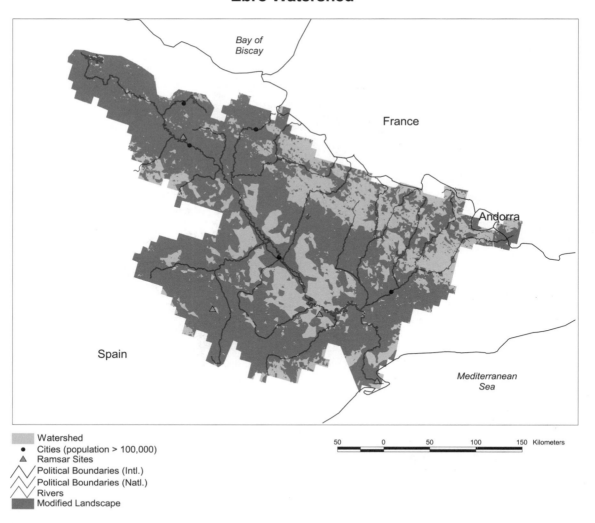

Watershed
● Cities (population > 100,000)
▲ Ramsar Sites
Political Boundaries (Intl.)
Political Boundaries (Natl.)
Rivers
Modified Landscape

Basin area:	82,593 km²	Forest:	10%
Population density:	38 people per km²	Cropland:	57%
Urban growth rate:	-	Cropland irrigated:	0%
Large cities:	5	Developed:	16%
Total fish species:	31 (intr: 6 diad: 6)	Shrub:	14%
Fish endemics:	0	Grassland:	2%
Threatened fish species:	3	Barren:	0%
Endemic bird areas:	0	Loss of original forest:	85%
Ramsar sites:	4	Deforestation rate:	-
Protected areas:	8%	Eroded area:	8%
Wetlands:	1%	Large dams:	1
Arid:	40%	Planned major dams:	-

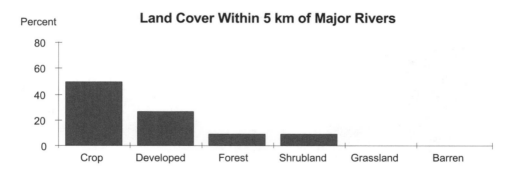

Land Cover Within 5 km of Major Rivers

Percent

2 - 44

© 1998 World Resources Institute

Elbe Watershed

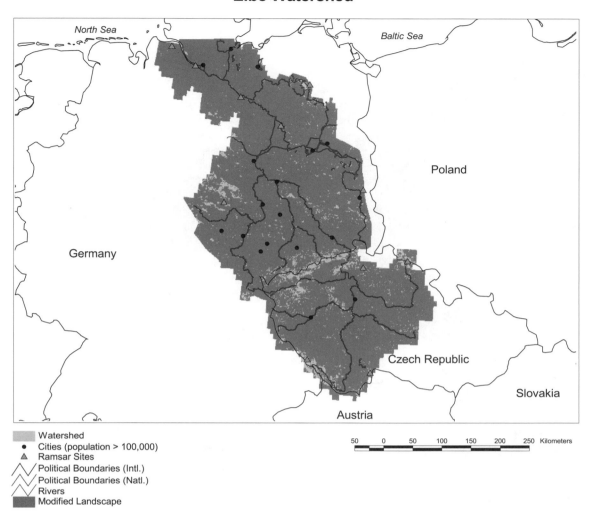

Watershed
● Cities (population > 100,000)
▲ Ramsar Sites
Political Boundaries (Intl.)
Political Boundaries (Natl.)
Rivers
Modified Landscape

Basin area:	149,002 km²	Forest:	5%
Population density:	164 people per km²	Cropland:	74%
Urban growth rate:	0.2%	Cropland irrigated:	0%
Large cities:	18	Developed:	21%
Total fish species:	51 (intr: 9 diad: 9)	Shrub:	0%
Fish endemics:	0	Grassland:	0%
Threatened fish species:	1	Barren:	0%
Endemic bird areas:	0	Loss of original forest:	75%
Ramsar sites:	11	Deforestation rate:	-
Protected areas:	13%	Eroded area:	4%
Wetlands:	2%	Large dams:	4
Arid:	0%	Planned major dams:	-

Land Cover Within 5 km of Major Rivers

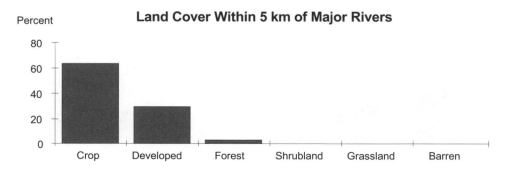

© 1998 World Resources Institute

Garonne Watershed

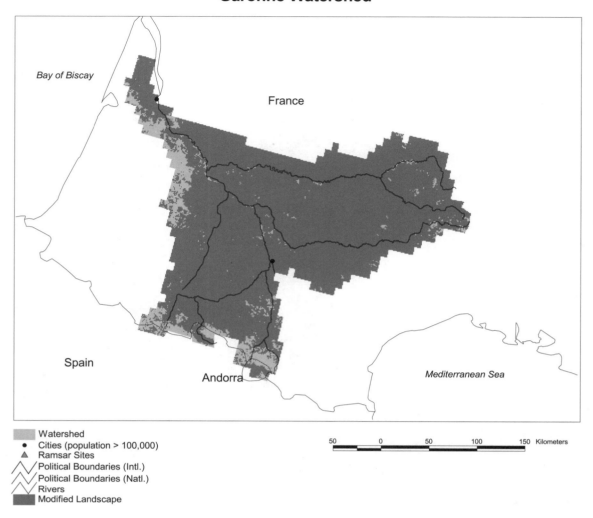

Watershed
● Cities (population > 100,000)
▲ Ramsar Sites
〰 Political Boundaries (Intl.)
〰 Political Boundaries (Natl.)
〰 Rivers
▓ Modified Landscape

50   0   50   100   150 Kilometers

Basin area:	53,536 km²	
Population density:	56 people per km²	
Urban growth rate:	-	
Large cities:	2	
Total fish species:	40 (intr: 6 diad: 9)	
Fish endemics:	0	
Threatened fish species:	1	
Endemic bird areas:	0	
Ramsar sites:	0	
Protected areas:	7%	
Wetlands:	0%	
Arid:	0%	

Forest:	7%
Cropland:	75%
Cropland irrigated:	0%
Developed:	16%
Shrub:	1%
Grassland:	1%
Barren:	0%
Loss of original forest:	85%
Deforestation rate:	-
Eroded area:	1%
Large dams:	0
Planned major dams:	-

Land Cover Within 5 km of Major Rivers

Percent

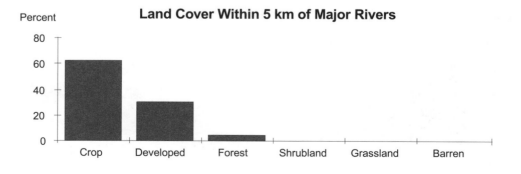

2 - 46

© 1998 World Resources Institute

Glama Watershed

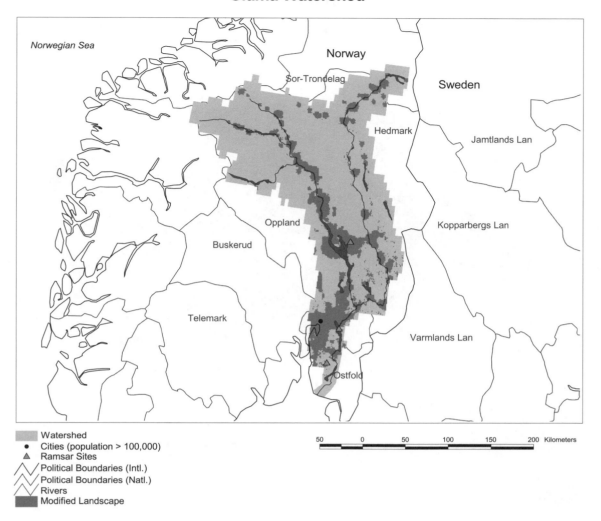

Watershed	
●	Cities (population > 100,000)
△	Ramsar Sites
	Political Boundaries (Intl.)
	Political Boundaries (Natl.)
	Rivers
	Modified Landscape

50 0 50 100 150 200 Kilometers

Basin area:	41,802 km²	Forest:	51%
Population density:	26 people per km²	Cropland:	1%
Urban growth rate:	-	Cropland irrigated:	0%
Large cities:	1	Developed:	19%
Total fish species:	31 (diad: 8)	Shrub:	18%
Fish endemics:	0	Grassland:	3%
Threatened fish species:	0	Barren:	1%
Endemic bird areas:	0	Loss of original forest:	6%
Ramsar sites:	3	Deforestation rate:	-
Protected areas:	4%	Eroded area:	0%
Wetlands:	2%	Large dams:	0
Arid:	0%	Planned major dams:	-

Land Cover Within 5 km of Major Rivers

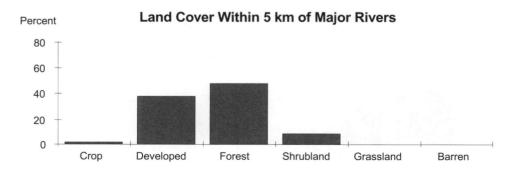

2 - 47

© 1998 World Resources Institute

Guadalquivir Watershed

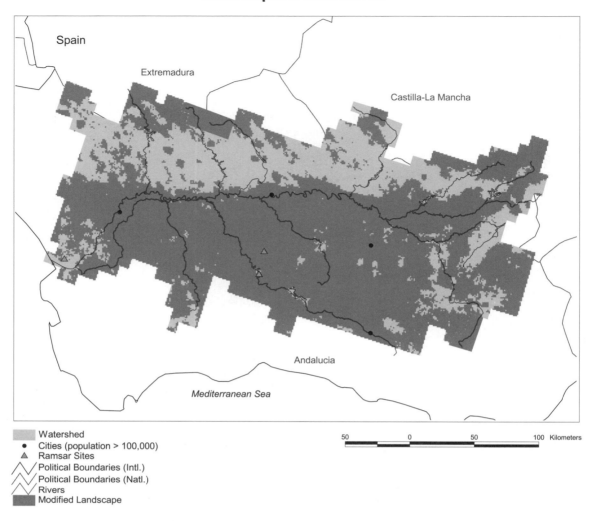

Watershed
● Cities (population > 100,000)
▲ Ramsar Sites
Political Boundaries (Intl.)
Political Boundaries (Natl.)
Rivers
Modified Landscape

Basin area:	52,664 km²		Forest:	3%
Population density:	68 people per km²		Cropland:	50%
Urban growth rate:	-		Cropland irrigated:	0%
Large cities:	4		Developed:	23%
Total fish species:	29 (intr: 6 diad: 6)		Shrub:	20%
Fish endemics:	1		Grassland:	4%
Threatened fish species:	5		Barren:	0%
Endemic bird areas:	0		Loss of original forest:	96%
Ramsar sites:	3		Deforestation rate:	-
Protected areas:	14%		Eroded area:	18%
Wetlands:	3%		Large dams:	0
Arid:	35%		Planned major dams:	-

Land Cover Within 5 km of Major Rivers

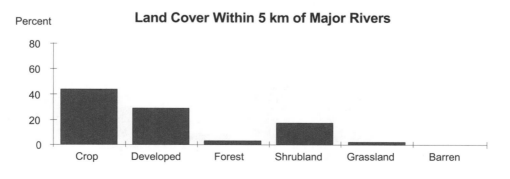

2 - 48

© 1998 World Resources Institute

Kemijoki Watershed

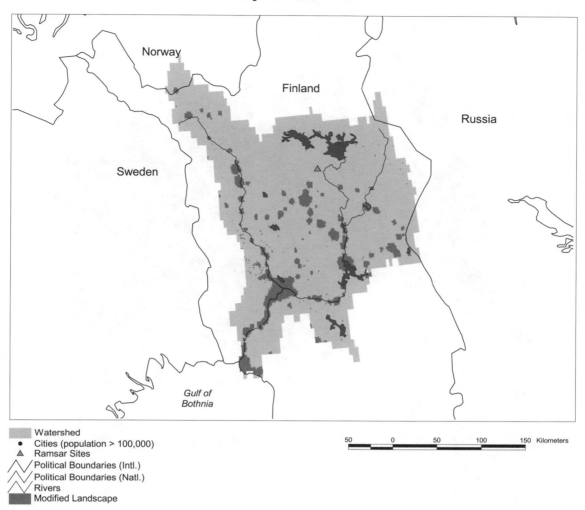

- ▨ Watershed
- ● Cities (population > 100,000)
- ▲ Ramsar Sites
- ⋀ Political Boundaries (Intl.)
- ⋀ Political Boundaries (Natl.)
- ⋀ Rivers
- ▨ Modified Landscape

Basin area:	52,452 km²	Forest:	76%
Population density:	2 people per km²	Cropland:	0%
Urban growth rate:	-	Cropland irrigated:	0%
Large cities:	0	Developed:	9%
Total fish species:	31 (intr: 4 diad: 3)	Shrub:	11%
Fish endemics:	0	Grassland:	1%
Threatened fish species:	0	Barren:	0%
Endemic bird areas:	0	Loss of original forest:	3%
Ramsar sites:	1	Deforestation rate:	-
Protected areas:	7%	Eroded area:	0%
Wetlands:	3%	Large dams:	3
Arid:	0%	Planned major dams:	-

Land Cover Within 5 km of Major Rivers

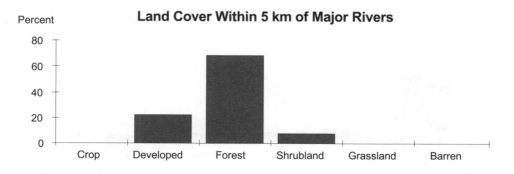

© 1998 World Resources Institute

Kura-Araks Watershed

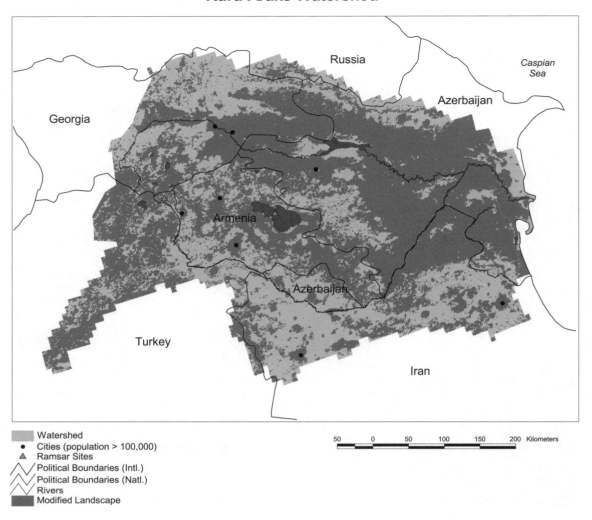

Watershed
● Cities (population > 100,000)
▲ Ramsar Sites
〜 Political Boundaries (Intl.)
〜 Political Boundaries (Natl.)
〜 Rivers
▨ Modified Landscape

| 50 | 0 | 50 | 100 | 150 | 200 | Kilometers |

Basin area:	205,040 km²		Forest:	13%
Population density:	72 people per km²		Cropland:	54%
Urban growth rate:	0.7%		Cropland irrigated:	6%
Large cities:	8		Developed:	7%
Total fish species:	47		Shrub:	6%
Fish endemics:	0		Grassland:	19%
Threatened fish species:	0		Barren:	0%
Endemic bird areas:	1		Loss of original forest:	80%
Ramsar sites:	2		Deforestation rate:	-
Protected areas:	4%		Eroded area:	10%
Wetlands:	1%		Large dams:	3
Arid:	25%		Planned major dams:	2

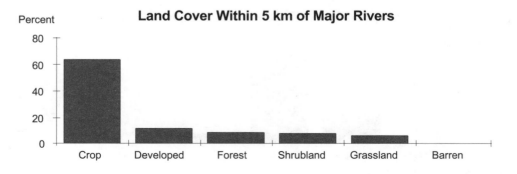

Land Cover Within 5 km of Major Rivers

Percent

© 1998 World Resources Institute

Loire Watershed

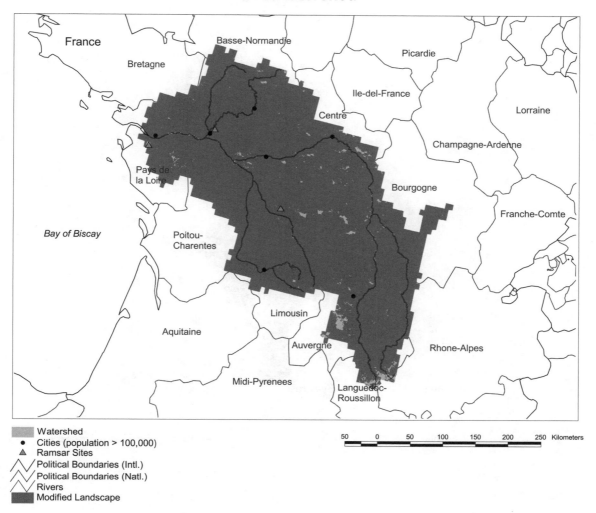

Watershed

● Cities (population > 100,000)

▲ Ramsar Sites

∧ Political Boundaries (Intl.)

∧ Political Boundaries (Natl.)

∧ Rivers

■ Modified Landscape

Basin area:	115,271 km²	Forest:	2%
Population density:	66 people per km²	Cropland:	82%
Urban growth rate:	-	Cropland irrigated:	0%
Large cities:	7	Developed:	16%
Total fish species:	43 (intr: 9 diad: 7)	Shrub:	0%
Fish endemics:	0	Grassland:	0%
Threatened fish species:	1	Barren:	0%
Endemic bird areas:	0	Loss of original forest:	89%
Ramsar sites:	3	Deforestation rate:	-
Protected areas:	10%	Eroded area:	0%
Wetlands:	1%	Large dams:	0
Arid:	0%	Planned major dams:	-

Land Cover Within 5 km of Major Rivers

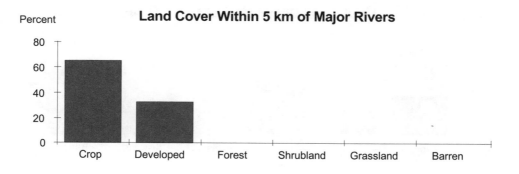

Percent

© 1998 World Resources Institute

Neva Watershed

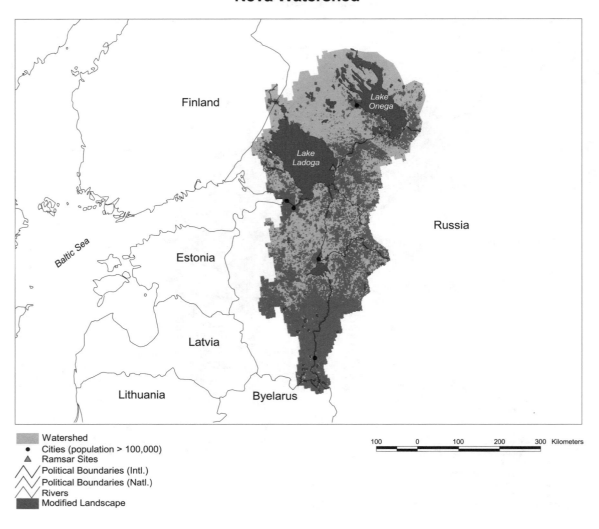

Watershed	
●	Cities (population > 100,000)
△	Ramsar Sites
	Political Boundaries (Intl.)
	Political Boundaries (Natl.)
	Rivers
	Modified Landscape

100 0 100 200 300 Kilometers

Basin area:	204,467 km²	Forest:	46%
Population density:	35 people per km²	Cropland:	41%
Urban growth rate:	-	Cropland irrigated:	0%
Large cities:	5	Developed:	10%
Total fish species:	40	Shrub:	0%
Fish endemics:	-	Grassland:	0%
Threatened fish species:	0	Barren:	0%
Endemic bird areas:	0	Loss of original forest:	41%
Ramsar sites:	2	Deforestation rate:	-
Protected areas:	1%	Eroded area:	3%
Wetlands:	22%	Large dams:	3
Arid:	0%	Planned major dams:	-

Land Cover Within 5 km of Major Rivers

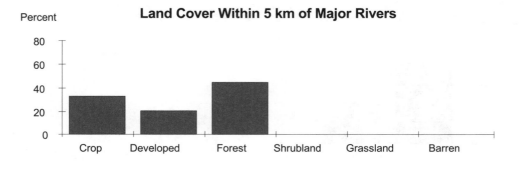

2 - 52

© 1998 World Resources Institute

North Dvina Watershed

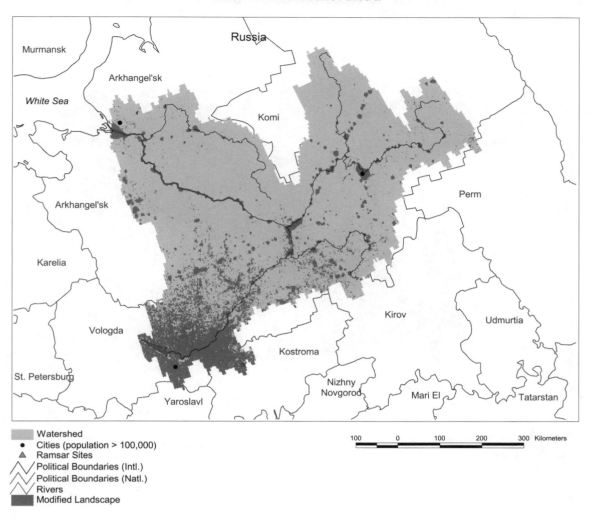

Watershed			
● Cities (population > 100,000)			
▲ Ramsar Sites			
Political Boundaries (Intl.)			
Political Boundaries (Natl.)			
Rivers			
Modified Landscape			

100   0   100   200   300 Kilometers

Basin area:	357,052 km²		Forest:	82%
Population density:	5 people per km²		Cropland:	11%
Urban growth rate:	-		Cropland irrigated:	0%
Large cities:	3		Developed:	5%
Total fish species:	33 (intr: 0 diad: 7)		Shrub:	0%
Fish endemics:	0		Grassland:	0%
Threatened fish species:	0		Barren:	0%
Endemic bird areas:	0		Loss of original forest:	15%
Ramsar sites:	0		Deforestation rate:	-
Protected areas:	0%		Eroded area:	4%
Wetlands:	2%		Large dams:	1
Arid:	0%		Planned major dams:	-

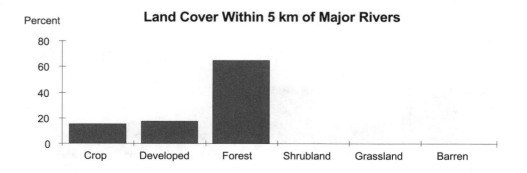

Land Cover Within 5 km of Major Rivers

Percent

2 - 53

© 1998 World Resources Institute

North Dvina Watershed: Sukhona Subbasin

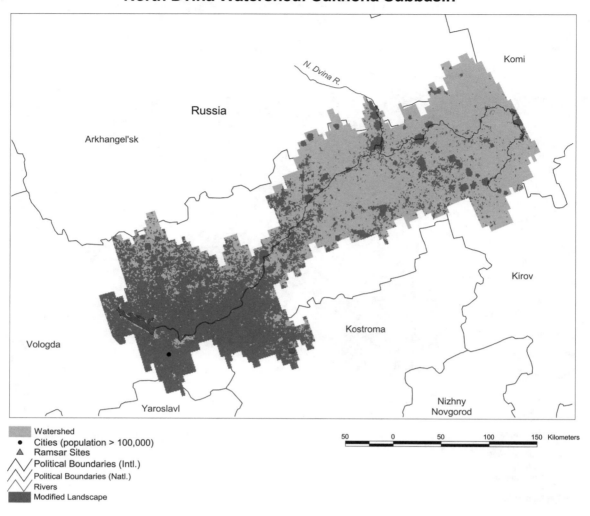

Legend:
- Watershed
- • Cities (population > 100,000)
- ▲ Ramsar Sites
- Political Boundaries (Intl.)
- Political Boundaries (Natl.)
- Rivers
- Modified Landscape

Basin area:	91,160 km²	Forest:	55%
Population density:	11 people per km²	Cropland:	37%
Urban growth rate:	-	Cropland irrigated:	0%
Large cities:	1	Developed:	6%
Total fish species:	29 (intr: 2 diad: 4)	Shrub:	0%
Fish endemics:	0	Grassland:	0%
Threatened fish species:	0	Barren:	0%
Endemic bird areas:	0	Loss of original forest:	35%
Ramsar sites:	0	Deforestation rate:	-
Protected areas:	0%	Eroded area:	7%
Wetlands:	1%	Large dams:	1
Arid:	0%	Planned major dams:	-

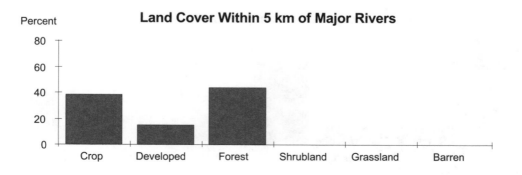

Land Cover Within 5 km of Major Rivers

Percent

Crop, Developed, Forest, Shrubland, Grassland, Barren

© 1998 World Resources Institute

North Dvina Watershed: Vychegda Subbasin

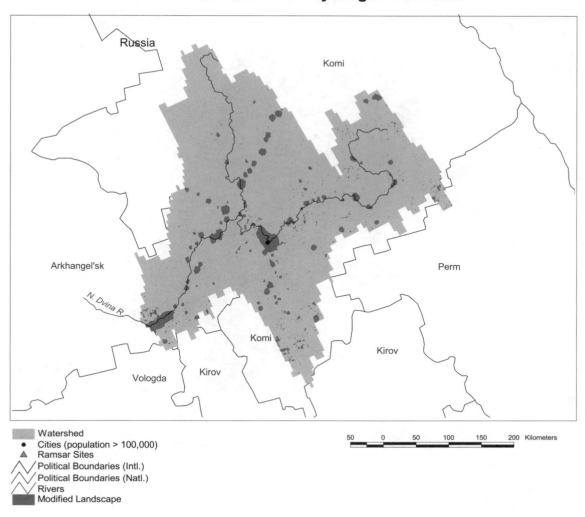

Watershed	
●	Cities (population > 100,000)
▲	Ramsar Sites
	Political Boundaries (Intl.)
	Political Boundaries (Natl.)
	Rivers
	Modified Landscape

50 0 50 100 150 200 Kilometers

Basin area:	122,053 km²	Forest:	93%
Population density:	3 people per km²	Cropland:	1%
Urban growth rate:	-	Cropland irrigated:	2%
Large cities:	1	Developed:	5%
Total fish species:	28 (intr: 1 diad: 4)	Shrub:	0%
Fish endemics:	0	Grassland:	0%
Threatened fish species:	0	Barren:	0%
Endemic bird areas:	0	Loss of original forest:	7%
Ramsar sites:	0	Deforestation rate:	-
Protected areas:	0%	Eroded area:	6%
Wetlands:	1%	Large dams:	0
Arid:	0%	Planned major dams:	-

Land Cover Within 5 km of Major Rivers

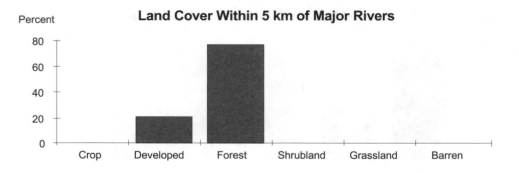

2 - 55

© 1998 World Resources Institute

Oder Watershed

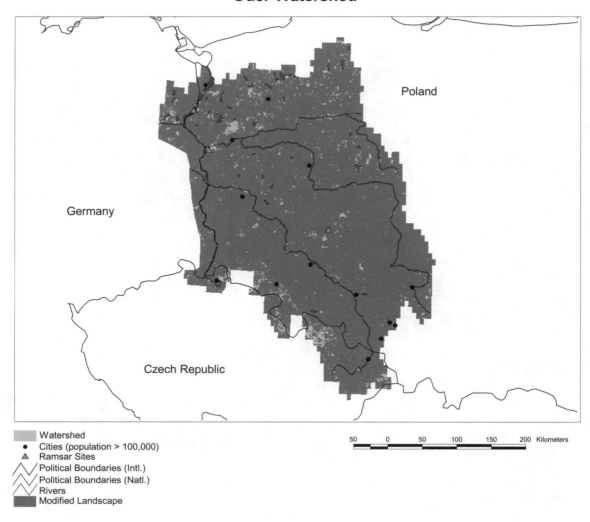

Watershed	
●	Cities (population > 100,000)
▲	Ramsar Sites
	Political Boundaries (Intl.)
	Political Boundaries (Natl.)
	Rivers
	Modified Landscape

50 0 50 100 150 200 Kilometers

Basin area:	124,123 km²	Forest:	3%
Population density:	117 people per km²	Cropland:	79%
Urban growth rate:	-	Cropland irrigated:	0%
Large cities:	14	Developed:	17%
Total fish species:	44 (intr: 9 diad: 9)	Shrub:	0%
Fish endemics:	0	Grassland:	0%
Threatened fish species:	1	Barren:	0%
Endemic bird areas:	0	Loss of original forest:	72%
Ramsar sites:	4	Deforestation rate:	-
Protected areas:	8%	Eroded area:	2%
Wetlands:	0%	Large dams:	0
Arid:	0%	Planned major dams:	-

Land Cover Within 5 km of Major Rivers

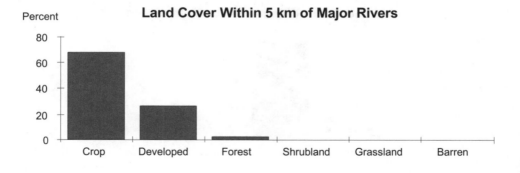

Percent

© 1998 World Resources Institute

Po Watershed

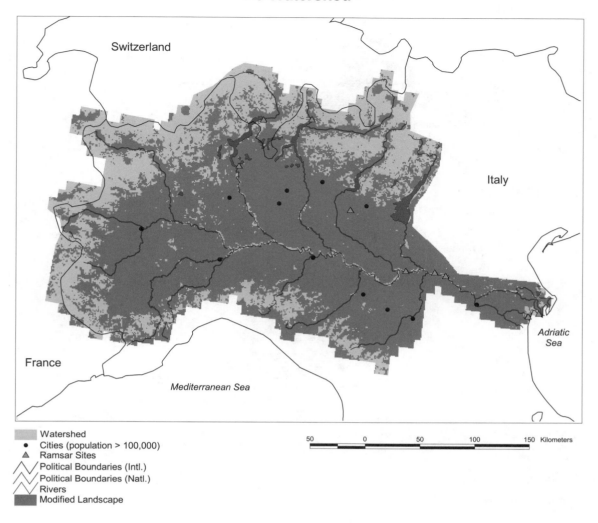

| Watershed |
| ● Cities (population > 100,000) |
| △ Ramsar Sites |
| Political Boundaries (Intl.) |
| Political Boundaries (Natl.) |
| Rivers |
| Modified Landscape |

50   0   50   100   150 Kilometers

Basin area:	76,987 km²	Forest:	14%
Population density:	215 people per km²	Cropland:	48%
Urban growth rate:	0.0%	Cropland irrigated:	3%
Large cities:	12	Developed:	22%
Total fish species:	47 (intr: 18 diad: 7)	Shrub:	8%
Fish endemics:	0	Grassland:	3%
Threatened fish species:	5	Barren:	0%
Endemic bird areas:	0	Loss of original forest:	81%
Ramsar sites:	9	Deforestation rate:	-
Protected areas:	9%	Eroded area:	5%
Wetlands:	2%	Large dams:	8
Arid:	0%	Planned major dams:	-

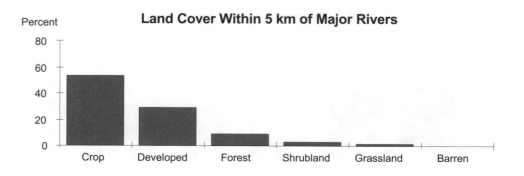

Land Cover Within 5 km of Major Rivers

Percent

Crop — Developed — Forest — Shrubland — Grassland — Barren

2 - 57

© 1998 World Resources Institute

Rhine - Meuse Watershed

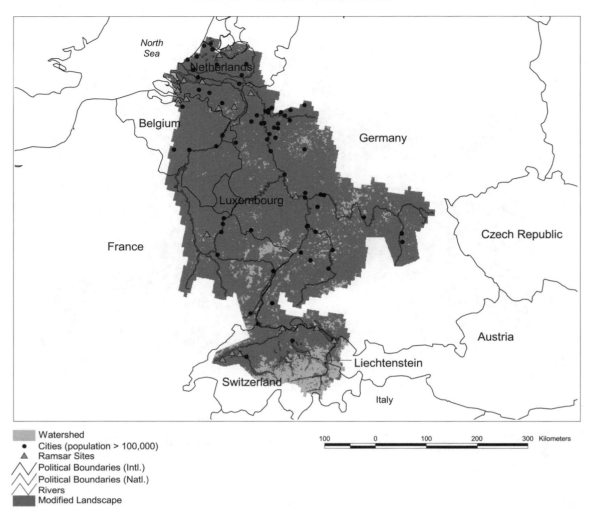

Watershed	(light shaded)
●	Cities (population > 100,000)
△	Ramsar Sites
⋀	Political Boundaries (Intl.)
⋀	Political Boundaries (Natl.)
⋀	Rivers
	Modified Landscape

Basin area:	19,8731 km²	Forest:	7%
Population density:	304 people per km²	Cropland:	64%
Urban growth rate:	0.7%	Cropland irrigated:	0%
Large cities:	68	Developed:	26%
Total fish species:	60 (intr:17 diad: 10)	Shrub:	1%
Fish endemics:	0	Grassland:	0%
Threatened fish species:	1	Barren:	0%
Endemic bird areas:	0	Loss of original forest:	71%
Ramsar sites:	20	Deforestation rate:	-
Protected areas:	18%	Eroded area:	1%
Wetlands:	1%	Large dams:	6
Arid:	0%	Planned major dams:	-

Land Cover Within 5 km of Major Rivers

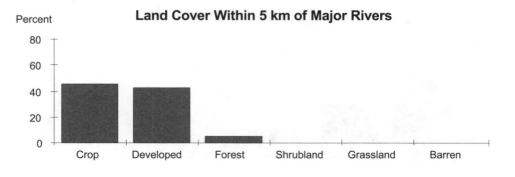

© 1998 World Resources Institute

Rhone Watershed

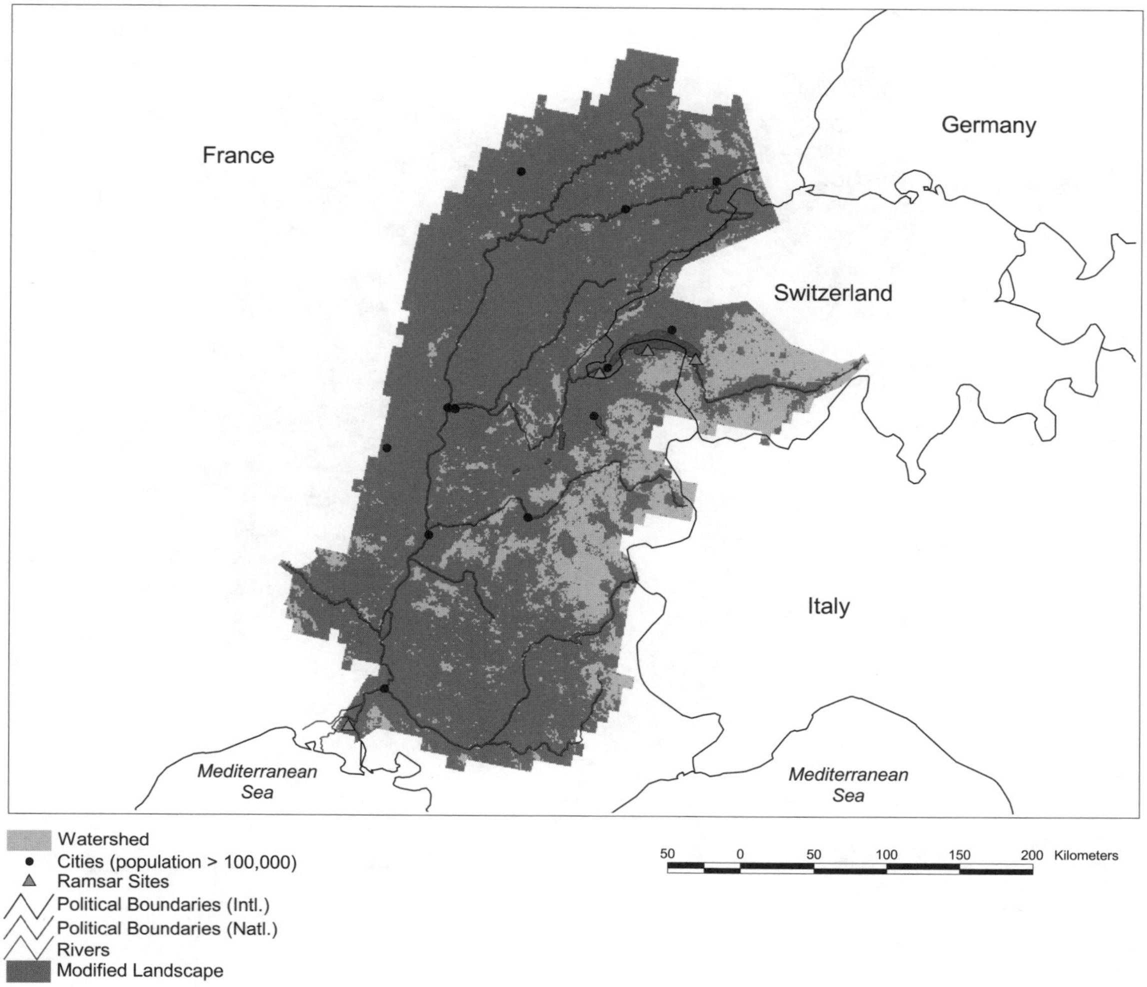
France
Germany
Switzerland
Italy
Mediterranean Sea
Mediterranean Sea
Watershed
Cities (population > 100,000)
Ramsar Sites
Political Boundaries (Intl.)
Political Boundaries (Natl.)
Rivers
Modified Landscape
50 0 50 100 150 200 Kilometers

Basin area:	100,531 km²
Population density:	97 people per km²
Urban growth rate:	0.6%
Large cities:	12
Total fish species:	58 (diad: 5)
Fish endemics:	1
Threatened fish species:	2
Endemic bird areas:	0
Ramsar sites:	4
Protected areas:	14%
Wetlands:	1%
Arid:	0%

Forest:	11%
Cropland:	61%
Cropland irrigated:	0%
Developed:	21%
Shrub:	3%
Grassland:	2%
Barren:	0%
Loss of original forest:	69%
Deforestation rate:	-
Eroded area:	5%
Large dams:	10
Planned major dams:	-

Land Cover Within 5 km of Major Rivers

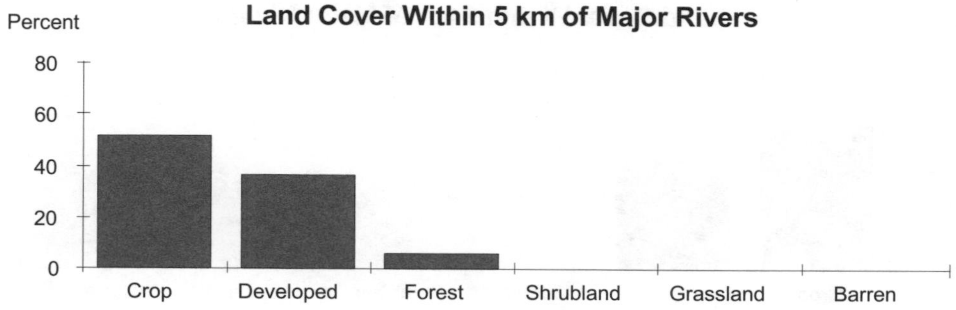
Percent
80
60
40
20
0
Crop
Developed
Forest
Shrubland
Grassland
Barren

© 1998 World Resources Institute

Seine Watershed

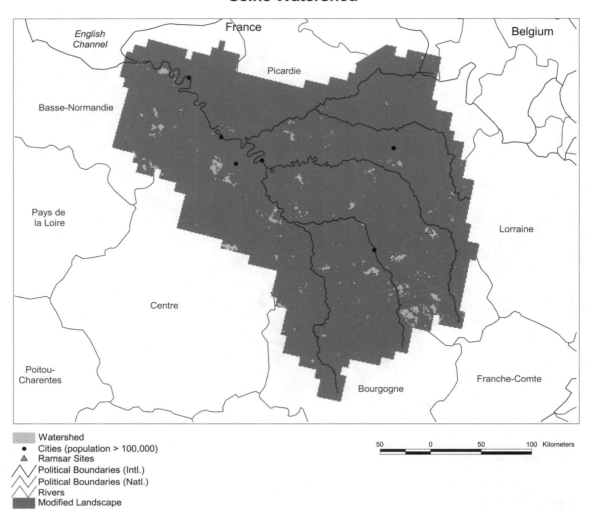

Watershed
● Cities (population > 100,000)
▲ Ramsar Sites
Political Boundaries (Intl.)
Political Boundaries (Natl.)
Rivers
Modified Landscape

Basin area:	78,910 km²	Forest:	2%
Population density:	201 people per km²	Cropland:	78%
Urban growth rate:	0.2%	Cropland irrigated:	0%
Large cities:	6	Developed:	20%
Total fish species:	39 (intr: 8 diad: 9)	Shrub:	0%
Fish endemics:	0	Grassland:	0%
Threatened fish species:	1	Barren:	0%
Endemic bird areas:	0	Loss of original forest:	93%
Ramsar sites:	1	Deforestation rate:	-
Protected areas:	5%	Eroded area:	0%
Wetlands:	0%	Large dams:	0
Arid:	0%	Planned major dams:	-

Land Cover Within 5 km of Major Rivers

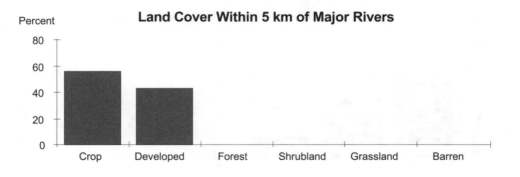

© 1998 World Resources Institute

Tagus Watershed

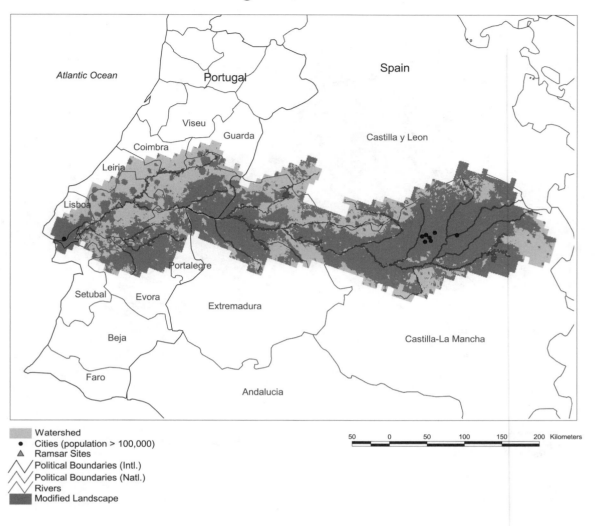

Watershed	
●	Cities (population > 100,000)
▲	Ramsar Sites
	Political Boundaries (Intl.)
	Political Boundaries (Natl.)
	Rivers
	Modified Landscape

Basin area: 78,463 km²
Population density: 108 people per km²
Urban growth rate: 0.6%
Large cities: 8
Total fish species: 39 (diad: 6)
Fish endemics: 0
Threatened fish species: 3
Endemic bird areas: 0
Ramsar sites: 2
Protected areas: 4%
Wetlands: 2%
Arid: 31%

Forest: 5%
Cropland: 45%
Cropland irrigated: 1%
Developed: 19%
Shrub: 20%
Grassland: 10%
Barren: 0%
Loss of original forest: 89%
Deforestation rate: -
Eroded area: 7%
Large dams: 7
Planned major dams: -

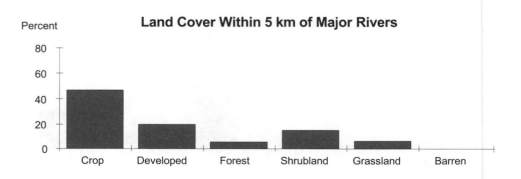

Land Cover Within 5 km of Major Rivers

Percent

© 1998 World Resources Institute

Tigris & Euphrates Watershed

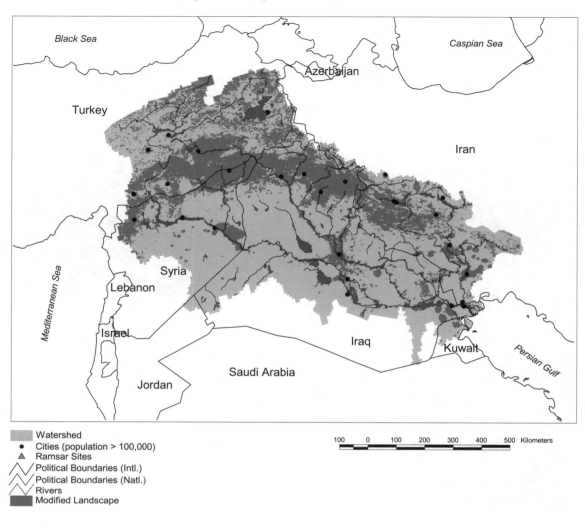

Watershed	
●	Cities (population > 100,000)
▲	Ramsar Sites
	Political Boundaries (Intl.)
	Political Boundaries (Natl.)
	Rivers
	Modified Landscape

Basin area: 765,831 km²
Population density: 58 people per km²
Urban growth rate: 3.9%
Large cities: 27
Total fish species: 92 (intr: 21)
Fish endemics: 28
Threatened fish species: 0
Endemic bird areas: 1
Ramsar sites: 0
Protected areas: 0%
Wetlands: 3%
Arid: 91%

Forest: 1%
Cropland: 25%
Cropland irrigated: 2%
Developed: 9%
Shrub: 32%
Grassland: 14%
Barren: 17%
Loss of original forest: 100%
Deforestation rate: -
Eroded area: 8%
Large dams: 19
Planned major dams: 7

Land Cover Within 5 km of Major Rivers

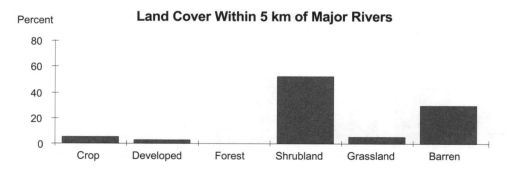

2 - 62

© 1998 World Resources Institute

Ural Watershed

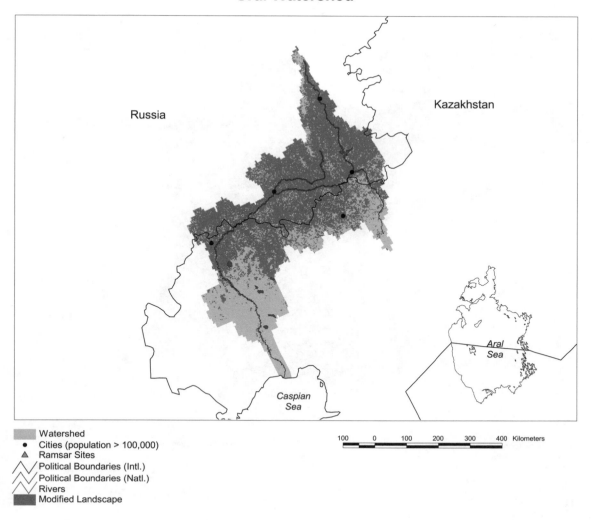

- ░ Watershed
- ● Cities (population > 100,000)
- ▲ Ramsar Sites
- ⋀ Political Boundaries (Intl.)
- ⋀ Political Boundaries (Natl.)
- ⋀ Rivers
- ▓ Modified Landscape

100   0   100   200   300   400   Kilometers

Basin area:	244,280 km²	Forest:	3%
Population density:	13 people per km²	Cropland:	58%
Urban growth rate:	-	Cropland irrigated:	0%
Large cities:	5	Developed:	6%
Total fish species:	48	Shrub:	0%
Fish endemics:	0	Grassland:	33%
Threatened fish species:	6	Barren:	0%
Endemic bird areas:	0	Loss of original forest:	32%
Ramsar sites:	0	Deforestation rate:	-
Protected areas:	1%	Eroded area:	5%
Wetlands:	0%	Large dams:	1
Arid:	100%	Planned major dams:	-

Land Cover Within 5 km of Major Rivers

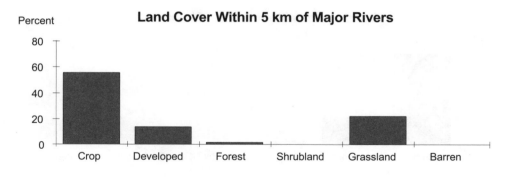

Percent

2 - 63

© 1998 World Resources Institute

Vistula Watershed

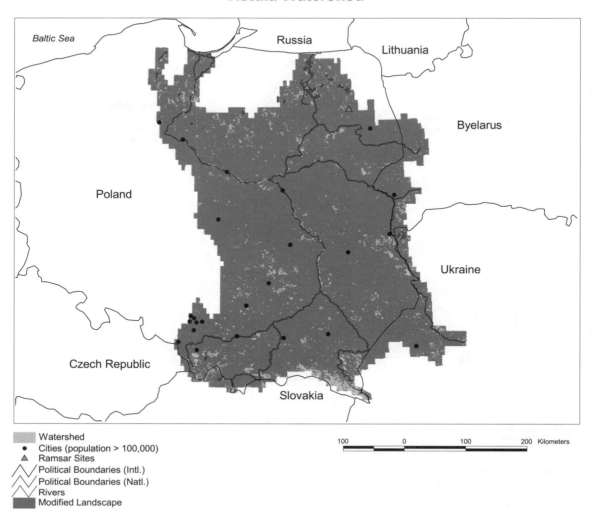

Watershed
● Cities (population > 100,000)
▲ Ramsar Sites
〰 Political Boundaries (Intl.)
〰 Political Boundaries (Natl.)
〰 Rivers
▨ Modified Landscape

100　　0　　100　　200　Kilometers

Basin area: 180,247 km²
Population density: 131 people per km²
Urban growth rate: 0.4%
Large cities: 24
Total fish species: 59 (intr: 13 diad: 9)
Fish endemics: 0
Threatened fish species: 1
Endemic bird areas: 0
Ramsar sites: 2
Protected areas: 10%
Wetlands: 3%
Arid: 0%

Forest: 4%
Cropland: 80%
Cropland irrigated: 0%
Developed: 15%
Shrub: 0%
Grassland: 0%
Barren: 0%
Loss of original forest: 82%
Deforestation rate: -
Eroded area: 9%
Large dams: 0
Planned major dams: -

Land Cover Within 5 km of Major Rivers

Percent

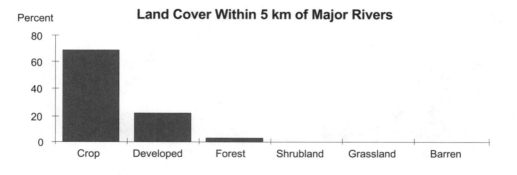

2 - 64

© 1998 World Resources Institute

Volga Watershed

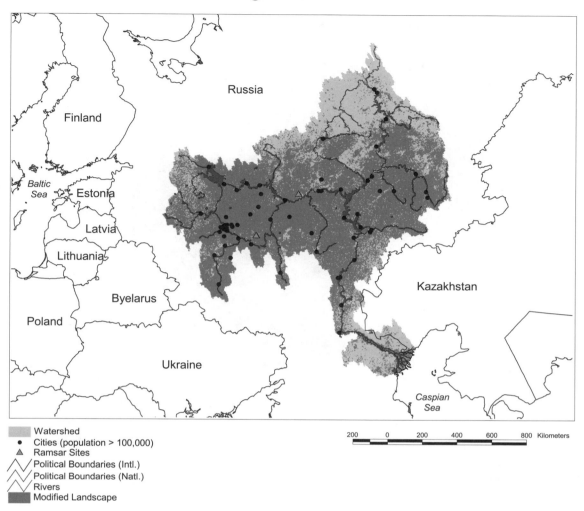

Watershed
● Cities (population > 100,000)
△ Ramsar Sites
〜 Political Boundaries (Intl.)
〜 Political Boundaries (Natl.)
〜 Rivers
▨ Modified Landscape

200 0 200 400 600 800 Kilometers

Basin area:	1,410,994 km²	Forest:	23%
Population density:	42 people per km²	Cropland:	59%
Urban growth rate:	0.0%	Cropland irrigated:	0%
Large cities:	61	Developed:	10%
Total fish species:	88 (diad: 4)	Shrub:	1%
Fish endemics:	0	Grassland:	6%
Threatened fish species:	5	Barren:	0%
Endemic bird areas:	0	Loss of original forest:	52%
Ramsar sites:	2	Deforestation rate:	-
Protected areas:	1%	Eroded area:	11%
Wetlands:	2%	Large dams:	14
Arid:	20%	Planned major dams:	-

Land Cover Within 5 km of Major Rivers

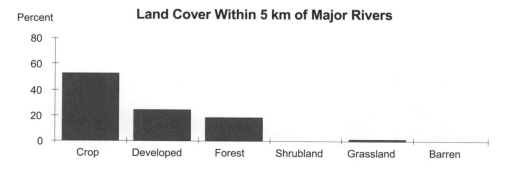

Percent

© 1998 World Resources Institute

Volga Watershed: Kama Subbasin

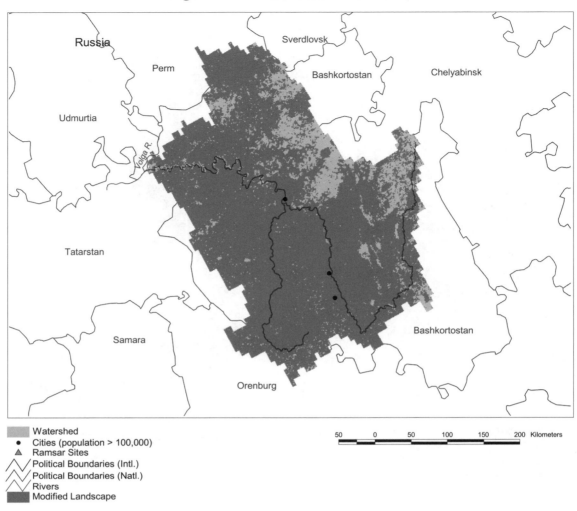

Watershed
● Cities (population > 100,000)
▲ Ramsar Sites
Political Boundaries (Intl.)
Political Boundaries (Natl.)
Rivers
Modified Landscape

50   0   50   100   150   200 Kilometers

Basin area:	105,861 km²	Forest:	13%
Population density:	28 people per km²	Cropland:	76%
Urban growth rate:	0.1%	Cropland irrigated:	0%
Large cities:	3	Developed:	10%
Total fish species:	41 (intr: 1 diad: 3)	Shrub:	0%
Fish endemics:	0	Grassland:	0%
Threatened fish species:	3	Barren:	0%
Endemic bird areas:	0	Loss of original forest:	38%
Ramsar sites:	0	Deforestation rate:	-
Protected areas:	2%	Eroded area:	10%
Wetlands:	0%	Large dams:	1
Arid:	39%	Planned major dams:	-

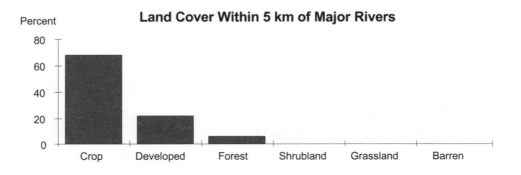

Land Cover Within 5 km of Major Rivers

2 - 66

© 1998 World Resources Institute

Volga Watershed: Oka Subbasin

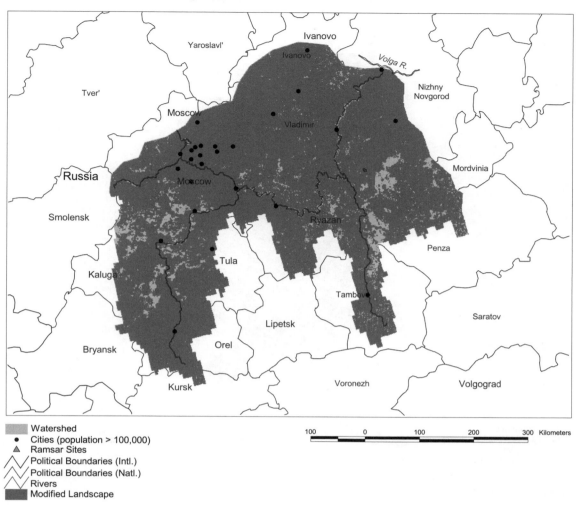

Watershed
● Cities (population > 100,000)
▲ Ramsar Sites
Political Boundaries (Intl.)
Political Boundaries (Natl.)
Rivers
Modified Landscape

Basin area:	221,342 km²	Forest:	5%
Population density:	96 people per km²	Cropland:	79%
Urban growth rate:	0.0%	Cropland irrigated:	0%
Large cities:	26	Developed:	15%
Total fish species:	35 (intr: 3)	Shrub:	0%
Fish endemics:	-	Grassland:	0%
Threatened fish species:	0	Barren:	0%
Endemic bird areas:	0	Loss of original forest:	94%
Ramsar sites:	1	Deforestation rate:	-
Protected areas:	2%	Eroded area:	10%
Wetlands:	0%	Large dams:	0
Arid:	0%	Planned major dams:	-

Land Cover Within 5 km of Major Rivers

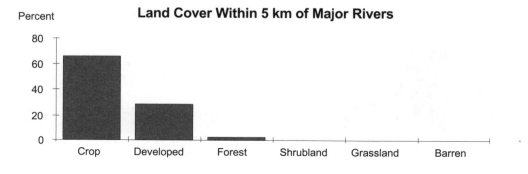

© 1998 World Resources Institute

Weser Watershed

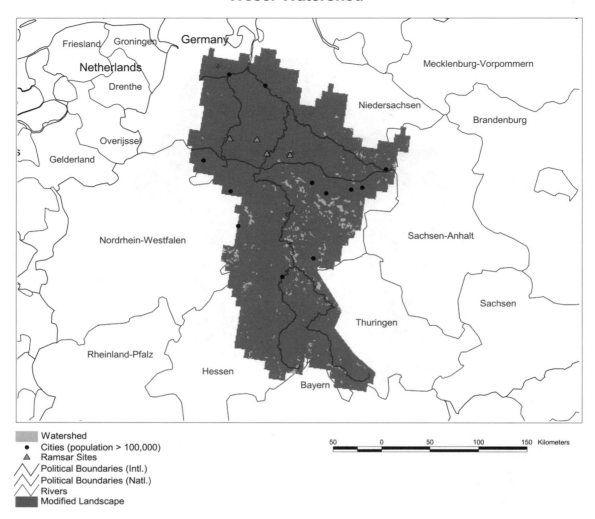

Watershed
● Cities (population > 100,000)
▲ Ramsar Sites
〜 Political Boundaries (Intl.)
〜 Political Boundaries (Natl.)
〜 Rivers
■ Modified Landscape

50   0   50   100   150 Kilometers

Basin area:	45,127 km²	Forest:	3%
Population density:	198 people per km²	Cropland:	77%
Urban growth rate:	0.5%	Cropland irrigated:	0%
Large cities:	12	Developed:	20%
Total fish species:	48 (intr: 7 diad: 9)	Shrub:	0%
Fish endemics:	0	Grassland:	0%
Threatened fish species:	1	Barren:	0%
Endemic bird areas:	0	Loss of original forest:	78%
Ramsar sites:	4	Deforestation rate:	-
Protected areas:	19%	Eroded area:	0%
Wetlands:	0%	Large dams:	0
Arid:	0%	Planned major dams:	-

Land Cover Within 5 km of Major Rivers

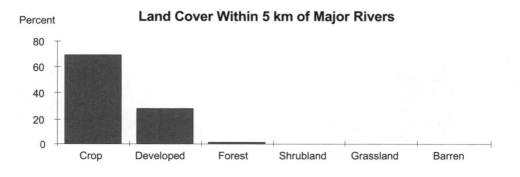

Percent

© 1998 World Resources Institute

WATERSHED PROFILES

FOR

ASIA AND OCEANIA

Amu Darya Watershed

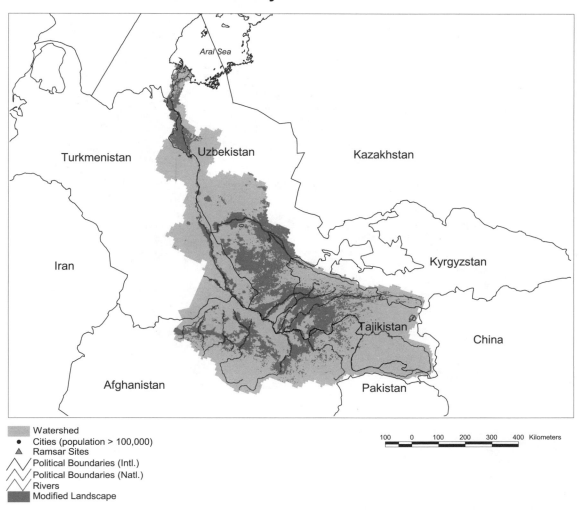

Aral Sea

Turkmenistan
Uzbekistan
Kazakhstan
Iran
Kyrgyzstan
Tajikistan
China
Afghanistan
Pakistan

- ▦ Watershed
- ● Cities (population > 100,000)
- ▲ Ramsar Sites
- ⋀ Political Boundaries (Intl.)
- ⋀ Political Boundaries (Natl.)
- ⋀ Rivers
- ▦ Modified Landscape

100 0 100 200 300 400 Kilometers

Basin area:	534,764 km²	Forest:	0%
Population density:	33 people per km²	Cropland:	22%
Urban growth rate:	-	Cropland irrigated:	35%
Large cities:	9	Developed:	5%
Total fish species:	68 (intr: 28)	Shrub:	39%
Fish endemics:	3	Grassland:	17%
Threatened fish species:	2	Barren:	14%
Endemic bird areas:	0	Loss of original forest:	99%
Ramsar sites:	0	Deforestation rate:	-
Protected areas:	1%	Eroded area:	3%
Wetlands:	0%	Large dams:	6
Arid:	72%	Planned major dams:	-

Land Cover Within 5 km of Major Rivers

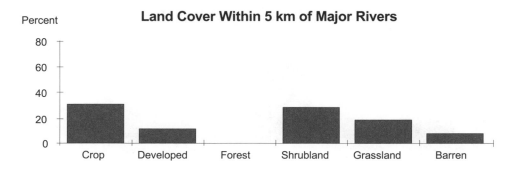

Percent

Crop Developed Forest Shrubland Grassland Barren

© 1998 World Resources Institute

Amur Watershed

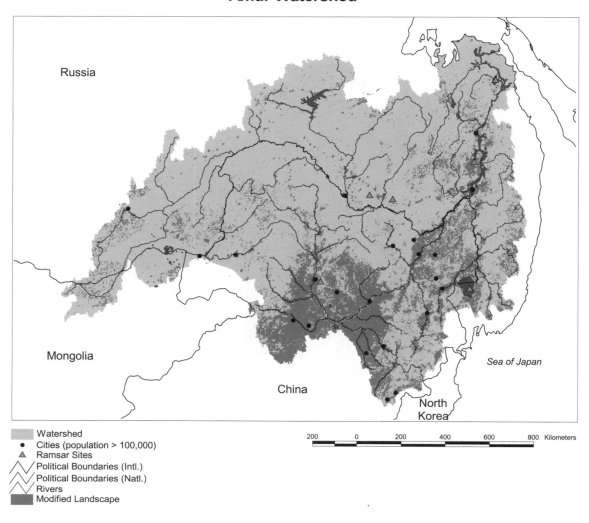

Watershed	(light shaded)
●	Cities (population > 100,000)
▲	Ramsar Sites
/\/	Political Boundaries (Intl.)
/\/	Political Boundaries (Natl.)
/\/	Rivers
	Modified Landscape

Basin area:	1,929,981 km²		Forest:	68%
Population density:	35 people per km²		Cropland:	18%
Urban growth rate:	3.0%		Cropland irrigated:	8%
Large cities:	22		Developed:	3%
Total fish species:	120		Shrub:	0%
Fish endemics:	6		Grassland:	8%
Threatened fish species:	2		Barren:	0%
Endemic bird areas:	0		Loss of original forest:	33%
Ramsar sites:	7		Deforestation rate:	-
Protected areas:	2%		Eroded area:	0%
Wetlands:	4%		Large dams:	5
Arid:	15%		Planned major dams:	-

Land Cover Within 5 km of Major Rivers

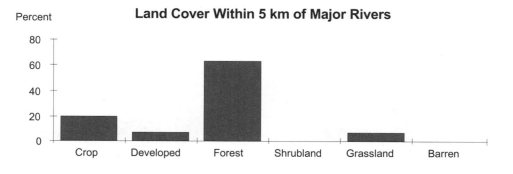

© 1998 World Resources Institute

Amur Watershed: Songhua Jiang Subbasin

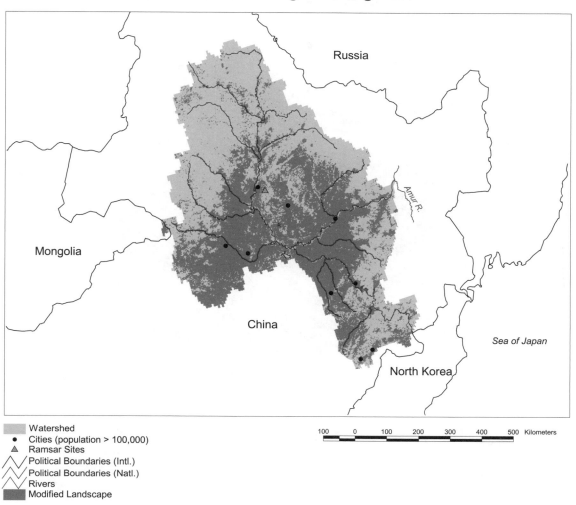

Watershed		
•	Cities (population > 100,000)	
▲	Ramsar Sites	
∿	Political Boundaries (Intl.)	
∿	Political Boundaries (Natl.)	
∿	Rivers	
	Modified Landscape	

Basin area:	459,745 km²	Forest:	51%
Population density:	105 people per km²	Cropland:	41%
Urban growth rate:	3.5%	Cropland irrigated:	3%
Large cities:	9	Developed:	5%
Total fish species:	-	Shrub:	0%
Fish endemics:	0	Grassland:	2%
Threatened fish species:	0	Barren:	0%
Endemic bird areas:	0	Loss of original forest:	34%
Ramsar sites:	1	Deforestation rate:	-
Protected areas:	2%	Eroded area:	0%
Wetlands:	3%	Large dams:	3
Arid:	7%	Planned major dams:	-

Land Cover Within 5 km of Major Rivers

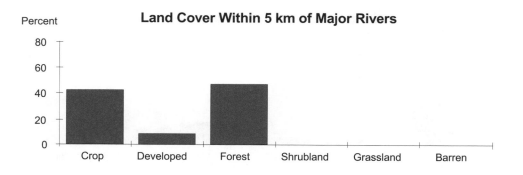

2 - 73

© 1998 World Resources Institute

Lake Balkhash Watershed

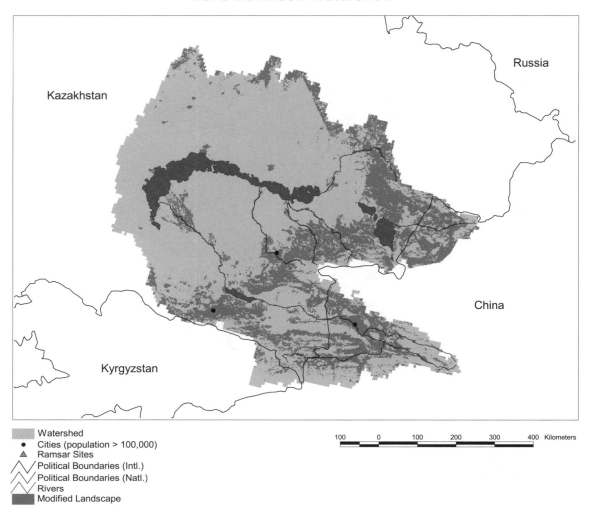

Watershed
● Cities (population > 100,000)
▲ Ramsar Sites
Political Boundaries (Intl.)
Political Boundaries (Natl.)
Rivers
Modified Landscape

| 100 | 0 | 100 | 200 | 300 | 400 | Kilometers |

Basin area:	512,010 km²	Forest:	4%
Population density:	11 people per km²	Cropland:	24%
Urban growth rate:	1.0%	Cropland irrigated:	21%
Large cities:	3	Developed:	2%
Total fish species:	36 (intr: 23)	Shrub:	20%
Fish endemics:	5	Grassland:	42%
Threatened fish species:	0	Barren:	6%
Endemic bird areas:	0	Loss of original forest:	26%
Ramsar sites:	0	Deforestation rate:	-
Protected areas:	7%	Eroded area:	1%
Wetlands:	5%	Large dams:	2
Arid:	92%	Planned major dams:	-

Land Cover Within 5 km of Major Rivers

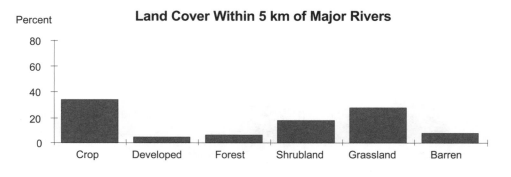

Percent

Crop Developed Forest Shrubland Grassland Barren

© 1998 World Resources Institute

Brahmaputra Watershed

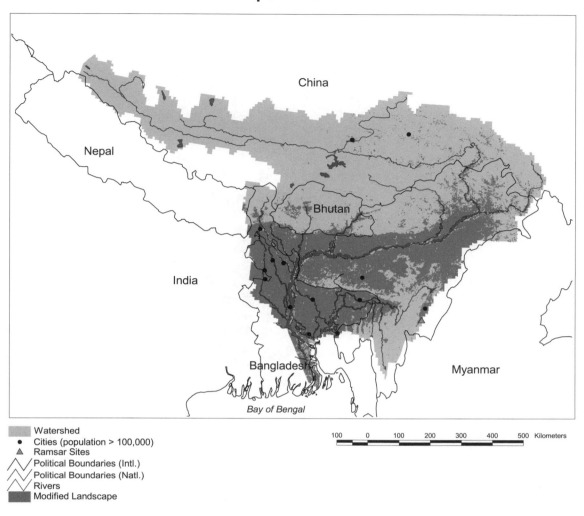

- ▨ Watershed
- ● Cities (population > 100,000)
- ▲ Ramsar Sites
- ⌇ Political Boundaries (Intl.)
- ⌇ Political Boundaries (Natl.)
- ⌇ Rivers
- ▨ Modified Landscape

100 0 100 200 300 400 500 Kilometers

Basin area:	651,334 km²	Forest:	19%
Population density:	174 people per km²	Cropland:	29%
Urban growth rate:	5.0%	Cropland irrigated:	47%
Large cities:	14	Developed:	3%
Total fish species:	126	Shrub:	16%
Fish endemics:	-	Grassland:	29%
Threatened fish species:	0	Barren:	2%
Endemic bird areas:	4	Loss of original forest:	73%
Ramsar sites:	1	Deforestation rate:	10%
Protected areas:	4%	Eroded area:	11%
Wetlands:	21%	Large dams:	0
Arid:	0%	Planned major dams:	-

Land Cover Within 5 km of Major Rivers

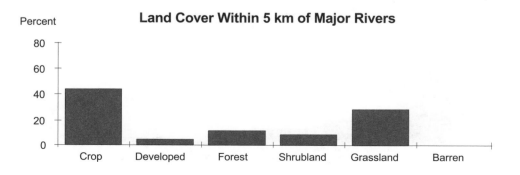

© 1998 World Resources Institute

Chao Phrya Watershed

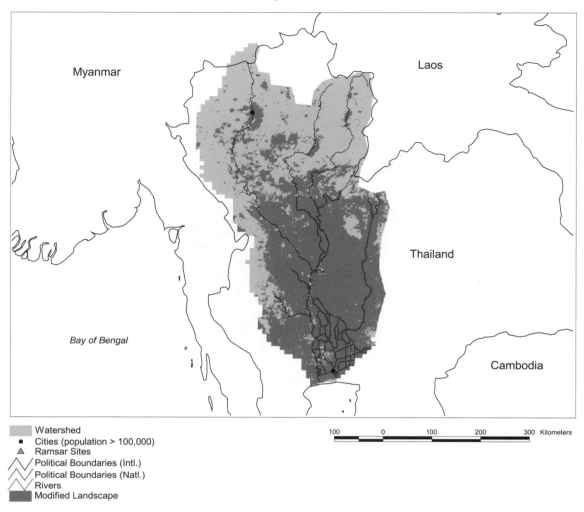

Myanmar

Laos

Thailand

Bay of Bengal

Cambodia

Watershed
● Cities (population > 100,000)
▲ Ramsar Sites
〰 Political Boundaries (Intl.)
〰 Political Boundaries (Natl.)
〰 Rivers
Modified Landscape

100   0   100   200   300 Kilometers

Basin area:	178,754 km²	Forest:	36%
Population density:	118 people per km²	Cropland:	46%
Urban growth rate:	2.0%	Cropland irrigated:	92%
Large cities:	2	Developed:	8%
Total fish species:	222	Shrub:	2%
Fish endemics:	34	Grassland:	8%
Threatened fish species:	5	Barren:	0%
Endemic bird areas:	0	Loss of original forest:	77%
Ramsar sites:	0	Deforestation rate:	26%
Protected areas:	12%	Eroded area:	24%
Wetlands:	8%	Large dams:	3
Arid:	0%	Planned major dams:	-

Land Cover Within 5 km of Major Rivers

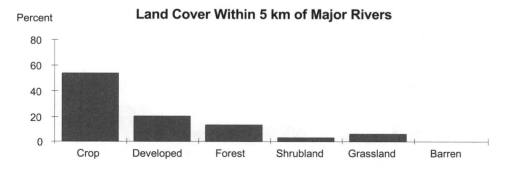

Percent

Crop	Developed	Forest	Shrubland	Grassland	Barren

© 1998 World Resources Institute

Fly Watershed

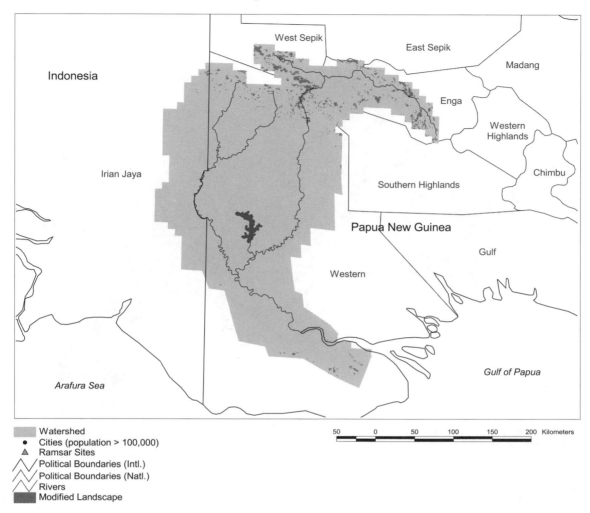

▨	Watershed
●	Cities (population > 100,000)
▲	Ramsar Sites
⋀	Political Boundaries (Intl.)
⋀	Political Boundaries (Natl.)
⋀	Rivers
▨	Modified Landscape

Basin area:	78,816 km²	Forest:	76%
Population density:	8 people per km²	Cropland:	2%
Urban growth rate:	-	Cropland irrigated:	27%
Large cities:	0	Developed:	-
Total fish species:	105 (intr: 4)	Shrub:	0%
Fish endemics:	5	Grassland:	19%
Threatened fish species:	0	Barren:	0%
Endemic bird areas:	3	Loss of original forest:	6%
Ramsar sites:	0	Deforestation rate:	3%
Protected areas:	0%	Eroded area:	0%
Wetlands:	42%	Large dams:	0
Arid:	0%	Planned major dams:	-

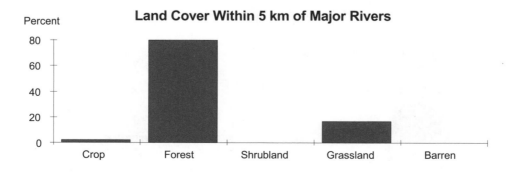

Land Cover Within 5 km of Major Rivers

© 1998 World Resources Institute

Ganges Watershed

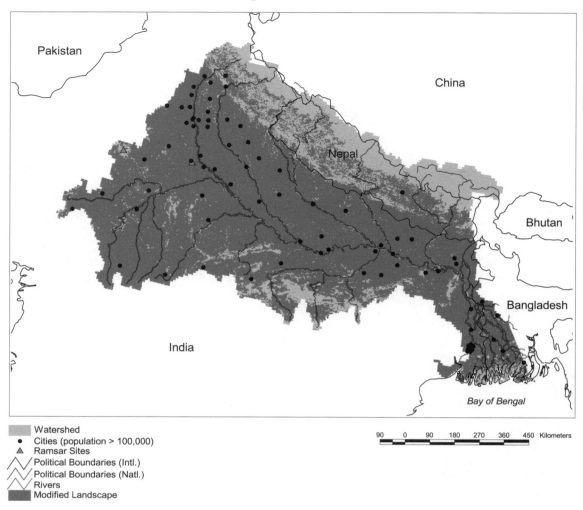

- Watershed
- • Cities (population > 100,000)
- ▲ Ramsar Sites
- Political Boundaries (Intl.)
- Political Boundaries (Natl.)
- Rivers
- Modified Landscape

90 0 90 180 270 360 450 Kilometers

Basin area:	1,016,104 km²	Forest:	4%
Population density:	375 people per km²	Cropland:	71%
Urban growth rate:	3.2%	Cropland irrigated:	15%
Large cities:	82	Developed:	8%
Total fish species:	141	Shrub:	6%
Fish endemics:	-	Grassland:	7%
Threatened fish species:	0	Barren:	1%
Endemic bird areas:	5	Loss of original forest:	85%
Ramsar sites:	4	Deforestation rate:	5%
Protected areas:	6%	Eroded area:	10%
Wetlands:	18%	Large dams:	6
Arid:	26%	Planned major dams:	6

Land Cover Within 5 km of Major Rivers

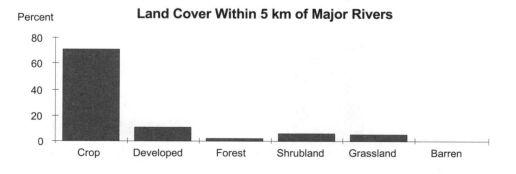

Percent

© 1998 World Resources Institute

Godavari Watershed

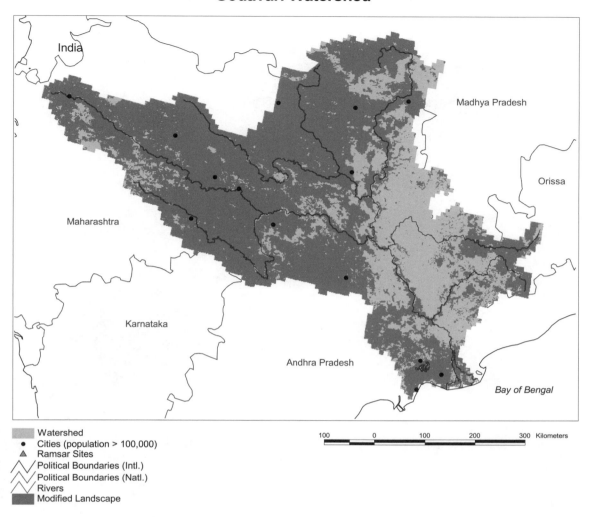

Watershed
● Cities (population > 100,000)
▲ Ramsar Sites
Political Boundaries (Intl.)
Political Boundaries (Natl.)
Rivers
Modified Landscape

Basin area:	319,808 km²	Forest:	7%
Population density:	195 people per km²	Cropland:	63%
Urban growth rate:	3.3%	Cropland irrigated:	27%
Large cities:	14	Developed:	7%
Total fish species:	-	Shrub:	2%
Fish endemics:	-	Grassland:	20%
Threatened fish species:	0	Barren:	0%
Endemic bird areas:	0	Loss of original forest:	77%
Ramsar sites:	0	Deforestation rate:	11%
Protected areas:	4%	Eroded area:	15%
Wetlands:	1%	Large dams:	3
Arid:	43%	Planned major dams:	-

Land Cover Within 5 km of Major Rivers

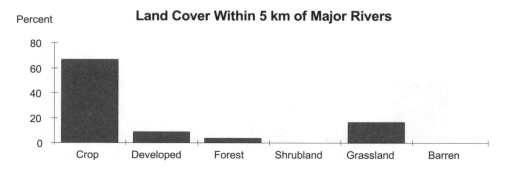

2 - 79

© 1998 World Resources Institute

Hong (Red River) Watershed

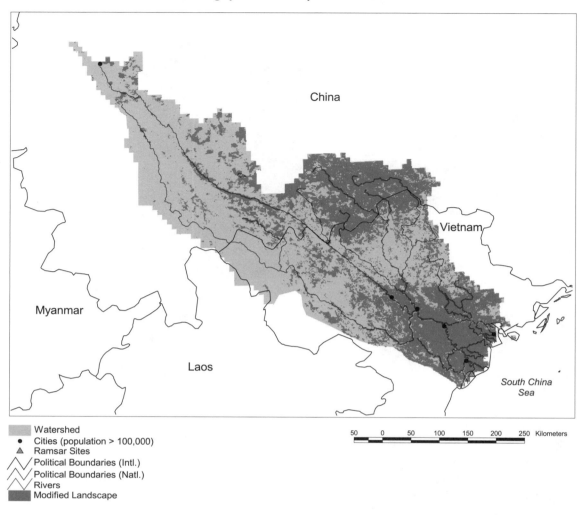

Watershed
● Cities (population > 100,000)
▲ Ramsar Sites
〰 Political Boundaries (Intl.)
〰 Political Boundaries (Natl.)
〰 Rivers
▨ Modified Landscape

Basin area:	170,977 km²	Forest:	43%
Population density:	180 people per km²	Cropland:	38%
Urban growth rate:	1.2%	Cropland irrigated:	52%
Large cities:	6	Developed:	3%
Total fish species:	180	Shrub:	11%
Fish endemics:	1	Grassland:	4%
Threatened fish species:	0	Barren:	0%
Endemic bird areas:	2	Loss of original forest:	80%
Ramsar sites:	1	Deforestation rate:	14%
Protected areas:	4%	Eroded area:	23%
Wetlands:	5%	Large dams:	3
Arid:	0%	Planned major dams:	-

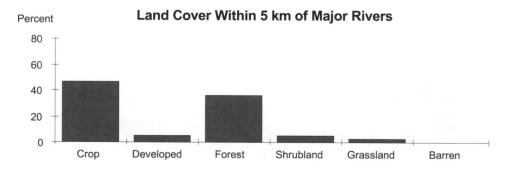

Land Cover Within 5 km of Major Rivers

Percent

© 1998 World Resources Institute

Hwang He Watershed

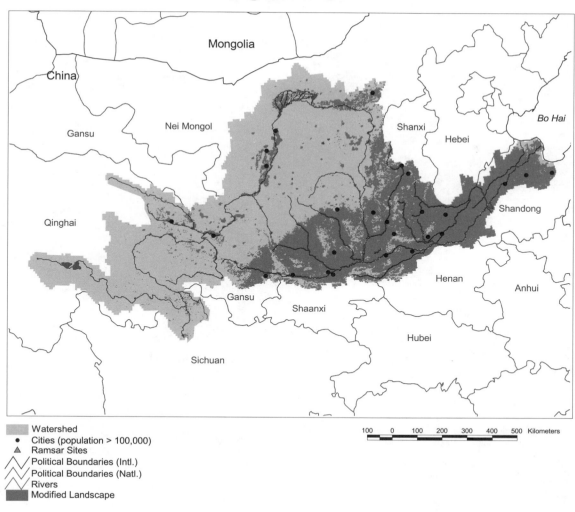

- ▨ Watershed
- ● Cities (population > 100,000)
- ▲ Ramsar Sites
- ∿ Political Boundaries (Intl.)
- ∿ Political Boundaries (Natl.)
- ∿ Rivers
- ▰ Modified Landscape

Basin area:	945,065 km²		Forest:	3%
Population density:	162 people per km²		Cropland:	29%
Urban growth rate:	2.9%		Cropland irrigated:	32%
Large cities:	27		Developed:	7%
Total fish species:	160		Shrub:	19%
Fish endemics:	-		Grassland:	39%
Threatened fish species:	0		Barren:	2%
Endemic bird areas:	4		Loss of original forest:	78%
Ramsar sites:	0		Deforestation rate:	-
Protected areas:	1%		Eroded area:	20%
Wetlands:	1%		Large dams:	6
Arid:	38%		Planned major dams:	4

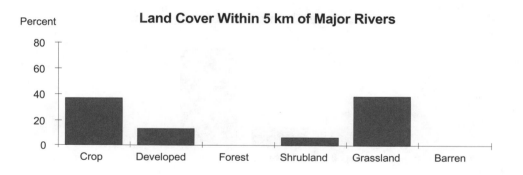

Land Cover Within 5 km of Major Rivers

2 - 81

© 1998 World Resources Institute

Indigirka Watershed

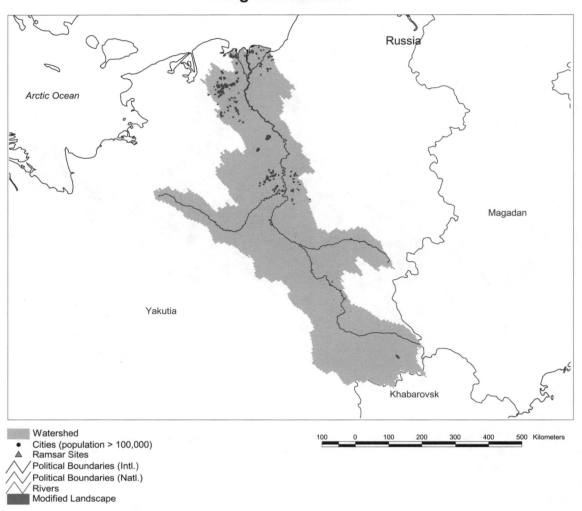

Russia

Arctic Ocean

Magadan

Yakutia

Khabarovsk

- Watershed
- • Cities (population > 100,000)
- ▲ Ramsar Sites
- Political Boundaries (Intl.)
- Political Boundaries (Natl.)
- Rivers
- Modified Landscape

100 0 100 200 300 400 500 Kilometers

Basin area:	274,818 km²	Forest:	21%
Population density:	<1 person per km²	Cropland:	0%
Urban growth rate:	-	Cropland irrigated:	0%
Large cities:	0	Developed:	0%
Total fish species:	-	Shrub:	63%
Fish endemics:	-	Grassland:	3%
Threatened fish species:	0	Barren:	2%
Endemic bird areas:	0	Loss of original forest:	52%
Ramsar sites:	0	Deforestation rate:	-
Protected areas:	0%	Eroded area:	0%
Wetlands:	3%	Large dams:	0
Arid:	0%	Planned major dams:	-

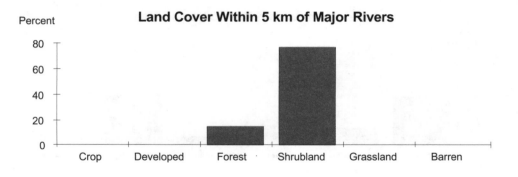

Percent

Land Cover Within 5 km of Major Rivers

80

60

40

20

0

Crop   Developed   Forest   Shrubland   Grassland   Barren

© 1998 World Resources Institute

Indus Watershed

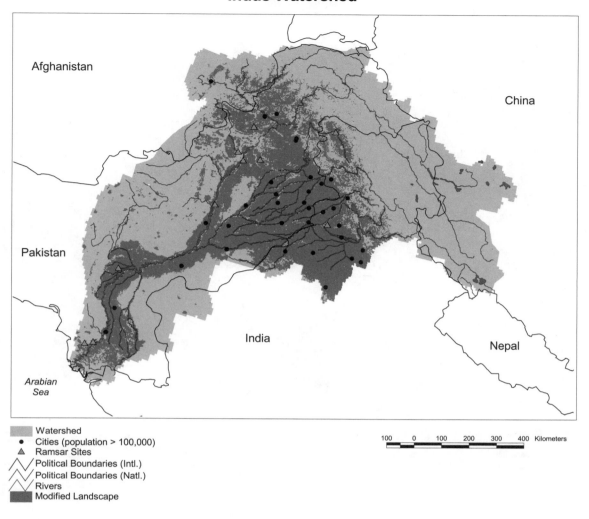

Watershed
● Cities (population > 100,000)
▲ Ramsar Sites
Political Boundaries (Intl.)
Political Boundaries (Natl.)
Rivers
Modified Landscape

Basin area:	1,081,733 km²	Forest:	0%
Population density:	145 people per km²	Cropland:	29%
Urban growth rate:	4.1%	Cropland irrigated:	25%
Large cities:	34	Developed:	6%
Total fish species:	147	Shrub:	40%
Fish endemics:	22	Grassland:	6%
Threatened fish species:	0	Barren:	15%
Endemic bird areas:	1	Loss of original forest:	90%
Ramsar sites:	10	Deforestation rate:	20%
Protected areas:	4%	Eroded area:	4%
Wetlands:	4%	Large dams:	10
Arid:	63%	Planned major dams:	1

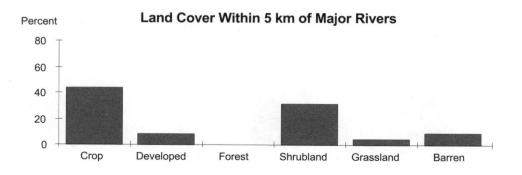

Land Cover Within 5 km of Major Rivers

2 - 83

© 1998 World Resources Institute

Irrawaddy Watershed

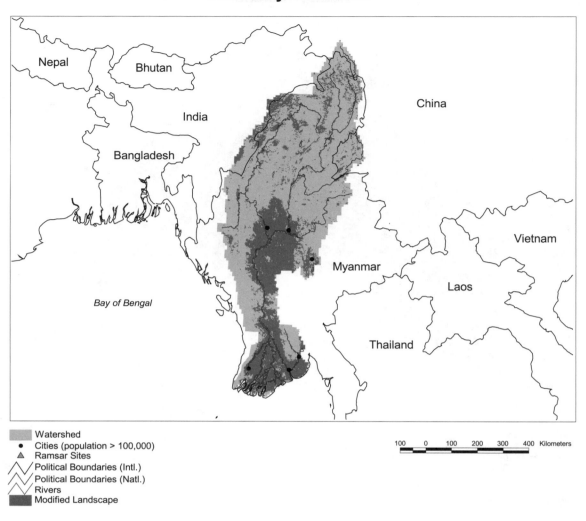

Watershed
- Cities (population > 100,000)
▲ Ramsar Sites
Political Boundaries (Intl.)
Political Boundaries (Natl.)
Rivers
Modified Landscape

100 0 100 200 300 400 Kilometers

Basin area:	413,674 km²		Forest:	56%
Population density:	80 people per km²		Cropland:	31%
Urban growth rate:	2.8%		Cropland irrigated:	78%
Large cities:	6		Developed:	2%
Total fish species:	79		Shrub:	2%
Fish endemics:	-		Grassland:	7%
Threatened fish species:	0		Barren:	0%
Endemic bird areas:	4		Loss of original forest:	61%
Ramsar sites:	0		Deforestation rate:	15%
Protected areas:	1%		Eroded area:	9%
Wetlands:	6%		Large dams:	0
Arid:	0%		Planned major dams:	-

Land Cover Within 5 km of Major Rivers

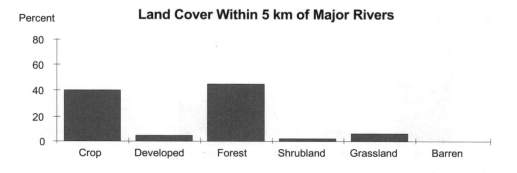

Percent

Crop   Developed   Forest   Shrubland   Grassland   Barren

© 1998 World Resources Institute

Kapuas Watershed

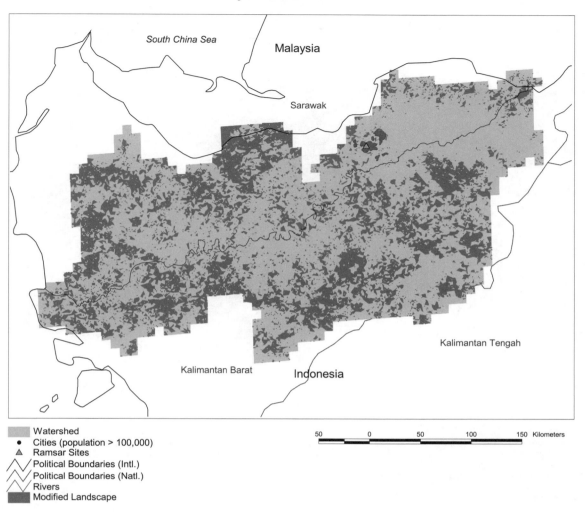

Watershed
● Cities (population > 100,000)
▲ Ramsar Sites
/\/ Political Boundaries (Intl.)
/\/ Political Boundaries (Natl.)
/\/ Rivers
▨ Modified Landscape

50   0   50   100   150 Kilometers

Basin area:	88,745 km²	Forest:	65%
Population density:	22 people per km²	Cropland:	33%
Urban growth rate:	-	Cropland irrigated:	57%
Large cities:	0	Developed:	-
Total fish species:	320	Shrub:	0%
Fish endemics:	35	Grassland:	0%
Threatened fish species:	0	Barren:	0%
Endemic bird areas:	1	Loss of original forest:	47%
Ramsar sites:	1	Deforestation rate:	8%
Protected areas:	6%	Eroded area:	12%
Wetlands:	2%	Large dams:	0
Arid:	0%	Planned major dams:	-

Land Cover Within 5 km of Major Rivers

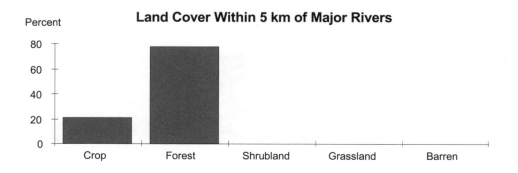

Percent

2 - 85

© 1998 World Resources Institute

Kolyma Basin

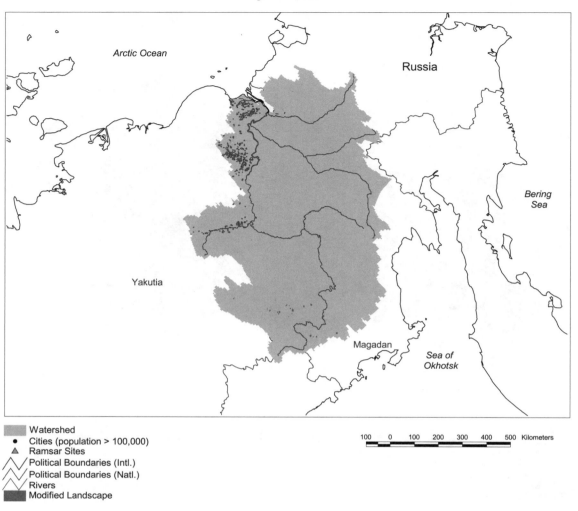

Watershed		
•	Cities (population > 100,000)	
▲	Ramsar Sites	
	Political Boundaries (Intl.)	
	Political Boundaries (Natl.)	
	Rivers	
	Modified Landscape	

100   0   100   200   300   400   500 Kilometers

Basin area:	679,908 km²		Forest:	31%
Population density:	< 1 person per km²		Cropland:	0%
Urban growth rate:	-		Cropland irrigated:	0%
Large cities:	0		Developed:	-
Total fish species:	29		Shrub:	42%
Fish endemics:	0		Grassland:	3%
Threatened fish species:	0		Barren:	1%
Endemic bird areas:	0		Loss of original forest:	56%
Ramsar sites:	0		Deforestation rate:	-
Protected areas:	0%		Eroded area:	0%
Wetlands:	1%		Large dams:	1
Arid:	0%		Planned major dams:	-

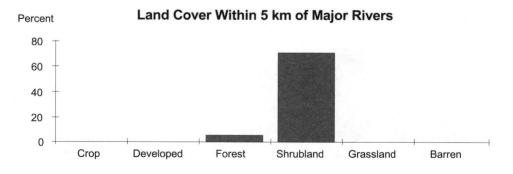

Land Cover Within 5 km of Major Rivers

2 - 86

© 1998 World Resources Institute

Krishna Watershed

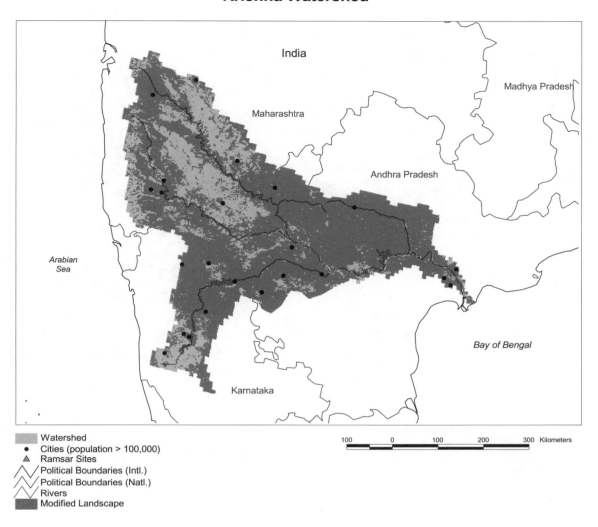

Watershed
● Cities (population > 100,000)
▲ Ramsar Sites
〜 Political Boundaries (Intl.)
〜 Political Boundaries (Natl.)
〜 Rivers
Modified Landscape

100   0   100   200   300 Kilometers

Basin area:	226,026 km²	Forest:	3%
Population density:	248 people per km²	Cropland:	67%
Urban growth rate:	3.8%	Cropland irrigated:	39%
Large cities:	23	Developed:	8%
Total fish species:	-	Shrub:	17%
Fish endemics:	-	Grassland:	5%
Threatened fish species:	0	Barren:	0%
Endemic bird areas:	1	Loss of original forest:	80%
Ramsar sites:	0	Deforestation rate:	7%
Protected areas:	4%	Eroded area:	20%
Wetlands:	16%	Large dams:	5
Arid:	41%	Planned major dams:	1

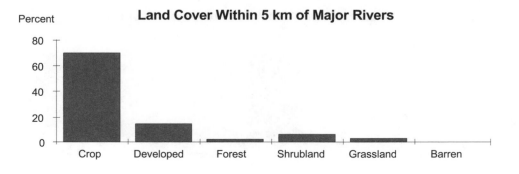

Land Cover Within 5 km of Major Rivers

Percent

© 1998 World Resources Institute

Lena Watershed

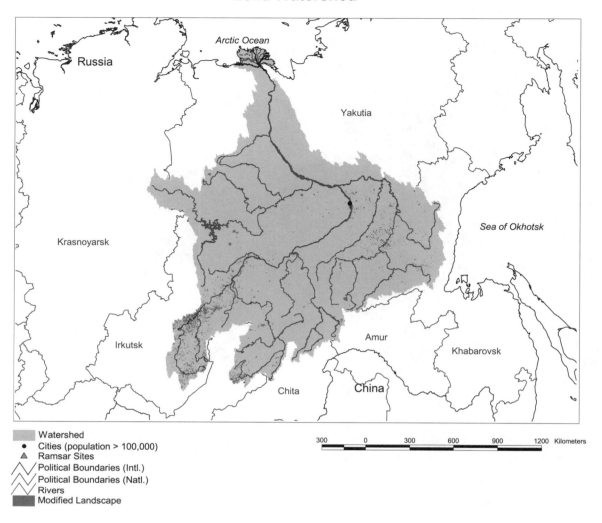

Watershed			
●	Cities (population > 100,000)		
▲	Ramsar Sites		
	Political Boundaries (Intl.)		
	Political Boundaries (Natl.)		
	Rivers		
	Modified Landscape		

Basin area:	2,306,772 km²	Forest:	84%
Population density:	1 person per km²	Cropland:	2%
Urban growth rate:	-	Cropland irrigated:	10%
Large cities:	1	Developed:	1%
Total fish species:	43	Shrub:	9%
Fish endemics:	0	Grassland:	3%
Threatened fish species:	0	Barren:	0%
Endemic bird areas:	0	Loss of original forest:	19%
Ramsar sites:	0	Deforestation rate:	-
Protected areas:	1%	Eroded area:	0%
Wetlands:	1%	Large dams:	2
Arid:	1%	Planned major dams:	-

Land Cover Within 5 km of Major Rivers

2 - 88

© 1998 World Resources Institute

Lena Watershed: Viljuj Subbasin

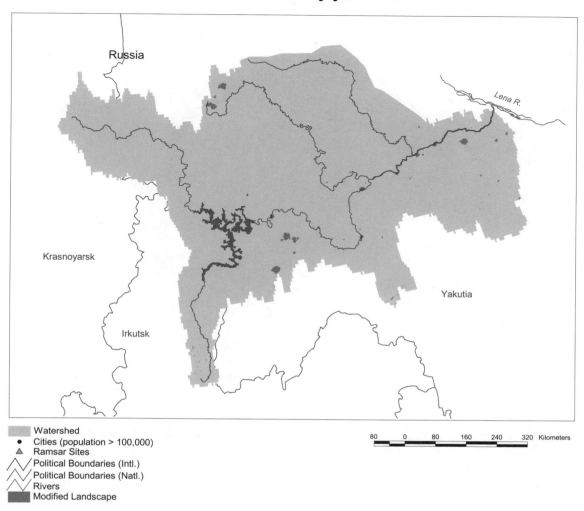

Russia

Krasnoyarsk

Lena R.

Irkutsk

Yakutia

	Watershed
•	Cities (population > 100,000)
▲	Ramsar Sites
⋀	Political Boundaries (Intl.)
⋀	Political Boundaries (Natl.)
⋀	Rivers
■	Modified Landscape

80   0   80   160   240   320 Kilometers

Basin area:	507,874 km²	Forest:	96%
Population density:	1 person per km²	Cropland:	0%
Urban growth rate:	-	Cropland irrigated:	61%
Large cities:	0	Developed:	1%
Total fish species:	-	Shrub:	1%
Fish endemics:	-	Grassland:	1%
Threatened fish species:	0	Barren:	0%
Endemic bird areas:	0	Loss of original forest:	14%
Ramsar sites:	0	Deforestation rate:	-
Protected areas:	0%	Eroded area:	0%
Wetlands:	2%	Large dams:	2
Arid:	0%	Planned major dams:	-

Land Cover Within 5 km of Major Rivers

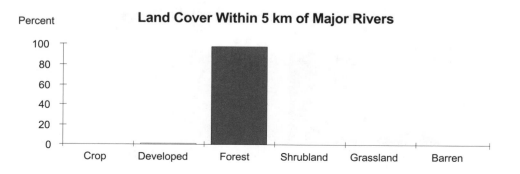

Percent

© 1998 World Resources Institute

Mahakam Watershed

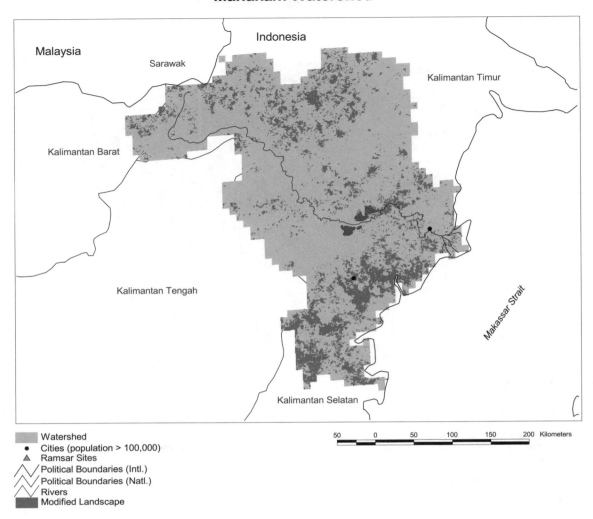

Watershed	
●	Cities (population > 100,000)
▲	Ramsar Sites
	Political Boundaries (Intl.)
	Political Boundaries (Natl.)
	Rivers
	Modified Landscape

Basin area:	98,189 km²	Forest:	80%
Population density:	18 people per km²	Cropland:	18%
Urban growth rate:	-	Cropland irrigated:	22%
Large cities:	2	Developed:	-
Total fish species:	-	Shrub:	0%
Fish endemics:	-	Grassland:	1%
Threatened fish species:	2	Barren:	0%
Endemic bird areas:	1	Loss of original forest:	11%
Ramsar sites:	0	Deforestation rate:	8%
Protected areas:	4%	Eroded area:	19%
Wetlands:	8%	Large dams:	0
Arid:	0%	Planned major dams:	-

Land Cover Within 5 km of Major Rivers

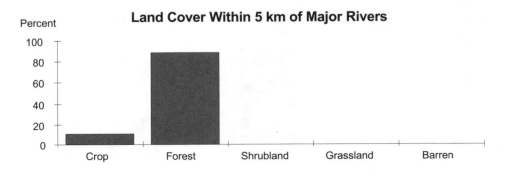

© 1998 World Resources Institute

Mahanadi Watershed

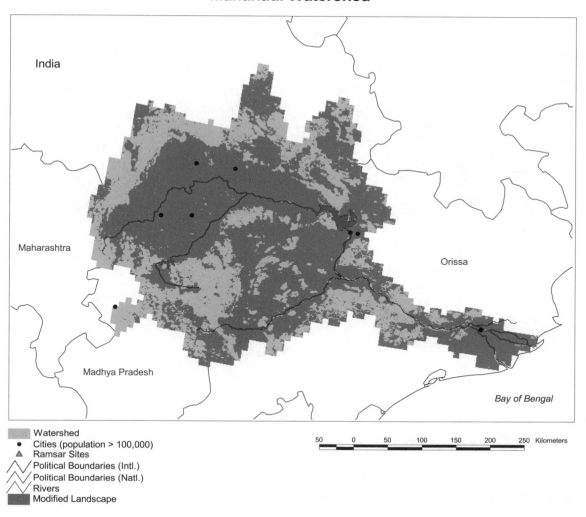

- ▨ Watershed
- ● Cities (population > 100,000)
- ▲ Ramsar Sites
- ∿ Political Boundaries (Intl.)
- ∿ Political Boundaries (Natl.)
- ∿ Rivers
- ▨ Modified Landscape

Basin area:	145,818 km²
Population density:	192 people per km²
Urban growth rate:	2.9%
Large cities:	8
Total fish species:	-
Fish endemics:	-
Threatened fish species:	0
Endemic bird areas:	0
Ramsar sites:	0
Protected areas:	4%
Wetlands:	0%
Arid:	0%

Forest:	8%
Cropland:	59%
Cropland irrigated:	26%
Developed:	6%
Shrub:	0%
Grassland:	26%
Barren:	0%
Loss of original forest:	79%
Deforestation rate:	7%
Eroded area:	10%
Large dams:	1
Planned major dams:	-

Land Cover Within 5 km of Major Rivers

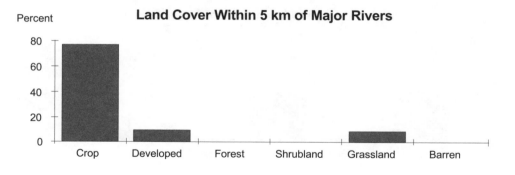

© 1998 World Resources Institute

Mekong Watershed

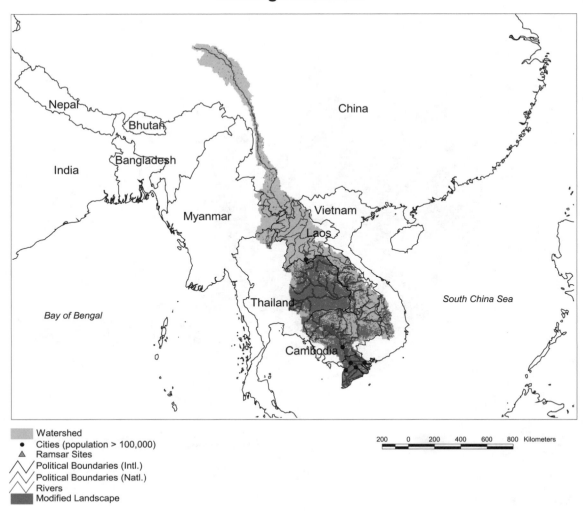

Watershed
● Cities (population > 100,000)
▲ Ramsar Sites
Political Boundaries (Intl.)
Political Boundaries (Natl.)
Rivers
Modified Landscape

200 0 200 400 600 800 Kilometers

Basin area:	805,627 km²	Forest:	41%
Population density:	78 people per km²	Cropland:	38%
Urban growth rate:	-	Cropland irrigated:	76%
Large cities:	6	Developed:	2%
Total fish species:	244	Shrub:	4%
Fish endemics:	62	Grassland:	13%
Threatened fish species:	7	Barren:	0%
Endemic bird areas:	7	Loss of original forest:	69%
Ramsar sites:	0	Deforestation rate:	16%
Protected areas:	5%	Eroded area:	21%
Wetlands:	9%	Large dams:	4
Arid:	0%	Planned major dams:	2

Land Cover Within 5 km of Major Rivers

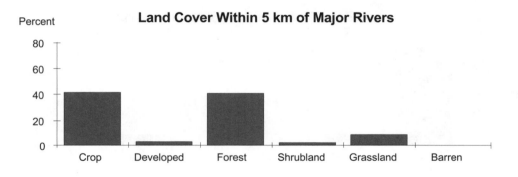

© 1998 World Resources Institute

Murray-Darling Watershed

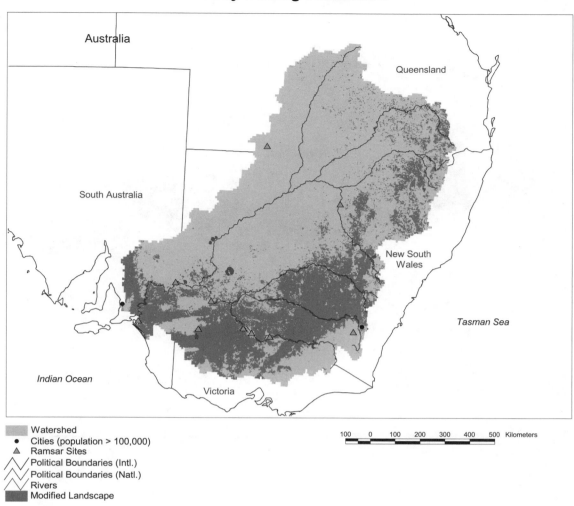

Australia
South Australia
Queensland
New South Wales
Tasman Sea
Indian Ocean
Victoria

	Watershed
●	Cities (population > 100,000)
△	Ramsar Sites
	Political Boundaries (Intl.)
	Political Boundaries (Natl.)
	Rivers
	Modified Landscape

100 0 100 200 300 400 500 Kilometers

Basin area:	1,050,111 km²	Forest:	8%
Population density:	2 people per km²	Cropland:	29%
Urban growth rate:	0.5%	Cropland irrigated:	0%
Large cities:	2	Developed:	-
Total fish species:	33 (intr: 8 diad: 5)	Shrub:	25%
Fish endemics:	7	Grassland:	38%
Threatened fish species:	5	Barren:	0%
Endemic bird areas:	2	Loss of original forest:	64%
Ramsar sites:	10	Deforestation rate:	-
Protected areas:	4%	Eroded area:	1%
Wetlands:	3%	Large dams:	12
Arid:	67%	Planned major dams:	-

Land Cover Within 5 km of Major Rivers

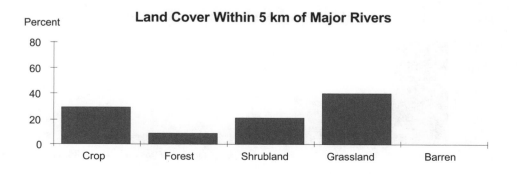

Percent

Crop   Forest   Shrubland   Grassland   Barren

© 1998 World Resources Institute

Narmada Watershed

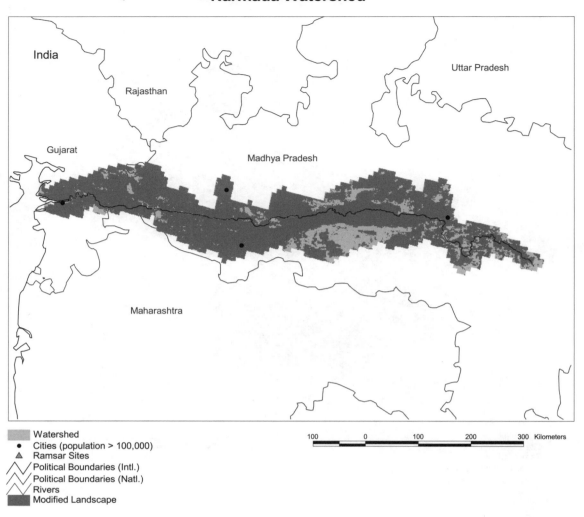

Watershed
● Cities (population > 100,000)
▲ Ramsar Sites
⋀ Political Boundaries (Intl.)
⋀ Political Boundaries (Natl.)
⋀ Rivers
▮ Modified Landscape

100   0   100   200   300 Kilometers

Basin area:	96,260 km²	Forest:	1%
Population density:	192 people per km²	Cropland:	76%
Urban growth rate:	2.0%	Cropland irrigated:	2%
Large cities:	4	Developed:	8%
Total fish species:	77	Shrub:	1%
Fish endemics:	-	Grassland:	15%
Threatened fish species:	0	Barren:	0%
Endemic bird areas:	0	Loss of original forest:	71%
Ramsar sites:	0	Deforestation rate:	9%
Protected areas:	4%	Eroded area:	28%
Wetlands:	1%	Large dams:	3
Arid:	26%	Planned major dams:	1

Land Cover Within 5 km of Major Rivers

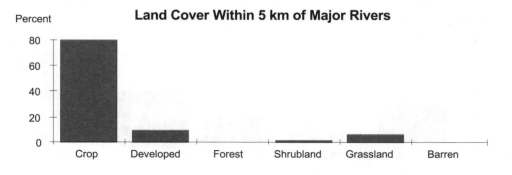

© 1998 World Resources Institute

Ob Watershed

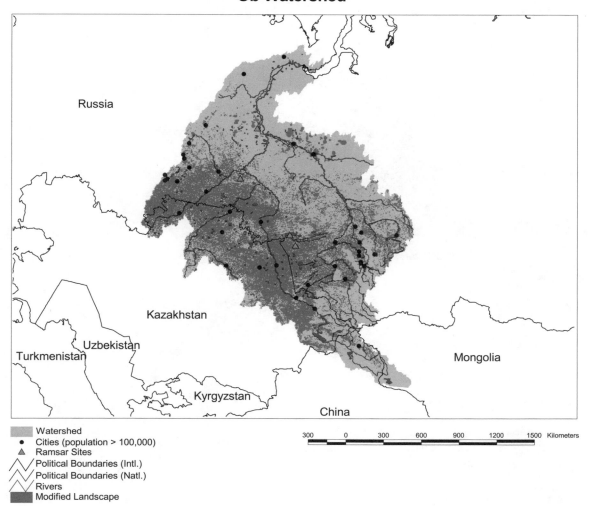

Russia

Kazakhstan

Turkmenistan · Uzbekistan

Kyrgyzstan

China

Mongolia

▨	Watershed
●	Cities (population > 100,000)
▲	Ramsar Sites
⋀⋁	Political Boundaries (Intl.)
⋀⋁	Political Boundaries (Natl.)
⋀⋁	Rivers
▨	Modified Landscape

300   0   300   600   900   1200   1500 Kilometers

Basin area:	2,972,497 km²	Forest:	30%
Population density:	9 people per km²	Cropland:	36%
Urban growth rate:	0.1%	Cropland irrigated:	3%
Large cities:	39	Developed:	5%
Total fish species:	43	Shrub:	5%
Fish endemics:	0	Grassland:	10%
Threatened fish species:	0	Barren:	1%
Endemic bird areas:	-	Loss of original forest:	39%
Ramsar sites:	4	Deforestation rate:	-
Protected areas:	2%	Eroded area:	3%
Wetlands:	11%	Large dams:	5
Arid:	42%	Planned major dams:	1

Land Cover Within 5 km of Major Rivers

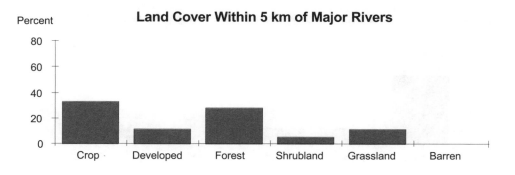

Percent

Crop   Developed   Forest   Shrubland   Grassland   Barren

© 1998 World Resources Institute

Ob Watershed: Irtysh Subbasin

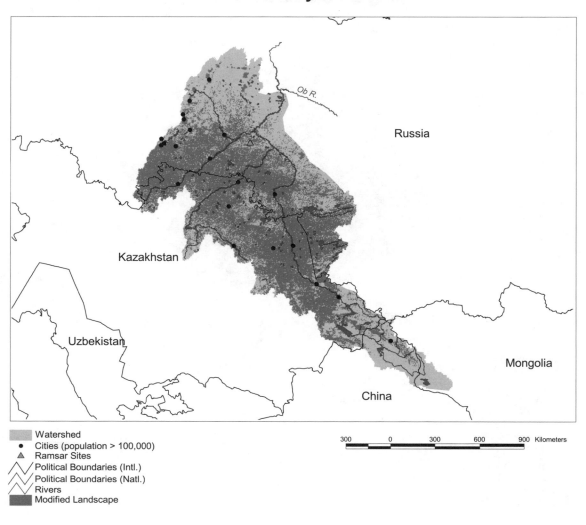

- ▨ Watershed
- • Cities (population > 100,000)
- ▲ Ramsar Sites
- ᐯᐱ Political Boundaries (Intl.)
- ᐯᐱ Political Boundaries (Natl.)
- ᐯᐱ Rivers
- ▨ Modified Landscape

Basin area:	1,673,470 km²	Forest:	17%
Population density:	12 people per km²	Cropland:	51%
Urban growth rate:	0.1%	Cropland irrigated:	3%
Large cities:	21	Developed:	5%
Total fish species:	-	Shrub:	4%
Fish endemics:	-	Grassland:	14%
Threatened fish species:	0	Barren:	1%
Endemic bird areas:	0	Loss of original forest:	52%
Ramsar sites:	3	Deforestation rate:	-
Protected areas:	2%	Eroded area:	3%
Wetlands:	8%	Large dams:	4
Arid:	69%	Planned major dams:	-

Land Cover Within 5 km of Major Rivers

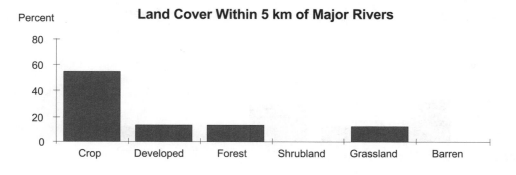

© 1998 World Resources Institute

Salween Watershed

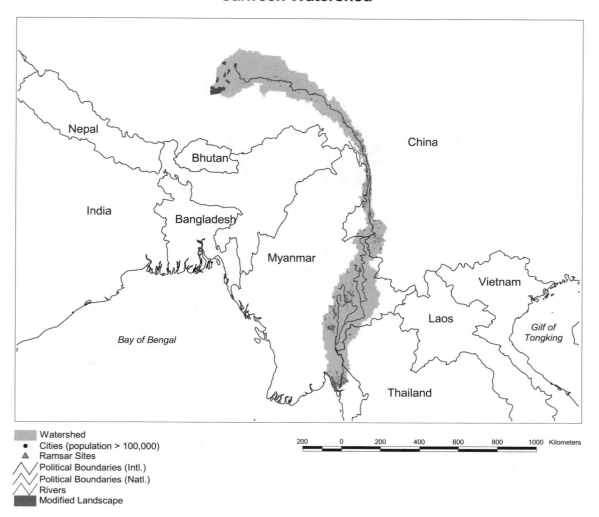

Watershed
● Cities (population > 100,000)
▲ Ramsar Sites
Political Boundaries (Intl.)
Political Boundaries (Natl.)
Rivers
Modified Landscape

Basin area:	271,866 km²	Forest:	44%
Population density:	76 people per km²	Cropland:	6%
Urban growth rate:	-	Cropland irrigated:	60%
Large cities:	0	Developed:	0%
Total fish species:	143	Shrub:	11%
Fish endemics:	47	Grassland:	37%
Threatened fish species:	2	Barren:	1%
Endemic bird areas:	3	Loss of original forest:	72%
Ramsar sites:	0	Deforestation rate:	10%
Protected areas:	2%	Eroded area:	4%
Wetlands:	10%	Large dams:	0
Arid:	0%	Planned major dams:	-

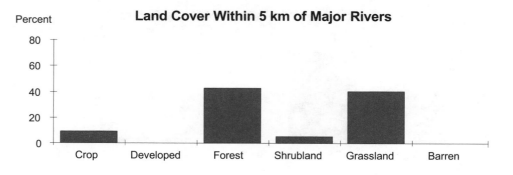

Land Cover Within 5 km of Major Rivers

© 1998 World Resources Institute

Sepik Watershed

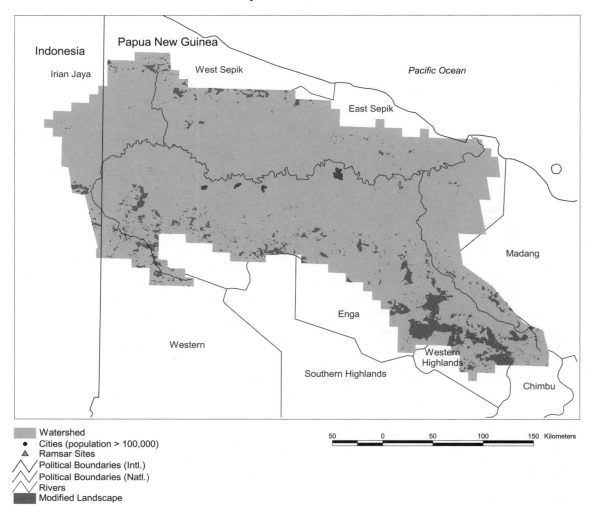

Watershed
● Cities (population > 100,000)
▲ Ramsar Sites
∿ Political Boundaries (Intl.)
∿ Political Boundaries (Natl.)
∿ Rivers
■ Modified Landscape

Basin area:	101,821 km²	Forest:	77%
Population density:	9 people per km²	Cropland:	7%
Urban growth rate:	-	Cropland irrigated:	8%
Large cities:	0	Developed:	-
Total fish species:	57 (intr: 4 diad: 4)	Shrub:	0%
Fish endemics:	0	Grassland:	14%
Threatened fish species:	0	Barren:	0%
Endemic bird areas:	3	Loss of original forest:	24%
Ramsar sites:	0	Deforestation rate:	3%
Protected areas:	0%	Eroded area:	0%
Wetlands:	33%	Large dams:	0
Arid:	0%	Planned major dams:	-

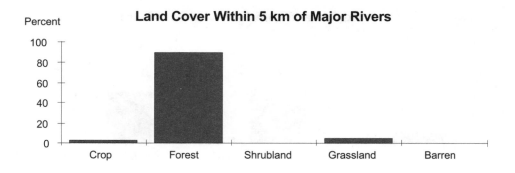

Land Cover Within 5 km of Major Rivers

Percent

© 1998 World Resources Institute

Syr Darya Watershed

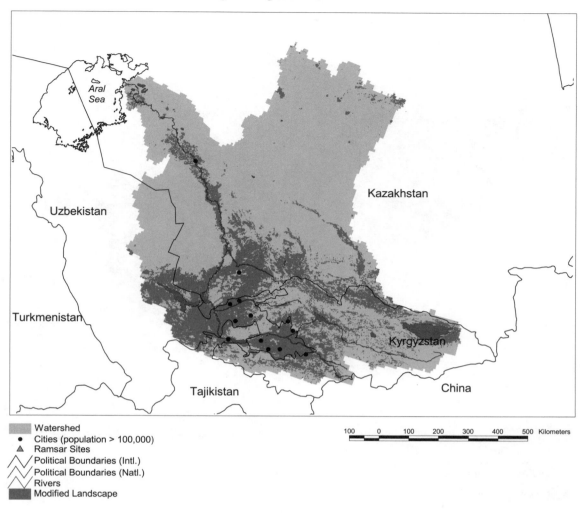

Watershed	
●	Cities (population > 100,000)
▲	Ramsar Sites
	Political Boundaries (Intl.)
	Political Boundaries (Natl.)
	Rivers
	Modified Landscape

100   0   100   200   300   400   500 Kilometers

Basin area:	782,669 km²	Forest:	3%
Population density:	26 people per km²	Cropland:	22%
Urban growth rate:	1.8%	Cropland irrigated:	27%
Large cities:	16	Developed:	4%
Total fish species:	48	Shrub:	31%
Fish endemics:	4	Grassland:	36%
Threatened fish species:	1	Barren:	4%
Endemic bird areas:	0	Loss of original forest:	45%
Ramsar sites:	1	Deforestation rate:	-
Protected areas:	1%	Eroded area:	0%
Wetlands:	2%	Large dams:	7
Arid:	89%	Planned major dams:	1

Land Cover Within 5 km of Major Rivers

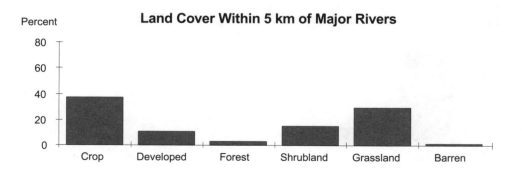

2 - 99

© 1998 World Resources Institute

Tapti Watershed

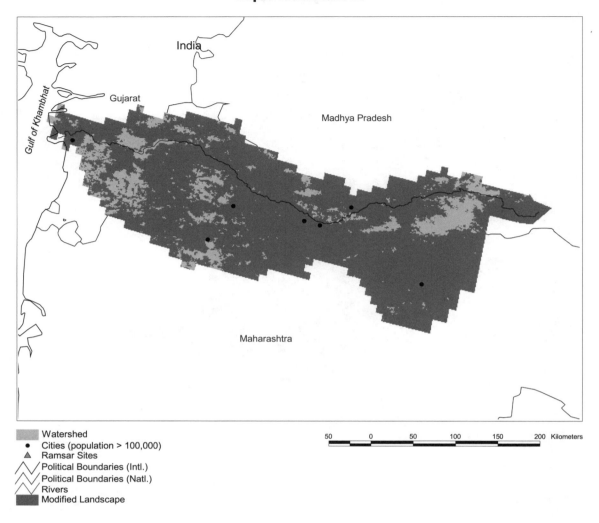

Watershed			
● Cities (population > 100,000)			
▲ Ramsar Sites			
Political Boundaries (Intl.)			
Political Boundaries (Natl.)			
Rivers			
Modified Landscape			

Basin area:	74,620 km²	Forest:	0%
Population density:	233 people per km²	Cropland:	78%
Urban growth rate:	4.2%	Cropland irrigated:	27%
Large cities:	7	Developed:	8%
Total fish species:	-	Shrub:	4%
Fish endemics:	-	Grassland:	10%
Threatened fish species:	0	Barren:	0%
Endemic bird areas:	0	Loss of original forest:	61%
Ramsar sites:	0	Deforestation rate:	10%
Protected areas:	4%	Eroded area:	23%
Wetlands:	1%	Large dams:	2
Arid:	64%	Planned major dams:	-

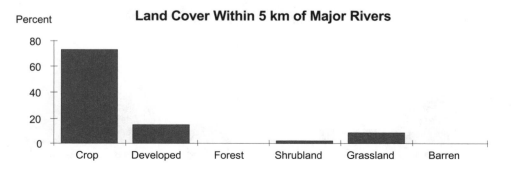

Percent

Land Cover Within 5 km of Major Rivers

© 1998 World Resources Institute

Tarim Watershed

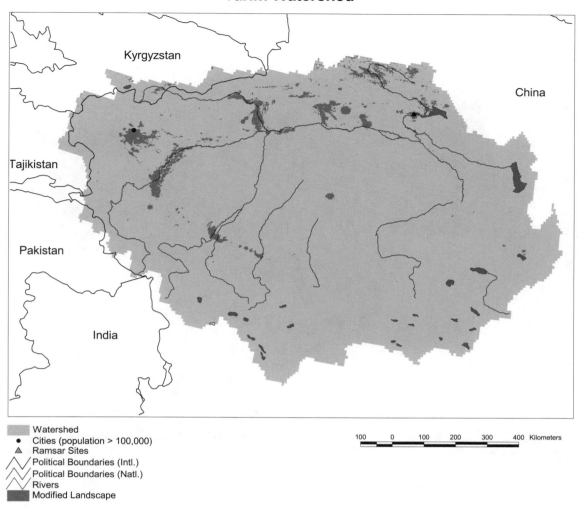

Watershed
● Cities (population > 100,000)
▲ Ramsar Sites
Political Boundaries (Intl.)
Political Boundaries (Natl.)
Rivers
Modified Landscape

100 0 100 200 300 400 Kilometers

Basin area:	1,152,447 km²	Forest:	0%
Population density:	10 people per km²	Cropland:	2%
Urban growth rate:	-	Cropland irrigated:	74%
Large cities:	2	Developed:	1%
Total fish species:	14	Shrub:	31%
Fish endemics:	3	Grassland:	5%
Threatened fish species:	0	Barren:	61%
Endemic bird areas:	1	Loss of original forest:	69%
Ramsar sites:	0	Deforestation rate:	-
Protected areas:	21%	Eroded area:	0%
Wetlands:	16%	Large dams:	0
Arid:	61%	Planned major dams:	-

Land Cover Within 5 km of Major Rivers

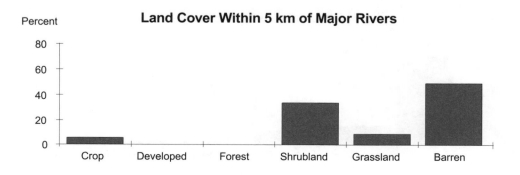

Percent

80
60
40
20
0

Crop Developed Forest Shrubland Grassland Barren

© 1998 World Resources Institute

Xi Jiang (Pearl River) Watershed

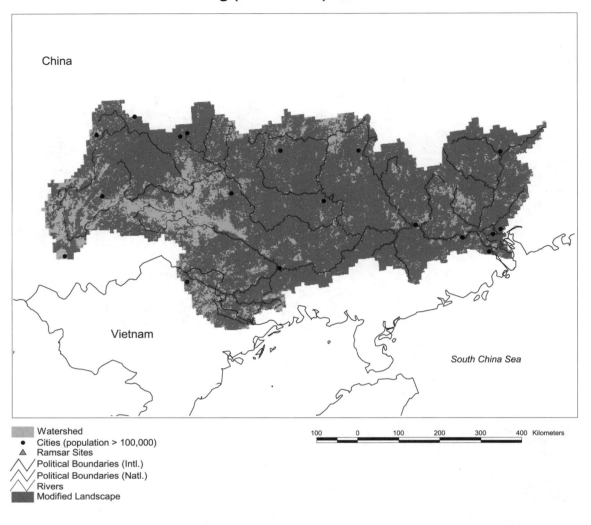

China

Vietnam

South China Sea

	Watershed
•	Cities (population > 100,000)
▲	Ramsar Sites
/\/\	Political Boundaries (Intl.)
/\/\	Political Boundaries (Natl.)
/\/	Rivers
	Modified Landscape

100   0   100   200   300   400 Kilometers

Basin area:	409,458 km²	Forest:	11%
Population density:	210 people per km²	Cropland:	76%
Urban growth rate:	3.0%	Cropland irrigated:	61%
Large cities:	18	Developed:	6%
Total fish species:	280-300	Shrub:	2%
Fish endemics:	120	Grassland:	3%
Threatened fish species:	1	Barren:	0%
Endemic bird areas:	4	Loss of original forest:	80%
Ramsar sites:	0	Deforestation rate:	-
Protected areas:	1%	Eroded area:	22%
Wetlands:	1%	Large dams:	7
Arid:	0%	Planned major dams:	2

Land Cover Within 5 km of Major Rivers

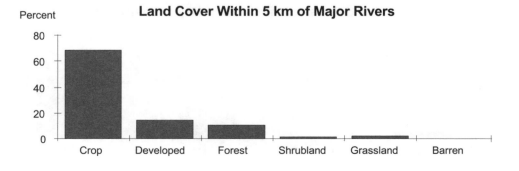

Percent

© 1998 World Resources Institute

Yalu Jiang Watershed

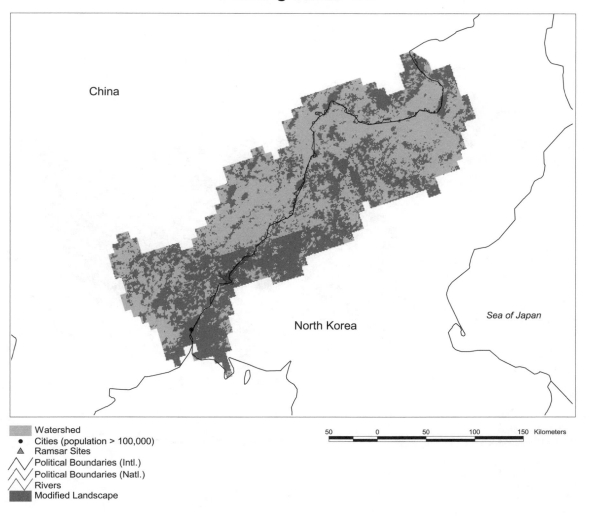

China

North Korea

Sea of Japan

Watershed
● Cities (population > 100,000)
▲ Ramsar Sites
Political Boundaries (Intl.)
Political Boundaries (Natl.)
Rivers
Modified Landscape

50   0   50   100   150 Kilometers

Basin area:	48,328 km²	Forest:	51%
Population density:	117 people per km²	Cropland:	41%
Urban growth rate:	2.7%	Cropland irrigated:	8%
Large cities:	1	Developed:	4%
Total fish species:	74	Shrub:	0%
Fish endemics:	4	Grassland:	2%
Threatened fish species:	0	Barren:	0%
Endemic bird areas:	0	Loss of original forest:	62%
Ramsar sites:	0	Deforestation rate:	-
Protected areas:	3%	Eroded area:	0%
Wetlands:	1%	Large dams:	3
Arid:	0%	Planned major dams:	-

Land Cover Within 5 km of Major Rivers

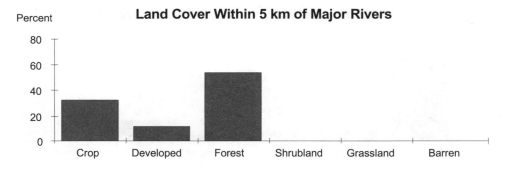

Percent

© 1998 World Resources Institute

Yangtze Watershed

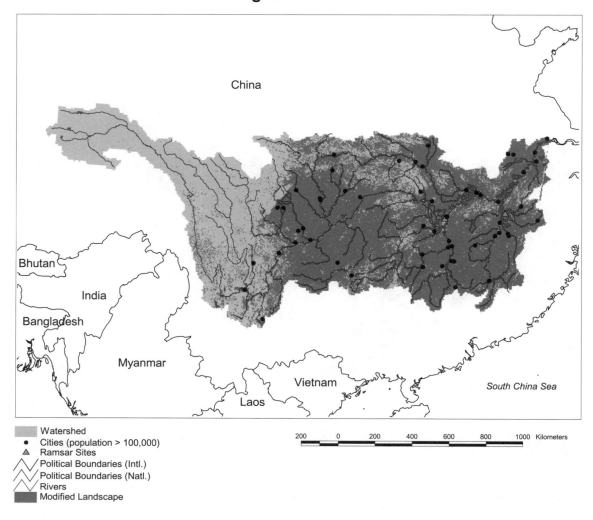

Watershed
● Cities (population > 100,000)
▲ Ramsar Sites
〰 Political Boundaries (Intl.)
〰 Political Boundaries (Natl.)
〰 Rivers
■ Modified Landscape

Basin area:	1,722,155 km²	Forest:	11%
Population density:	224 people per km²	Cropland:	56%
Urban growth rate:	2.4%	Cropland irrigated:	32%
Large cities:	56	Developed:	4%
Total fish species:	322	Shrub:	7%
Fish endemics:	-	Grassland:	22%
Threatened fish species:	3	Barren:	0%
Endemic bird areas:	6	Loss of original forest:	85%
Ramsar sites:	2	Deforestation rate:	-
Protected areas:	2%	Eroded area:	27%
Wetlands:	3%	Large dams:	17
Arid:	0%	Planned major dams:	11

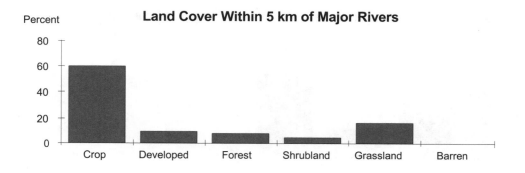

Land Cover Within 5 km of Major Rivers

© 1998 World Resources Institute

Yenisey Watershed

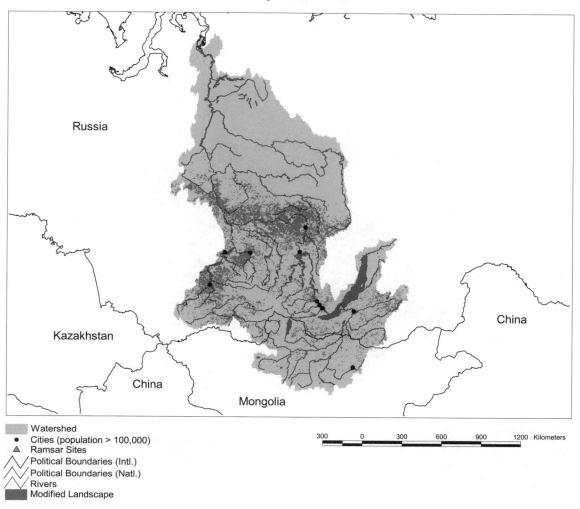

Watershed
● Cities (population > 100,000)
▲ Ramsar Sites
Political Boundaries (Intl.)
Political Boundaries (Natl.)
Rivers
Modified Landscape

300   0   300   600   900   1200 Kilometers

Basin area:	2,554,482 km²		Forest:	49%
Population density:	2 people per km²		Cropland:	13%
Urban growth rate:	0.2%		Cropland irrigated:	6%
Large cities:	10		Developed:	2%
Total fish species:	42		Shrub:	15%
Fish endemics:	2		Grassland:	18%
Threatened fish species:	1		Barren:	0%
Endemic bird areas:	0		Loss of original forest:	19%
Ramsar sites:	1		Deforestation rate:	-
Protected areas:	3%		Eroded area:	2%
Wetlands:	3%		Large dams:	12
Arid:	11%		Planned major dams:	-

Land Cover Within 5 km of Major Rivers

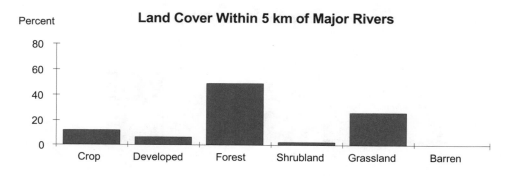

Percent

© 1998 World Resources Institute

Yenisey Watershed: Lake Baikal Subbasin

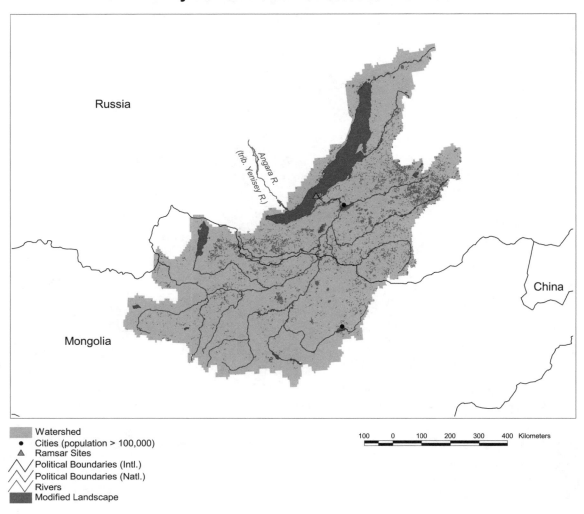

Watershed
● Cities (population > 100,000)
▲ Ramsar Sites
〰 Political Boundaries (Intl.)
〰 Political Boundaries (Natl.)
〰 Rivers
▪ Modified Landscape

100   0   100   200   300   400   Kilometers

Basin area:	597,253 km²	Forest:	33%
Population density:	3 people per km²	Cropland:	7%
Urban growth rate:	-	Cropland irrigated:	12%
Large cities:	2	Developed:	1%
Total fish species:	-	Shrub:	5%
Fish endemics:	-	Grassland:	52%
Threatened fish species:	-	Barren:	0%
Endemic bird areas:	0	Loss of original forest:	28%
Ramsar sites:	1	Deforestation rate:	-
Protected areas:	7%	Eroded area:	2%
Wetlands:	7%	Large dams:	0
Arid:	11%	Planned major dams:	-

Land Cover Within 5 km of Major Rivers

Percent

© 1998 World Resources Institute

WATERSHED PROFILES

FOR

NORTH AND CENTRAL AMERICA

Alabama & Tombigbee Watershed

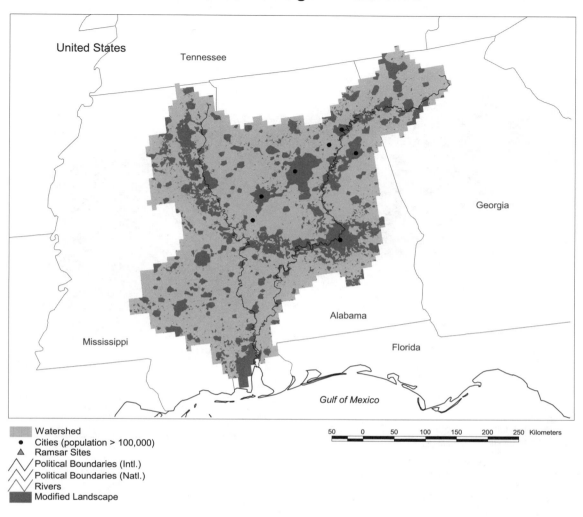

Watershed
● Cities (population > 100,000)
▲ Ramsar Sites
Political Boundaries (Intl.)
Political Boundaries (Natl.)
Rivers
Modified Landscape

Basin area:	138,130 km²		Forest:	72%
Population density:	30 people per km²		Cropland:	9%
Urban growth rate:	0.0%		Cropland irrigated:	0%
Large cities:	7		Developed:	18%
Total fish species:	122 (diad: 4)		Shrub:	0%
Fish endemics:	23		Grassland:	0%
Threatened fish species:	13		Barren:	0%
Endemic bird areas:	0		Loss of original forest:	25%
Ramsar sites:	0		Deforestation rate:	-
Protected areas:	0%		Eroded area:	4%
Wetlands:	4%		Large dams:	103
Arid:	0%		Planned major dams:	-

Land Cover Within 5 km of Major Rivers

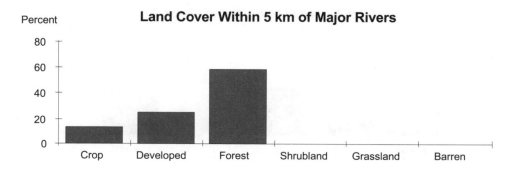

© 1998 World Resources Institute

Balsas Watershed

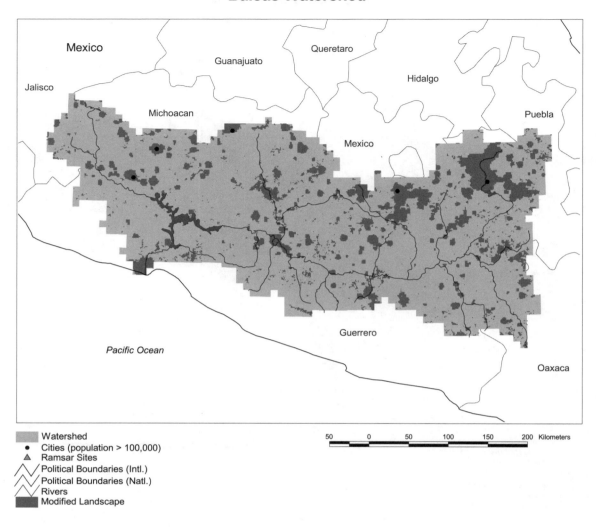

Watershed
• Cities (population > 100,000)
▲ Ramsar Sites
Political Boundaries (Intl.)
Political Boundaries (Natl.)
Rivers
Modified Landscape

Basin area:	117,109 km²		Forest:	49%
Population density:	85 people per km²		Cropland:	4%
Urban growth rate:	-		Cropland irrigated:	42%
Large cities:	5		Developed:	12%
Total fish species:	37		Shrub:	1%
Fish endemics:	7		Grassland:	34%
Threatened fish species:	0		Barren:	0%
Endemic bird areas:	5		Loss of original forest:	29%
Ramsar sites:	0		Deforestation rate:	10%
Protected areas:	2%		Eroded area:	56%
Wetlands:	0%		Large dams:	1
Arid:	12%		Planned major dams:	-

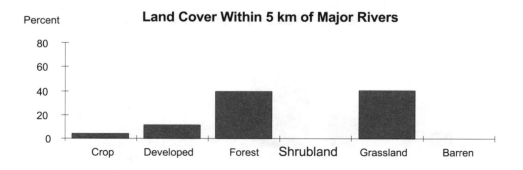

Land Cover Within 5 km of Major Rivers

© 1998 World Resources Institute

Brazos Watershed

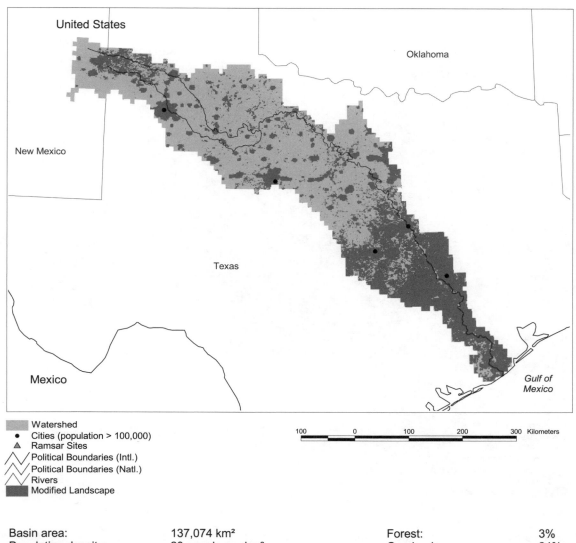

Watershed
● Cities (population > 100,000)
▲ Ramsar Sites
〰 Political Boundaries (Intl.)
〰 Political Boundaries (Natl.)
〰 Rivers
▮ Modified Landscape

Basin area:	137,074 km²	Forest:	3%
Population density:	20 people per km²	Cropland:	24%
Urban growth rate:	-	Cropland irrigated:	9%
Large cities:	5	Developed:	15%
Total fish species:	55 (diad: 1)	Shrub:	0%
Fish endemics:	1	Grassland:	57%
Threatened fish species:	1	Barren:	0%
Endemic bird areas:	0	Loss of original forest:	81%
Ramsar sites:	0	Deforestation rate:	-
Protected areas:	0%	Eroded area:	3%
Wetlands:	4%	Large dams:	132
Arid:	80%	Planned major dams:	-

Land Cover Within 5 km of Major Rivers

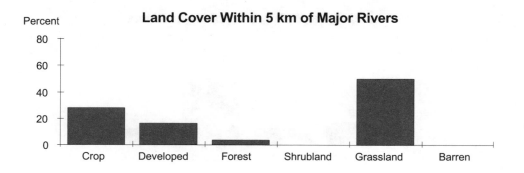

2 - 111

© 1998 World Resources Institute

Colorado Watershed

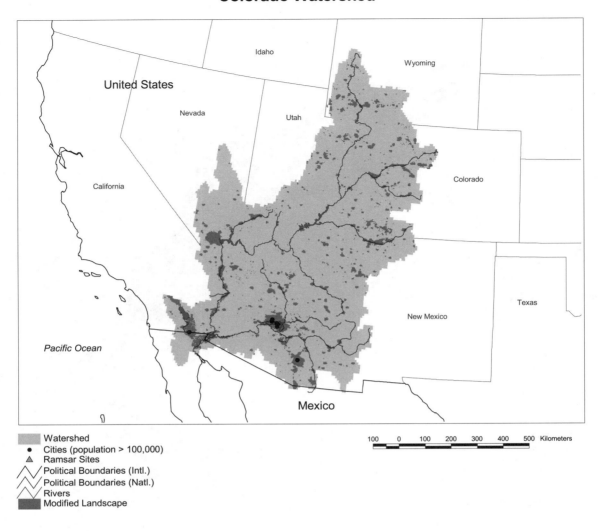

Watershed
● Cities (population > 100,000)
▲ Ramsar Sites
〰 Political Boundaries (Intl.)
〰 Political Boundaries (Natl.)
〰 Rivers
■ Modified Landscape

100   0   100   200   300   400   500   Kilometers

Basin area:	703,132 km²	Forest:	23%
Population density:	10 people per km²	Cropland:	1%
Urban growth rate:	2.1%	Cropland irrigated:	86%
Large cities:	7	Developed:	8%
Total fish species:	121	Shrub:	55%
Fish endemics:	42	Grassland:	12%
Threatened fish species:	8	Barren:	0%
Endemic bird areas:	1	Loss of original forest:	43%
Ramsar sites:	0	Deforestation rate:	-
Protected areas:	8%	Eroded area:	1%
Wetlands:	1%	Large dams:	265
Arid:	89%	Planned major dams:	-

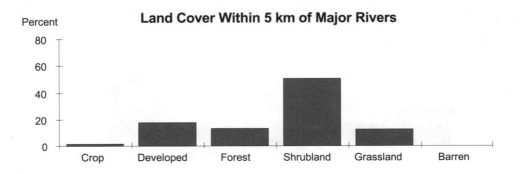

Land Cover Within 5 km of Major Rivers

Percent

80
60
40
20
0

Crop   Developed   Forest   Shrubland   Grassland   Barren

© 1998 World Resources Institute

Columbia Watershed

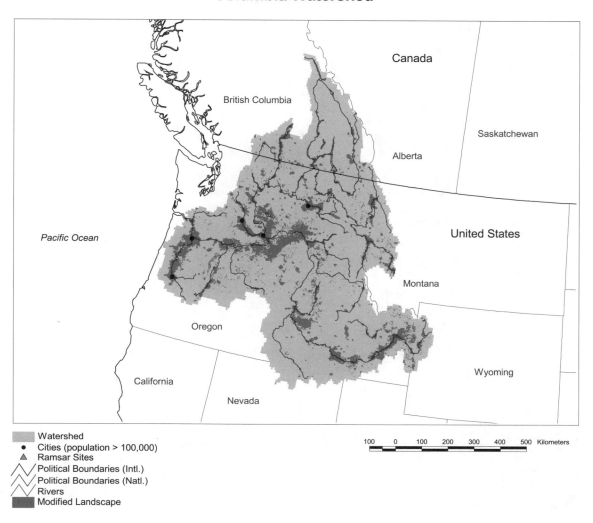

Watershed
● Cities (population > 100,000)
▲ Ramsar Sites
〈〉 Political Boundaries (Intl.)
〈〉 Political Boundaries (Natl.)
〈〉 Rivers
■ Modified Landscape

100 0 100 200 300 400 500 Kilometers

Basin area:	657,490 km²	Forest:	49%
Population density:	9 people per km²	Cropland:	6%
Urban growth rate:	1.1%	Cropland irrigated:	40%
Large cities:	5	Developed:	9%
Total fish species:	- (diad: 11)	Shrub:	22%
Fish endemics:	13	Grassland:	14%
Threatened fish species:	4	Barren:	0%
Endemic bird areas:	0	Loss of original forest:	22%
Ramsar sites:	1	Deforestation rate:	-
Protected areas:	8%	Eroded area:	5%
Wetlands:	2%	Large dams:	184
Arid:	49%	Planned major dams:	1

Land Cover Within 5 km of Major Rivers

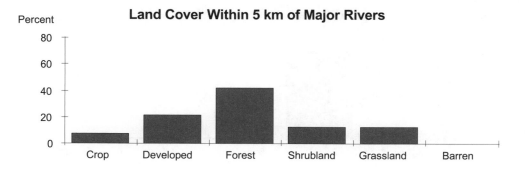

Percent

2 - 113

© 1998 World Resources Institute

Fraser Watershed

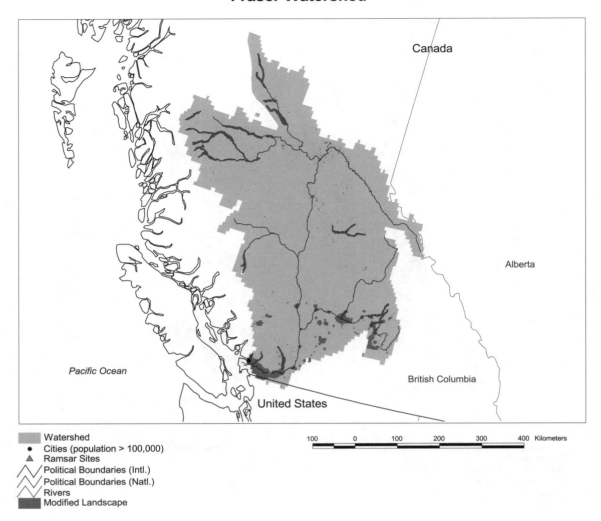

Watershed
● Cities (population > 100,000)
▲ Ramsar Sites
∿ Political Boundaries (Intl.)
∿ Political Boundaries (Natl.)
∿ Rivers
Modified Landscape

Basin area:	248,035 km²	Forest:	89%
Population density:	6 people per km²	Cropland:	1%
Urban growth rate:	-	Cropland irrigated:	12%
Large cities:	1	Developed:	-
Total fish species:	46 (diad: 11)	Shrub:	5%
Fish endemics:	0	Grassland:	2%
Threatened fish species:	0	Barren:	0%
Endemic bird areas:	0	Loss of original forest:	7%
Ramsar sites:	0	Deforestation rate:	-
Protected areas:	12%	Eroded area:	0%
Wetlands:	2%	Large dams:	3
Arid:	3%	Planned major dams:	-

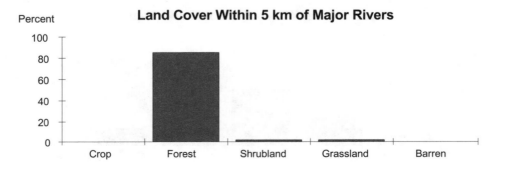

Land Cover Within 5 km of Major Rivers

Percent

© 1998 World Resources Institute

Fraser Watershed: Nechako Subbasin

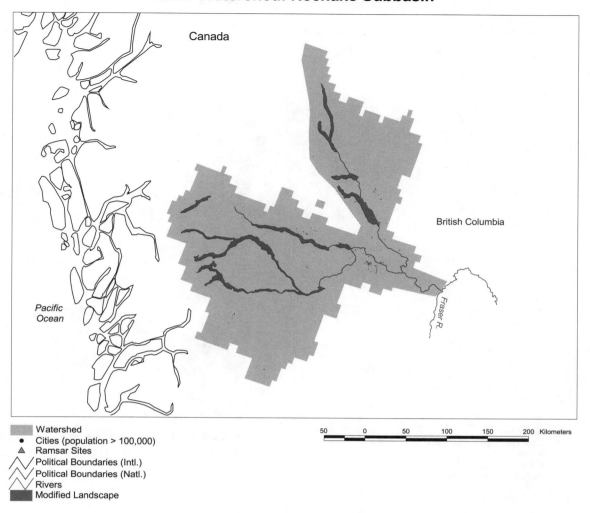

Canada

British Columbia

Pacific
Ocean

Fraser R.

	Watershed
●	Cities (population > 100,000)
▲	Ramsar Sites
∧	Political Boundaries (Intl.)
∧	Political Boundaries (Natl.)
∧	Rivers
	Modified Landscape

50   0   50   100   150   200 Kilometers

Basin area:	60,084 km²	Forest:	88%
Population density:	1 person per km²	Cropland:	0%
Urban growth rate:	-	Cropland irrigated:	59%
Large cities:	0	Developed:	-
Total fish species:	38 (intr: 2 diad: 0)	Shrub:	4%
Fish endemics:	0	Grassland:	1%
Threatened fish species:	0	Barren:	0%
Endemic bird areas:	0	Loss of original forest:	3%
Ramsar sites:	0	Deforestation rate:	-
Protected areas:	18%	Eroded area:	0%
Wetlands:	4%	Large dams:	2
Arid:	0%	Planned major dams:	-

Land Cover Within 5 km of Major Rivers

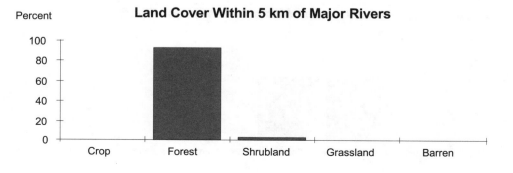

Percent

100
80
60
40
20
0

Crop   Forest   Shrubland   Grassland   Barren

© 1998 World Resources Institute

Hudson Watershed

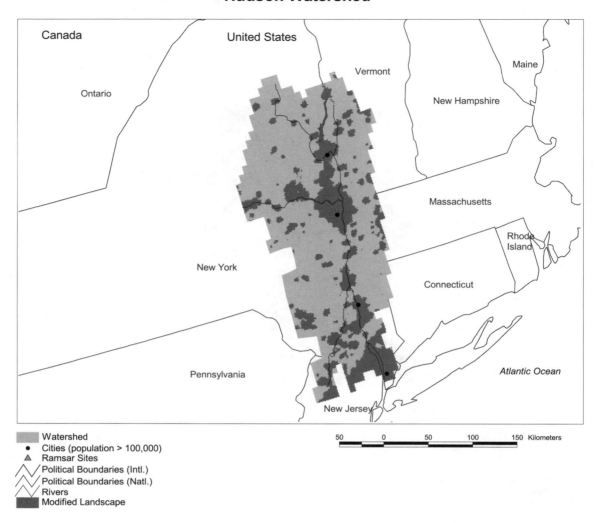

- ▨ Watershed
- ● Cities (population > 100,000)
- ▲ Ramsar Sites
- ⋀ Political Boundaries (Intl.)
- ⋀ Political Boundaries (Natl.)
- ⋀ Rivers
- ■ Modified Landscape

Basin area:	41,912 km²	Forest:	73%
Population density:	92 people per km²	Cropland:	0%
Urban growth rate:	0.4%	Cropland irrigated:	0%
Large cities:	4	Developed:	26%
Total fish species:	84 (intr: 4 diad: 9)	Shrub:	0%
Fish endemics:	0	Grassland:	0%
Threatened fish species:	1	Barren:	0%
Endemic bird areas:	0	Loss of original forest:	9%
Ramsar sites:	0	Deforestation rate:	-
Protected areas:	2%	Eroded area:	1%
Wetlands:	15%	Large dams:	53
Arid:	0%	Planned major dams:	-

Land Cover Within 5 km of Major Rivers

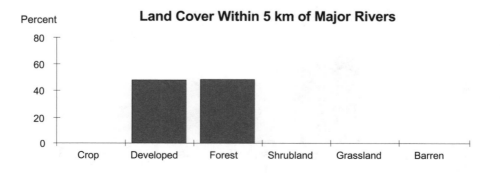

2 - 116

© 1998 World Resources Institute

Mackenzie Watershed

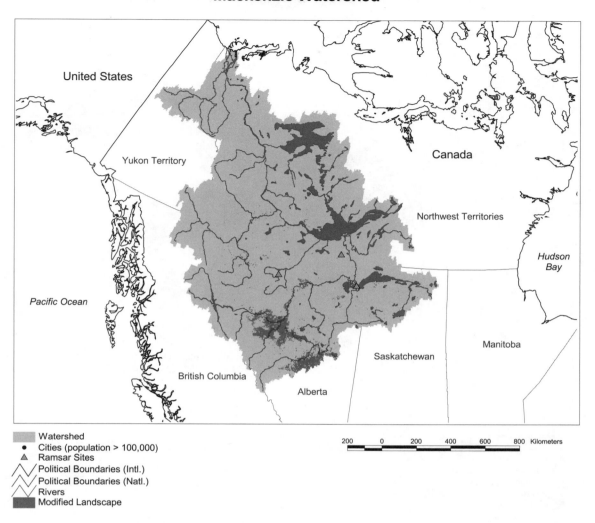

Watershed
● Cities (population > 100,000)
▲ Ramsar Sites
/\/ Political Boundaries (Intl.)
/\/ Political Boundaries (Natl.)
/\/ Rivers
■ Modified Landscape

Basin area:	1,743,058 km²	Forest:	63%
Population density:	< 1 person per km²	Cropland:	3%
Urban growth rate:	-	Cropland irrigated:	0%
Large cities:	0	Developed:	-
Total fish species:	53 (diad: 5)	Shrub:	18%
Fish endemics:	0	Grassland:	4%
Threatened fish species:	0	Barren:	1%
Endemic bird areas:	0	Loss of original forest:	7%
Ramsar sites:	3	Deforestation rate:	-
Protected areas:	5%	Eroded area:	0%
Wetlands:	18%	Large dams:	2
Arid:	0%	Planned major dams:	-

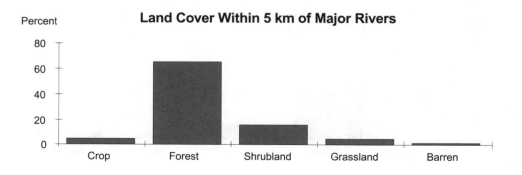

Land Cover Within 5 km of Major Rivers

© 1998 World Resources Institute

Mackenzie Watershed: Great Bear Lake Subbasin

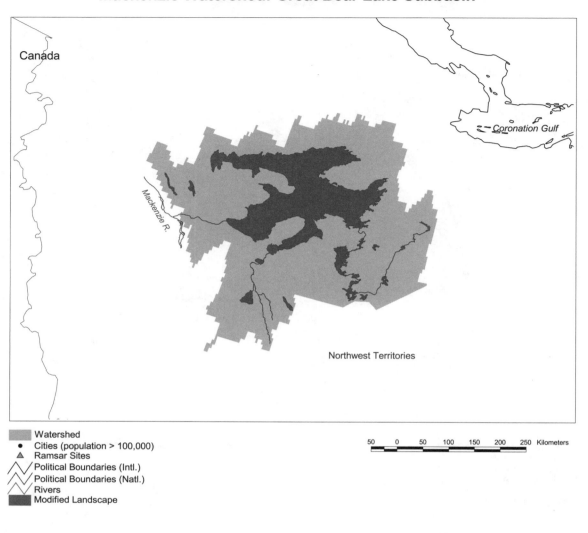

Watershed	
•	Cities (population > 100,000)
▲	Ramsar Sites
	Political Boundaries (Intl.)
	Political Boundaries (Natl.)
	Rivers
	Modified Landscape

50 0 50 100 150 200 250 Kilometers

Basin area:	162,207 km²	Forest:	32%
Population density:	< 1 person per km²	Cropland:	0%
Urban growth rate:	-	Cropland irrigated:	0%
Large cities:	0	Developed:	-
Total fish species:	16 (intr: 0 diad: 1)	Shrub:	12%
Fish endemics:	0	Grassland:	1%
Threatened fish species:	0	Barren:	7%
Endemic bird areas:	0	Loss of original forest:	1%
Ramsar sites:	0	Deforestation rate:	-
Protected areas:	0%	Eroded area:	0%
Wetlands:	11%	Large dams:	0
Arid:	0%	Planned major dams:	-

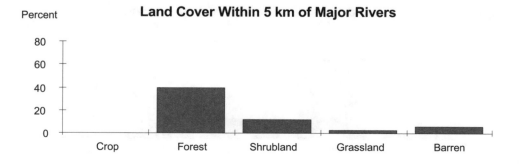

Percent

Land Cover Within 5 km of Major Rivers

2 - 118

© 1998 World Resources Institute

Mackenzie Watershed: Great Slave Lake Subbasin

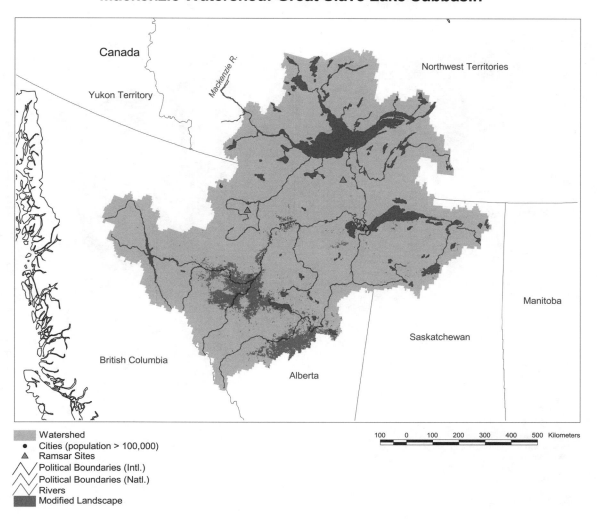

Watershed

● Cities (population > 100,000)

▲ Ramsar Sites

Political Boundaries (Intl.)

Political Boundaries (Natl.)

Rivers

Modified Landscape

Basin area:	972,404 km²	Forest:	77%
Population density:	< 1 person per km²	Cropland:	5%
Urban growth rate:	-	Cropland irrigated:	0%
Large cities:	0	Developed:	-
Total fish species:	24 (intr: 0 diad: 1)	Shrub:	8%
Fish endemics:	0	Grassland:	2%
Threatened fish species:	1	Barren:	1%
Endemic bird areas:	0	Loss of original forest:	8%
Ramsar sites:	3	Deforestation rate:	-
Protected areas:	7%	Eroded area:	0%
Wetlands:	24%	Large dams:	2
Arid:	0%	Planned major dams:	-

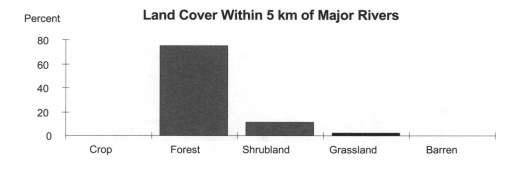

Land Cover Within 5 km of Major Rivers

Percent

© 1998 World Resources Institute

Mississippi Watershed

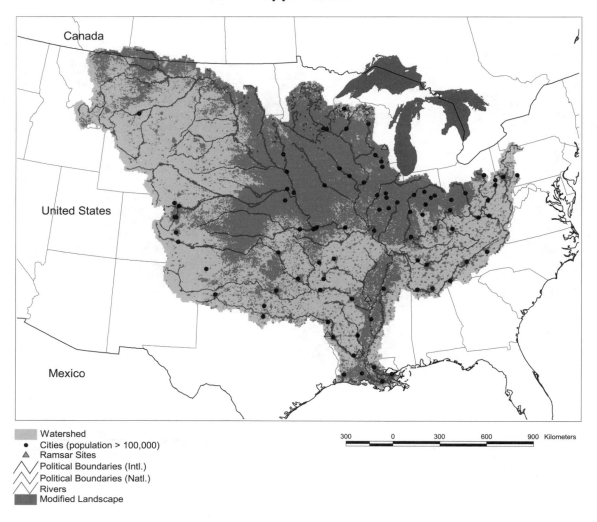

Watershed
● Cities (population > 100,000)
▲ Ramsar Sites
⋀ Political Boundaries (Intl.)
⋁ Political Boundaries (Natl.)
⋁ Rivers
▨ Modified Landscape

300   0   300   600   900 Kilometers

Basin area:	3,202,230 km²	Forest:	22%
Population density:	21 people per km²	Cropland:	35%
Urban growth rate:	1.0%	Cropland irrigated:	4%
Large cities:	87	Developed:	14%
Total fish species:	375 (diad: 2)	Shrub:	6%
Fish endemics:	85-127	Grassland:	22%
Threatened fish species:	6	Barren:	0%
Endemic bird areas:	0	Loss of original forest:	52%
Ramsar sites:	6	Deforestation rate:	-
Protected areas:	2%	Eroded area:	9%
Wetlands:	5%	Large dams:	2091
Arid:	36%	Planned major dams:	-

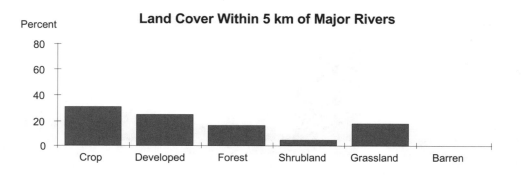

Land Cover Within 5 km of Major Rivers

Percent

2 - 120

© 1998 World Resources Institute

Mississippi Watershed: Arkansas Subbasin

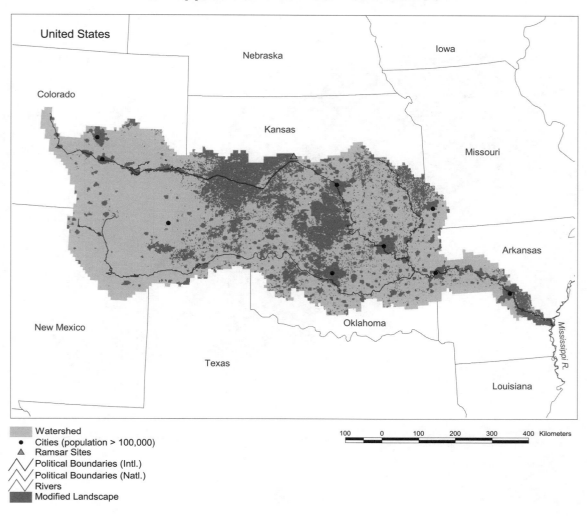

Watershed	
●	Cities (population > 100,000)
△	Ramsar Sites
	Political Boundaries (Intl.)
	Political Boundaries (Natl.)
	Rivers
	Modified Landscape

100   0   100   200   300   400 Kilometers

Basin area:	435,122 km²	Forest:	15%
Population density:	14 people per km²	Cropland:	17%
Urban growth rate:	1.9%	Cropland irrigated:	9%
Large cities:	9	Developed:	12%
Total fish species:	165 (intr: 21 diad: 2)	Shrub:	6%
Fish endemics:	21	Grassland:	50%
Threatened fish species:	0	Barren:	0%
Endemic bird areas:	0	Loss of original forest:	65%
Ramsar sites:	1	Deforestation rate:	-
Protected areas:	1%	Eroded area:	5%
Wetlands:	2%	Large dams:	387
Arid:	50%	Planned major dams:	-

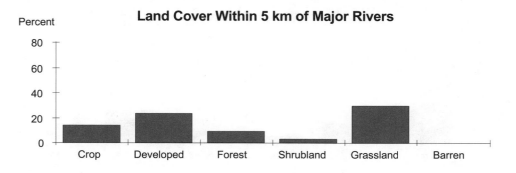

Land Cover Within 5 km of Major Rivers

2 - 121

© 1998 World Resources Institute

Mississippi Watershed: Missouri Subbasin

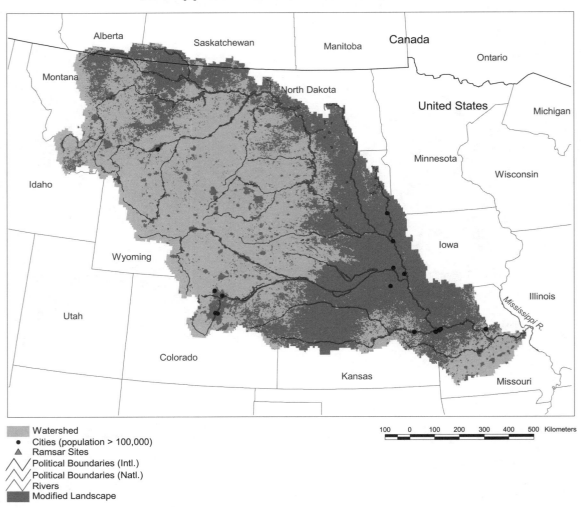

Watershed
● Cities (population > 100,000)
▲ Ramsar Sites
Political Boundaries (Intl.)
Political Boundaries (Natl.)
Rivers
Modified Landscape

100 0 100 200 300 400 500 Kilometers

Basin area:	1,331,810 km²	Forest:	11%
Population density:	8 people per km²	Cropland:	37%
Urban growth rate:	1.0%	Cropland irrigated:	7%
Large cities:	15	Developed:	9%
Total fish species:	155 (intr: 29 diad: 2)	Shrub:	13%
Fish endemics:	26	Grassland:	30%
Threatened fish species:	6	Barren:	0%
Endemic bird areas:	0	Loss of original forest:	54%
Ramsar sites:	0	Deforestation rate:	-
Protected areas:	3%	Eroded area:	6%
Wetlands:	5%	Large dams:	581
Arid:	64%	Planned major dams:	-

Land Cover Within 5 km of Major Rivers

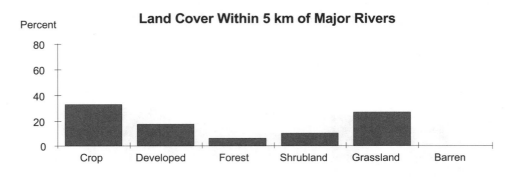

Percent

© 1998 World Resources Institute

Mississippi Watershed: Ohio Subbasin

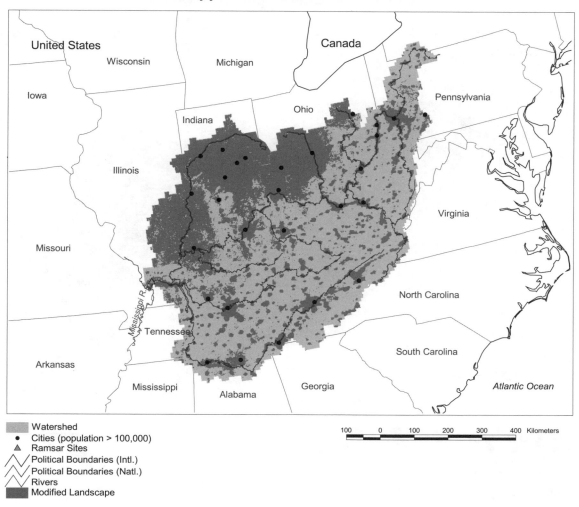

Watershed
● Cities (population > 100,000)
▲ Ramsar Sites
/\/\ Political Boundaries (Intl.)
/\/\ Political Boundaries (Natl.)
/\/ Rivers
Modified Landscape

Basin area:	490,603 km²	Forest:	57%
Population density:	50 people per km²	Cropland:	19%
Urban growth rate:	0.7%	Cropland irrigated:	0%
Large cities:	28	Developed:	23%
Total fish species:	281 (diad: 1)	Shrub:	0%
Fish endemics:	15	Grassland:	0%
Threatened fish species:	20	Barren:	0%
Endemic bird areas:	0	Loss of original forest:	44%
Ramsar sites:	1	Deforestation rate:	-
Protected areas:	1%	Eroded area:	6%
Wetlands:	1%	Large dams:	711
Arid:	0%	Planned major dams:	-

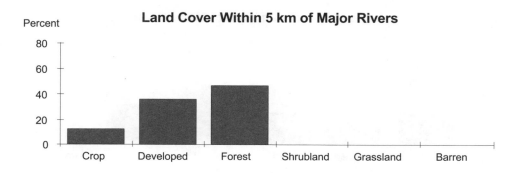

Land Cover Within 5 km of Major Rivers

© 1998 World Resources Institute

Mississippi Watershed: Red Subbasin

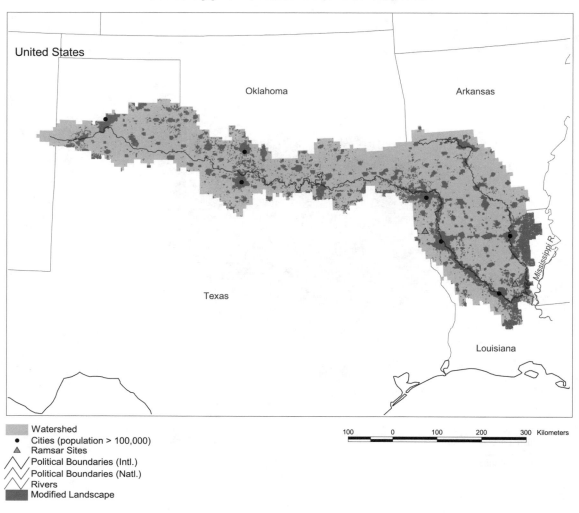

Legend:
- Watershed
- ● Cities (population > 100,000)
- △ Ramsar Sites
- Political Boundaries (Intl.)
- Political Boundaries (Natl.)
- Rivers
- Modified Landscape

Basin area:	187,944 km²	Forest:	42%
Population density:	14 people per km²	Cropland:	12%
Urban growth rate:	-	Cropland irrigated:	5%
Large cities:	7	Developed:	13%
Total fish species:	67 (intr: 5 diad: 2)	Shrub:	0%
Fish endemics:	0	Grassland:	33%
Threatened fish species:	6	Barren:	0%
Endemic bird areas:	0	Loss of original forest:	45%
Ramsar sites:	2	Deforestation rate:	-
Protected areas:	1%	Eroded area:	4%
Wetlands:	7%	Large dams:	101
Arid:	33%	Planned major dams:	-

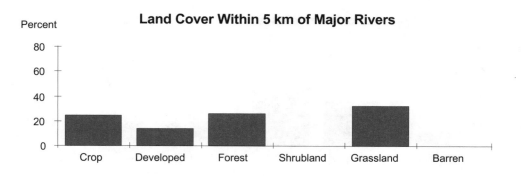

Land Cover Within 5 km of Major Rivers

© 1998 World Resources Institute

Nelson Watershed

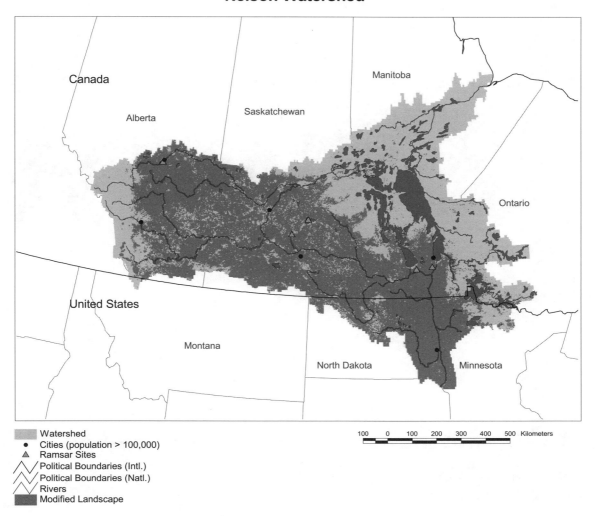

Watershed
● Cities (population > 100,000)
△ Ramsar Sites
〈 Political Boundaries (Intl.)
〈 Political Boundaries (Natl.)
〈 Rivers
■ Modified Landscape

Basin area:	1,093,442 km²	Forest:	34%
Population density:	5 people per km²	Cropland:	51%
Urban growth rate:	1.0%	Cropland irrigated:	0%
Large cities:	6	Developed:	-
Total fish species:	47 (intr: 3 diad: 1)	Shrub:	2%
Fish endemics:	0	Grassland:	5%
Threatened fish species:	1	Barren:	0%
Endemic bird areas:	0	Loss of original forest:	21%
Ramsar sites:	5	Deforestation rate:	-
Protected areas:	4%	Eroded area:	0%
Wetlands:	27%	Large dams:	13
Arid:	22%	Planned major dams:	-

Land Cover Within 5 km of Major Rivers

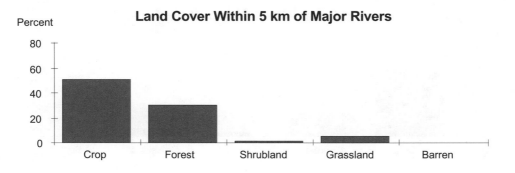

2 - 125

© 1998 World Resources Institute

Nelson Watershed: Saskatchewan Subbasin

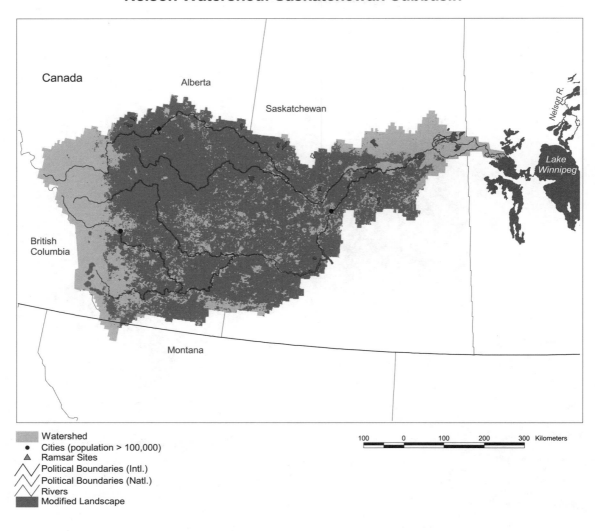

Watershed
● Cities (population > 100,000)
▲ Ramsar Sites
Political Boundaries (Intl.)
Political Boundaries (Natl.)
Rivers
Modified Landscape

100   0   100   200   300 Kilometers

Basin area:	370,884 km²	Forest:	22%
Population density:	7 people per km²	Cropland:	67%
Urban growth rate:	1.0%	Cropland irrigated:	0%
Large cities:	3	Developed:	-
Total fish species:	-	Shrub:	3%
Fish endemics:	-	Grassland:	7%
Threatened fish species:	-	Barren:	0%
Endemic bird areas:	0	Loss of original forest:	35%
Ramsar sites:	1	Deforestation rate:	-
Protected areas:	5%	Eroded area:	0%
Wetlands:	24%	Large dams:	3
Arid:	35%	Planned major dams:	-

Land Cover Within 5 km of Major Rivers

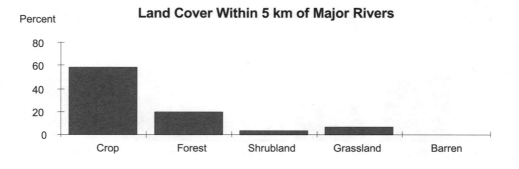

Percent

© 1998 World Resources Institute

Rio Grande Watershed

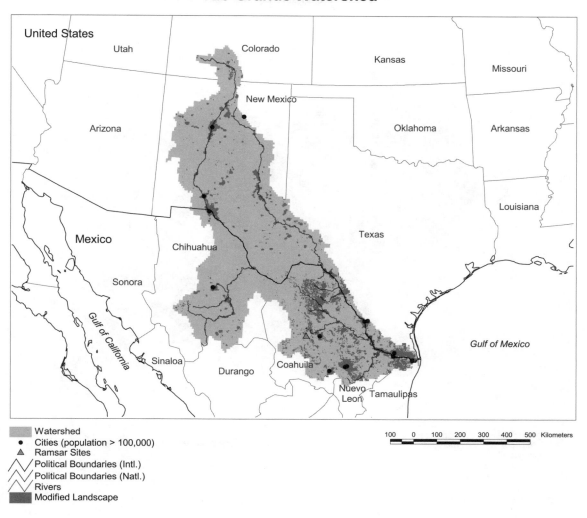

Watershed
● Cities (population > 100,000)
▲ Ramsar Sites
/\/ Political Boundaries (Intl.)
/\/ Political Boundaries (Natl.)
/\/ Rivers
■ Modified Landscape

Basin area:	608,023 km²	Forest:	14%
Population density:	16 people per km²	Cropland:	5%
Urban growth rate:	3.1%	Cropland irrigated:	2%
Large cities:	15	Developed:	7%
Total fish species:	121	Shrub:	43%
Fish endemics:	69	Grassland:	31%
Threatened fish species:	8	Barren:	0%
Endemic bird areas:	3	Loss of original forest:	52%
Ramsar sites:	1	Deforestation rate:	-
Protected areas:	2%	Eroded area:	2%
Wetlands:	1%	Large dams:	100
Arid:	96%	Planned major dams:	-

Land Cover Within 5 km of Major Rivers

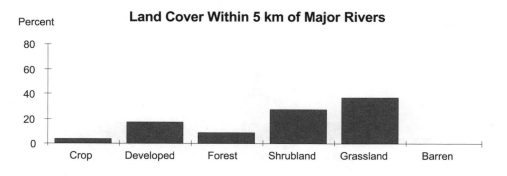

© 1998 World Resources Institute

Rio Grande de Santiago Watershed

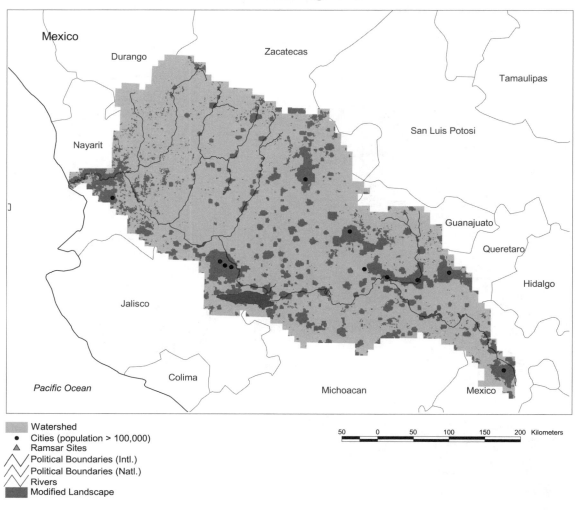

Watershed
● Cities (population > 100,000)
▲ Ramsar Sites
〰 Political Boundaries (Intl.)
〰 Political Boundaries (Natl.)
〰 Rivers
▬ Modified Landscape

50 0 50 100 150 200 Kilometers

Basin area:	136,628 km²	Forest:	63%
Population density:	101 people per km²	Cropland:	4%
Urban growth rate:	5.2%	Cropland irrigated:	11%
Large cities:	11	Developed:	15%
Total fish species:	-	Shrub:	1%
Fish endemics:	-	Grassland:	16%
Threatened fish species:	0	Barren:	0%
Endemic bird areas:	3	Loss of original forest:	52%
Ramsar sites:	0	Deforestation rate:	10%
Protected areas:	0%	Eroded area:	31%
Wetlands:	0%	Large dams:	1
Arid:	25%	Planned major dams:	1

Land Cover Within 5 km of Major Rivers

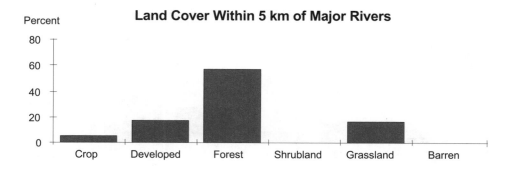

Percent

© 1998 World Resources Institute

Sacramento Watershed

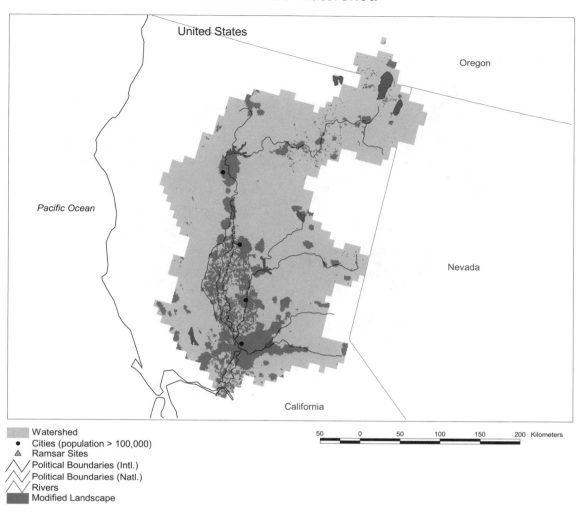

Watershed
● Cities (population > 100,000)
▲ Ramsar Sites
∿ Political Boundaries (Intl.)
∿ Political Boundaries (Natl.)
∿ Rivers
■ Modified Landscape

50 0 50 100 150 200 Kilometers

Basin area:	78,773 km²	Forest:	49%
Population density:	32 people per km²	Cropland:	6%
Urban growth rate:	2.0%	Cropland irrigated:	85%
Large cities:	4	Developed:	12%
Total fish species:	- (diad: 3)	Shrub:	7%
Fish endemics:	6	Grassland:	26%
Threatened fish species:	3	Barren:	0%
Endemic bird areas:	1	Loss of original forest:	26%
Ramsar sites:	0	Deforestation rate:	-
Protected areas:	3%	Eroded area:	4%
Wetlands:	3%	Large dams:	147
Arid:	27%	Planned major dams:	-

Land Cover Within 5 km of Major Rivers

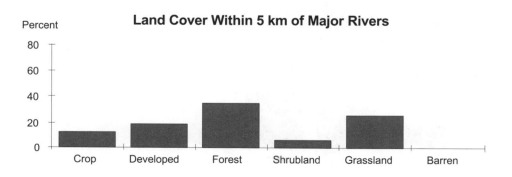

Percent

Crop Developed Forest Shrubland Grassland Barren

© 1998 World Resources Institute

St. Lawrence Watershed

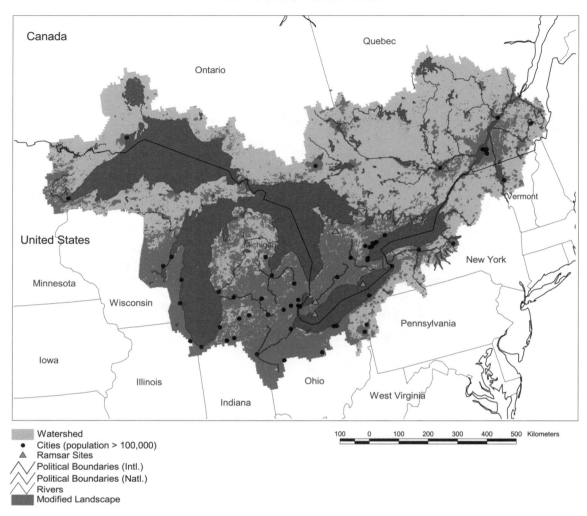

Watershed
● Cities (population > 100,000)
▲ Ramsar Sites
⋀ Political Boundaries (Intl.)
⋀ Political Boundaries (Natl.)
⋀ Rivers
▇ Modified Landscape

Basin area:	1,049,621 km²	Forest:	55%
Population density:	54 people per km²	Cropland:	20%
Urban growth rate:	0.8%	Cropland irrigated:	0%
Large cities:	60	Developed:	22%
Total fish species:	98 (intr: 5 diad: 5) *	Shrub:	0%
Fish endemics:	1*	Grassland:	0%
Threatened fish species:	1*	Barren:	0%
Endemic bird areas:	0	Loss of original forest:	31%
Ramsar sites:	7	Deforestation rate:	-
Protected areas:	10%	Eroded area:	3%
Wetlands:	10%	Large dams:	11
Arid:	0%	Planned major dams:	-

* St. Lawrence River only

Land Cover Within 5 km of Major Rivers

Percent

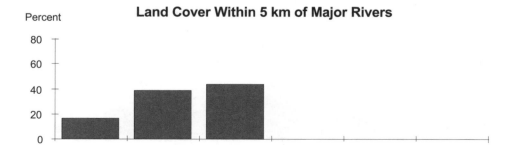

© 1998 World Resources Institute

St. Lawrence Watershed: Lakes Huron & Erie Subbasin

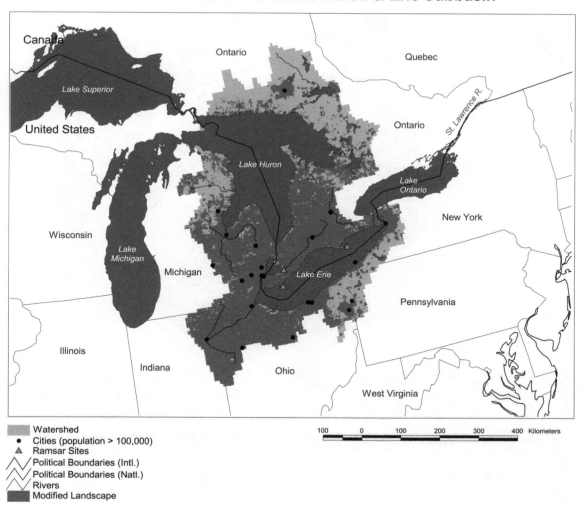

Legend:
- Watershed
- • Cities (population > 100,000)
- ▲ Ramsar Sites
- Political Boundaries (Intl.)
- Political Boundaries (Natl.)
- Rivers
- Modified Landscape

Basin area:	307,422 km²	Forest:	33%
Population density:	79 people per km²	Cropland:	38%
Urban growth rate:	0.7%	Cropland irrigated:	0%
Large cities:	22	Developed:	29%
Total fish species:	103 (intr: 4 diad: 3)	Shrub:	0%
Fish endemics:	0	Grassland:	0%
Threatened fish species:	6	Barren:	0%
Endemic bird areas:	0	Loss of original forest:	58%
Ramsar sites:	5	Deforestation rate:	-
Protected areas:	1%	Eroded area:	4%
Wetlands:	5%	Large dams:	1
Arid:	0%	Planned major dams:	-

Land Cover Within 5 km of Major Rivers

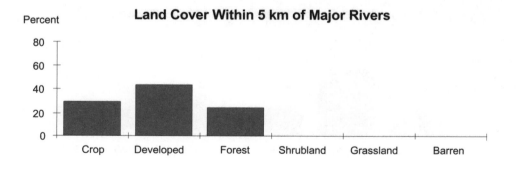

© 1998 World Resources Institute

St. Lawrence Watershed: Lake Michigan Subbasin

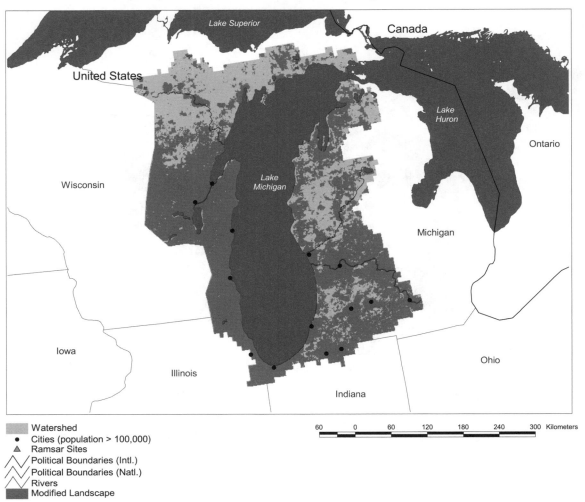

Watershed			
●	Cities (population > 100,000)		
▲	Ramsar Sites		
	Political Boundaries (Intl.)		
	Political Boundaries (Natl.)		
	Rivers		
	Modified Landscape		

Basin area:	176,384 km²	Forest:	31%
Population density:	89 people per km²	Cropland:	38%
Urban growth rate:	0.4%	Cropland irrigated:	0%
Large cities:	14	Developed:	32%
Total fish species:	87 (intr: 2 diad: 3)	Shrub:	0%
Fish endemics:	0	Grassland:	0%
Threatened fish species:	4	Barren:	0%
Endemic bird areas:	0	Loss of original forest:	50%
Ramsar sites:	0	Deforestation rate:	-
Protected areas:	1%	Eroded area:	10%
Wetlands:	21%	Large dams:	1
Arid:	0%	Planned major dams:	-

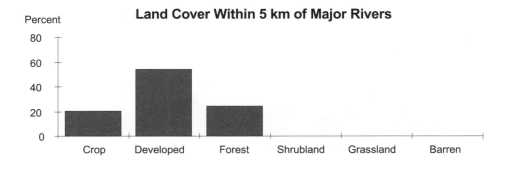

Land Cover Within 5 km of Major Rivers

© 1998 World Resources Institute

St. Lawrence Watershed: Lake Ontario Subbasin

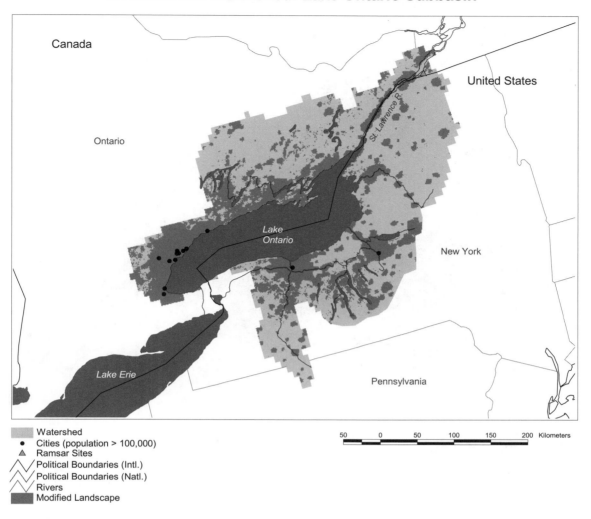

Canada

United States

Ontario

New York

St. Lawrence R.

Lake Ontario

Pennsylvania

Lake Erie

	Watershed
•	Cities (population > 100,000)
▲	Ramsar Sites
	Political Boundaries (Intl.)
	Political Boundaries (Natl.)
	Rivers
	Modified Landscape

50   0   50   100   150   200 Kilometers

Basin area:	96,846 km²	Forest:	61%
Population density:	97 people per km²	Cropland:	9%
Urban growth rate:	1.5%	Cropland irrigated:	0%
Large cities:	14	Developed:	29%
Total fish species:	99 (intr: 4 diad: 4)	Shrub:	0%
Fish endemics:	0	Grassland:	0%
Threatened fish species:	4	Barren:	0%
Endemic bird areas:	0	Loss of original forest:	39%
Ramsar sites:	1	Deforestation rate:	-
Protected areas:	17%	Eroded area:	1%
Wetlands:	10%	Large dams:	2
Arid:	0%	Planned major dams:	-

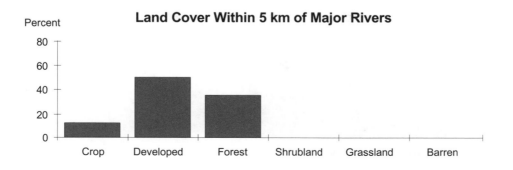

Land Cover Within 5 km of Major Rivers

Percent

80

60

40

20

0

Crop   Developed   Forest   Shrubland   Grassland   Barren

2 - 133

© 1998 World Resources Institute

St. Lawrence Watershed: Lake Superior Subbasin

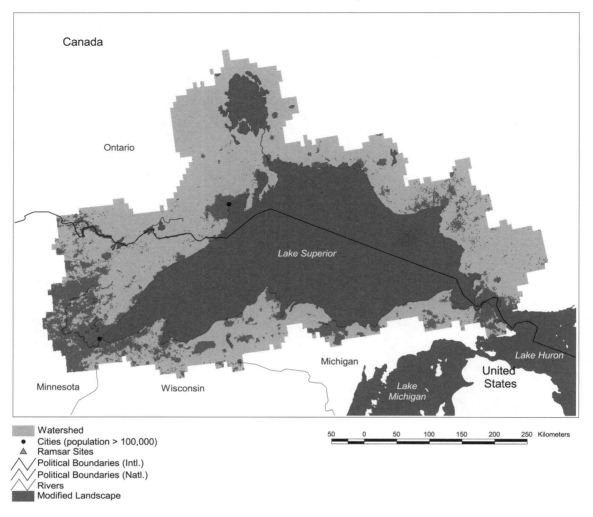

Canada

Ontario

Minnesota
Wisconsin
Michigan
Lake Superior
Lake Huron
United States
Lake Michigan

Watershed
● Cities (population > 100,000)
▲ Ramsar Sites
Political Boundaries (Intl.)
Political Boundaries (Natl.)
Rivers
Modified Landscape

50   0   50   100   150   200   250 Kilometers

Basin area:	219,442 km²		Forest:	72%
Population density:	4 people per km²		Cropland:	10%
Urban growth rate:	-		Cropland irrigated:	0%
Large cities:	2		Developed:	10%
Total fish species:	60 (intr: 2 diad: 3)		Shrub:	0%
Fish endemics:	0		Grassland:	0%
Threatened fish species:	4		Barren:	0%
Endemic bird areas:	0		Loss of original forest:	1%
Ramsar sites:	0		Deforestation rate:	-
Protected areas:	10%		Eroded area:	0%
Wetlands:	16%		Large dams:	1
Arid:	0%		Planned major dams:	-

Land Cover Within 5 km of Major Rivers

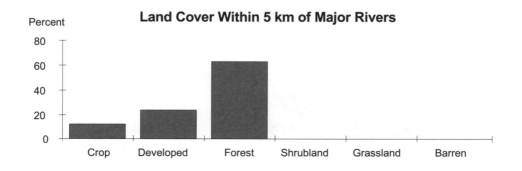

Percent

80	
60	
40	
20	
0	

Crop   Developed   Forest   Shrubland   Grassland   Barren

© 1998 World Resources Institute

Susquehanna Watershed

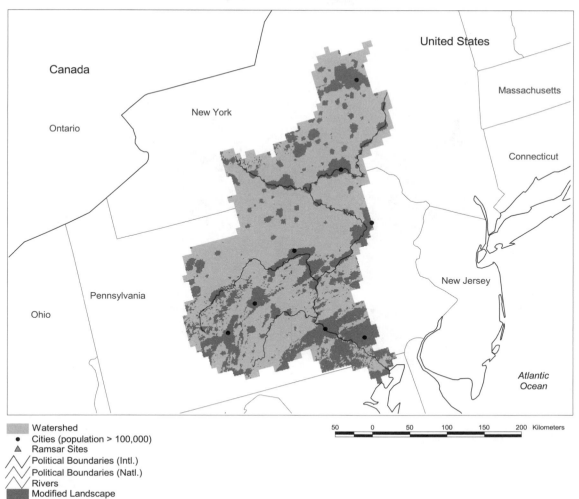

Watershed		
●	Cities (population > 100,000)	
▲	Ramsar Sites	
	Political Boundaries (Intl.)	
	Political Boundaries (Natl.)	
	Rivers	
	Modified Landscape	

Basin area:	78,673 km²	Forest:	71%
Population density:	57 people per km²	Cropland:	7%
Urban growth rate:	-	Cropland irrigated:	0%
Large cities:	8	Developed:	22%
Total fish species:	128 (intr: 17 diad: 4)	Shrub:	0%
Fish endemics:	0	Grassland:	0%
Threatened fish species:	0	Barren:	0%
Endemic bird areas:	0	Loss of original forest:	14%
Ramsar sites:	0	Deforestation rate:	-
Protected areas:	0%	Eroded area:	7%
Wetlands:	4%	Large dams:	124
Arid:	0%	Planned major dams:	-

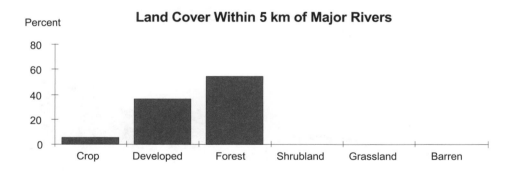

Land Cover Within 5 km of Major Rivers

© 1998 World Resources Institute

Thelon Watershed

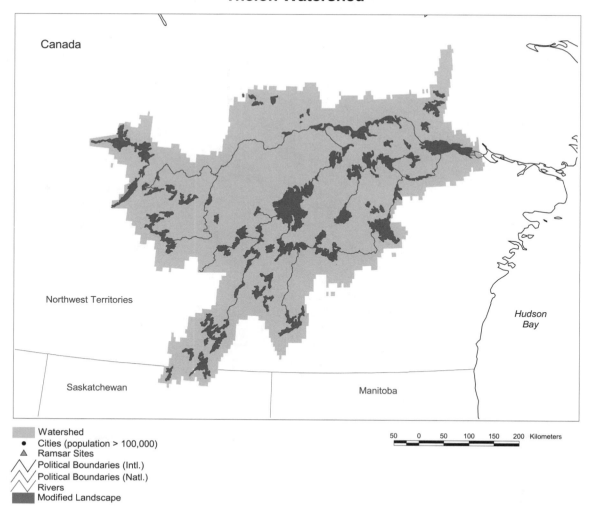

Canada

Northwest Territories

Saskatchewan

Manitoba

Hudson Bay

Watershed
● Cities (population > 100,000)
▲ Ramsar Sites
Political Boundaries (Intl.)
Political Boundaries (Natl.)
Rivers
Modified Landscape

50   0   50   100   150   200 Kilometers

Basin area:	239,332 km²	
Population density:	< 1 person per km²	
Urban growth rate:	-	
Large cities:	0	
Total fish species:	13 (intr: 0 diad: 1)	
Fish endemics:	0	
Threatened fish species:	0	
Endemic bird areas:	0	
Ramsar sites:	0	
Protected areas:	18%	
Wetlands:	11%	
Arid:	0%	

Forest:	6%
Cropland:	0%
Cropland irrigated:	0%
Developed:	-
Shrub:	0%
Grassland:	21%
Barren:	48%
Loss of original forest:	0%
Deforestation rate:	-
Eroded area:	0%
Large dams:	0
Planned major dams:	-

Land Cover Within 5 km of Major Rivers

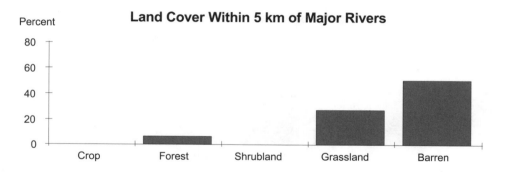

Percent

	Crop	Forest	Shrubland	Grassland	Barren

© 1998 World Resources Institute

Usumacinta Watershed

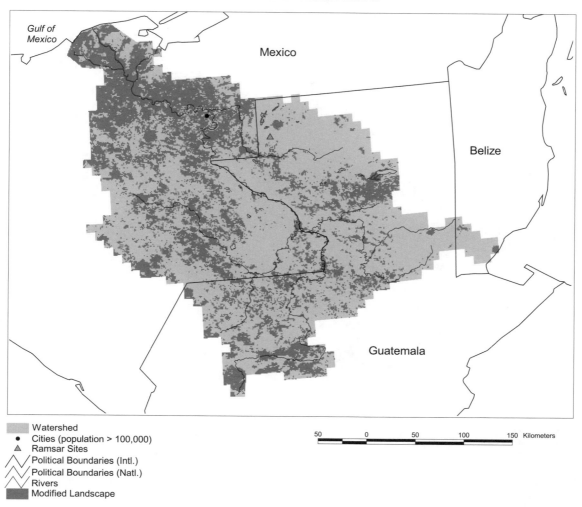

Watershed			
●	Cities (population > 100,000)		
△	Ramsar Sites		
	Political Boundaries (Intl.)		
	Political Boundaries (Natl.)		
	Rivers		
	Modified Landscape		

Basin area:	78,726 km²	Forest:	59%
Population density:	25 people per km²	Cropland:	30%
Urban growth rate:	-	Cropland irrigated:	0%
Large cities:	1	Developed:	3%
Total fish species:	70	Shrub:	0%
Fish endemics:	35	Grassland:	7%
Threatened fish species:	0	Barren:	0%
Endemic bird areas:	1	Loss of original forest:	37%
Ramsar sites:	1	Deforestation rate:	16%
Protected areas:	16%	Eroded area:	9%
Wetlands:	0%	Large dams:	0
Arid:	3%	Planned major dams:	-

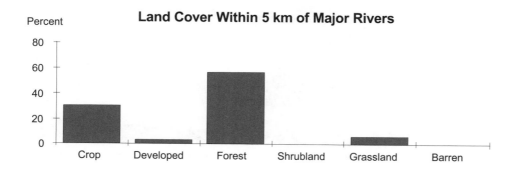

Land Cover Within 5 km of Major Rivers

© 1998 World Resources Institute

Yaqui Watershed

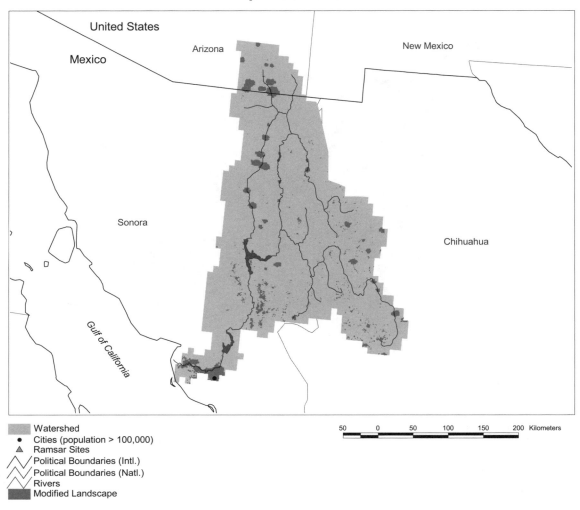

Watershed
● Cities (population > 100,000)
▲ Ramsar Sites
〜 Political Boundaries (Intl.)
〜 Political Boundaries (Natl.)
〜 Rivers
Modified Landscape

50   0   50   100   150   200   Kilometers

Basin area:	79,172 km²	
Population density:	7 people per km²	
Urban growth rate:	-	
Large cities:	1	
Total fish species:	62 (intr: 27 diad: 19)	
Fish endemics:	5	
Threatened fish species:	3	
Endemic bird areas:	2	
Ramsar sites:	0	
Protected areas:	9%	
Wetlands:	0%	
Arid:	100%	

Forest:	76%
Cropland:	2%
Cropland irrigated:	60%
Developed:	4%
Shrub:	4%
Grassland:	14%
Barren:	0%
Loss of original forest:	15%
Deforestation rate:	-
Eroded area:	6%
Large dams:	3
Planned major dams:	-

Land Cover Within 5 km of Major Rivers

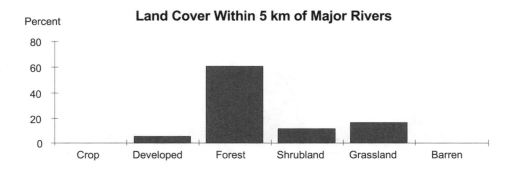

© 1998 World Resources Institute

Yukon Watershed

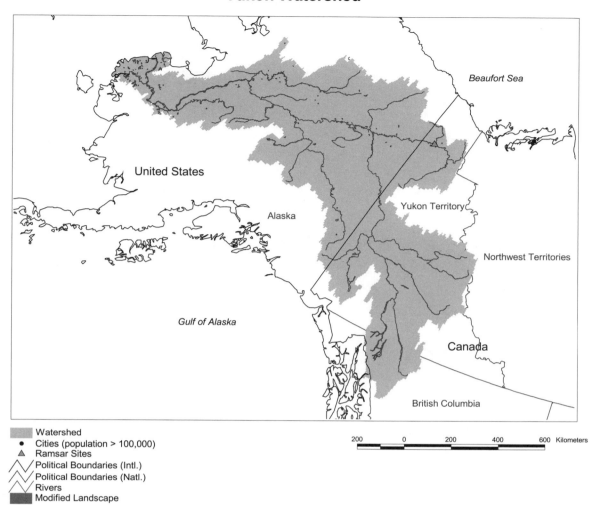

Watershed	
●	Cities (population > 100,000)
▲	Ramsar Sites
	Political Boundaries (Intl.)
	Political Boundaries (Natl.)
	Rivers
	Modified Landscape

Basin area:	847,642 km²	Forest:	51%
Population density:	< 1 person per km²	Cropland:	0%
Urban growth rate:	-	Cropland irrigated:	0%
Large cities:	0	Developed:	-
Total fish species:	33 (intr: 2 diad: 11)	Shrub:	26%
Fish endemics:	0	Grassland:	15%
Threatened fish species:	0	Barren:	2%
Endemic bird areas:	0	Loss of original forest:	23%
Ramsar sites:	1	Deforestation rate:	-
Protected areas:	29%	Eroded area:	0%
Wetlands:	14%	Large dams:	1
Arid:	0%	Planned major dams:	-

Land Cover Within 5 km of Major Rivers

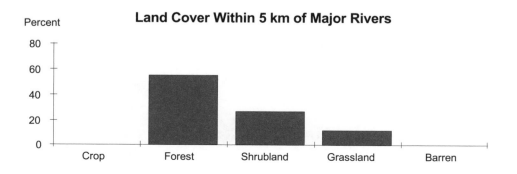

2 - 139

© 1998 World Resources Institute

WATERSHED PROFILES

FOR

SOUTH AMERICA

Amazon Watershed

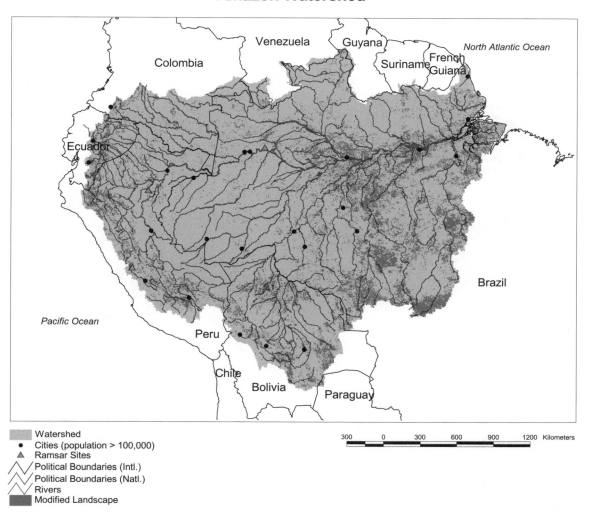

- ▨ Watershed
- ● Cities (population > 100,000)
- ▲ Ramsar Sites
- ∧ Political Boundaries (Intl.)
- ∧ Political Boundaries (Natl.)
- ∧ Rivers
- ▨ Modified Landscape

Basin area:	6,144,727 km²	Forest:	73%
Population density:	4 people per km²	Cropland:	15%
Urban growth rate:	3.5%	Cropland irrigated:	0%
Large cities:	24	Developed:	1%
Total fish species:	3000	Shrub:	2%
Fish endemics:	1800	Grassland:	8%
Threatened fish species:	0	Barren:	0%
Endemic bird areas:	24	Loss of original forest:	13%
Ramsar sites:	3	Deforestation rate:	5%
Protected areas:	7%	Eroded area:	1%
Wetlands:	8%	Large dams:	2
Arid:	4%	Planned major dams:	1

Land Cover Within 5 km of Major Rivers

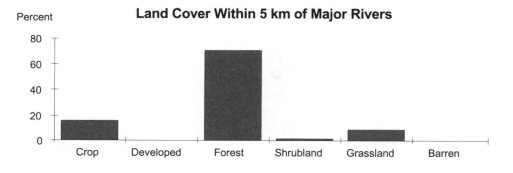

© 1998 World Resources Institute

Amazon Watershed: Ica - Putumayo Subbasin

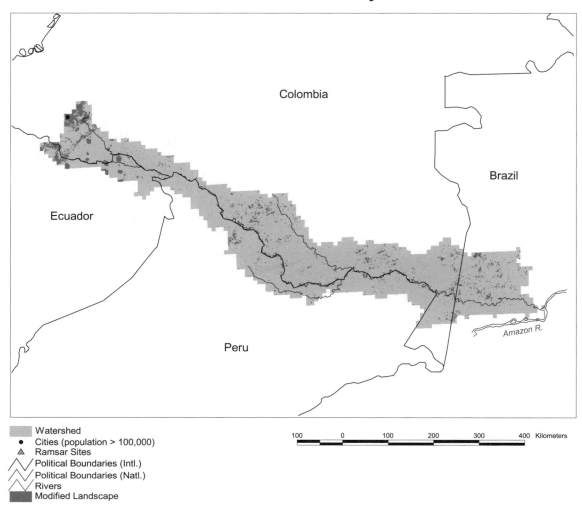

Colombia

Brazil

Ecuador

Peru

Amazon R.

- Watershed
- • Cities (population > 100,000)
- ▲ Ramsar Sites
- ⋀ Political Boundaries (Intl.)
- ⋀ Political Boundaries (Natl.)
- ⋀ Rivers
- ▬ Modified Landscape

100   0   100   200   300   400   Kilometers

Basin area:	139,300 km²	Forest:	87%
Population density:	3 people per km²	Cropland:	6%
Urban growth rate:	-	Cropland irrigated:	0%
Large cities:	1	Developed:	1%
Total fish species:	-	Shrub:	1%
Fish endemics:	-	Grassland:	4%
Threatened fish species:	0	Barren:	0%
Endemic bird areas:	5	Loss of original forest:	7%
Ramsar sites:	0	Deforestation rate:	3%
Protected areas:	3%	Eroded area:	0%
Wetlands:	10%	Large dams:	0
Arid:	0%	Planned major dams:	-

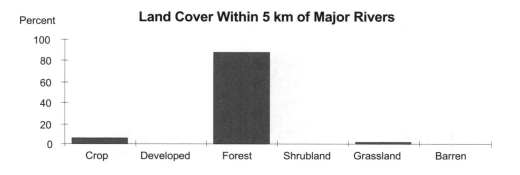

Land Cover Within 5 km of Major Rivers

Percent

Crop   Developed   Forest   Shrubland   Grassland   Barren

© 1998 World Resources Institute

Amazon Watershed: Japurá Subbasin

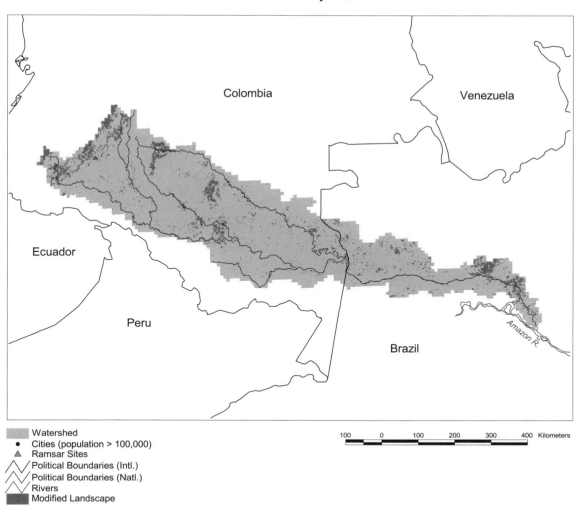

Watershed
● Cities (population > 100,000)
▲ Ramsar Sites
〰 Political Boundaries (Intl.)
〰 Political Boundaries (Natl.)
〰 Rivers
■ Modified Landscape

100 0 100 200 300 400 Kilometers

Basin area:	255,709 km²		Forest:	85%
Population density:	3 people per km²		Cropland:	8%
Urban growth rate:	-		Cropland irrigated:	0%
Large cities:	0		Developed:	< 1%
Total fish species:	-		Shrub:	1%
Fish endemics:	-		Grassland:	4%
Threatened fish species:	0		Barren:	0%
Endemic bird areas:	5		Loss of original forest:	17%
Ramsar sites:	0		Deforestation rate:	3%
Protected areas:	11%		Eroded area:	0%
Wetlands:	6%		Large dams:	0
Arid:	0%		Planned major dams:	-

Land Cover Within 5 km of Major Rivers

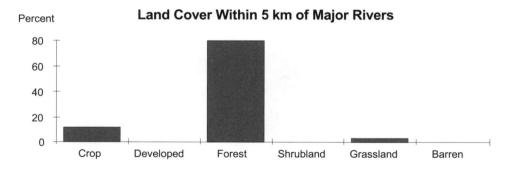

Percent

© 1998 World Resources Institute

Amazon Watershed: Juruá Subbasin

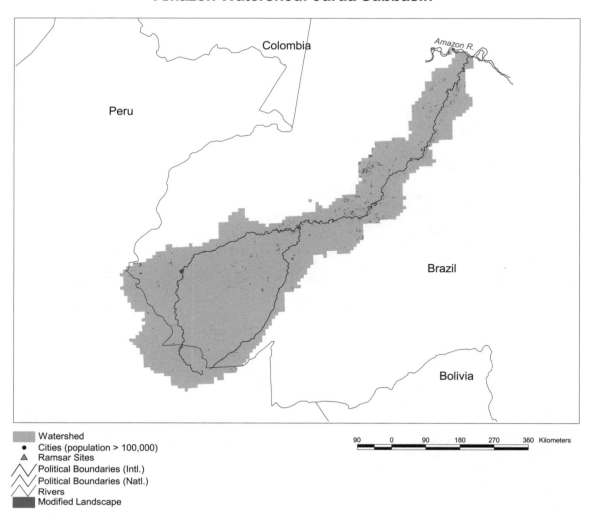

Watershed
● Cities (population > 100,000)
▲ Ramsar Sites
〰 Political Boundaries (Intl.)
〰 Political Boundaries (Natl.)
〰 Rivers
▨ Modified Landscape

90   0   90   180   270   360 Kilometers

Basin area:	225,828 km²	Forest:	95%
Population density:	1 person per km²	Cropland:	1%
Urban growth rate:	-	Cropland irrigated:	0%
Large cities:	0	Developed:	< 1%
Total fish species:	-	Shrub:	0%
Fish endemics:	-	Grassland:	3%
Threatened fish species:	0	Barren:	0%
Endemic bird areas:	1	Loss of original forest:	1%
Ramsar sites:	0	Deforestation rate:	2%
Protected areas:	4%	Eroded area:	0%
Wetlands:	12%	Large dams:	0
Arid:	5%	Planned major dams:	-

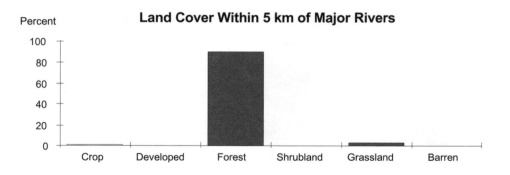

Land Cover Within 5 km of Major Rivers

Percent

© 1998 World Resources Institute

Amazon Watershed: Madeira Subbasin

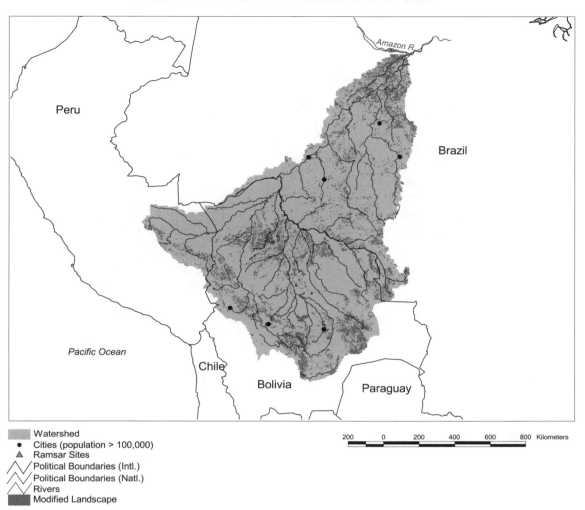

Watershed
● Cities (population > 100,000)
▲ Ramsar Sites
/\/ Political Boundaries (Intl.)
/\/ Political Boundaries (Natl.)
/\/ Rivers
■ Modified Landscape

200 0 200 400 600 800 Kilometers

Basin area:	1,485,218 km²	Forest:	66%
Population density:	5 people per km²	Cropland:	16%
Urban growth rate:	4.2%	Cropland irrigated:	0%
Large cities:	7	Developed:	1%
Total fish species:	398	Shrub:	3%
Fish endemics:	-	Grassland:	13%
Threatened fish species:	0	Barren:	0%
Endemic bird areas:	8	Loss of original forest:	17%
Ramsar sites:	0	Deforestation rate:	9%
Protected areas:	12%	Eroded area:	3%
Wetlands:	4%	Large dams:	0
Arid:	11%	Planned major dams:	-

Land Cover Within 5 km of Major Rivers

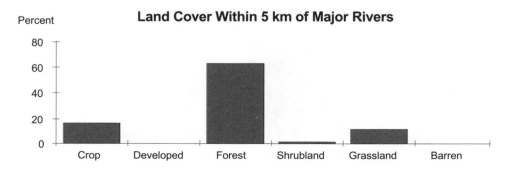

Percent

© 1998 World Resources Institute

Amazon Watershed: Rio Negro Subbasin

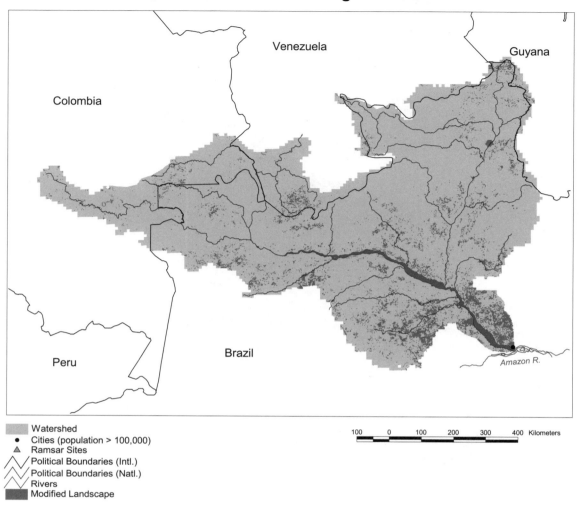

Watershed
● Cities (population > 100,000)
▲ Ramsar Sites
∿ Political Boundaries (Intl.)
∿ Political Boundaries (Natl.)
∿ Rivers
■ Modified Landscape

Basin area:	720114 km²	Forest:	82%
Population density:	2 people per km²	Cropland:	7%
Urban growth rate:	3.6%	Cropland irrigated:	0%
Large cities:	1	Developed:	< 1%
Total fish species:	600	Shrub:	1%
Fish endemics:	-	Grassland:	7%
Threatened fish species:	0	Barren:	0%
Endemic bird areas:	4	Loss of original forest:	17%
Ramsar sites:	0	Deforestation rate:	2%
Protected areas:	11%	Eroded area:	0%
Wetlands:	4%	Large dams:	0
Arid:	0%	Planned major dams:	-

Land Cover Within 5 km of Major Rivers

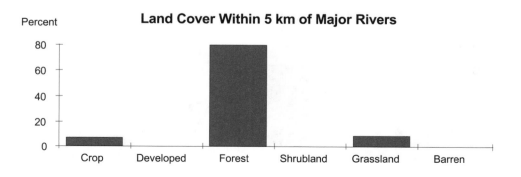

© 1998 World Resources Institute

Amazon Watershed: Purus Subbasin

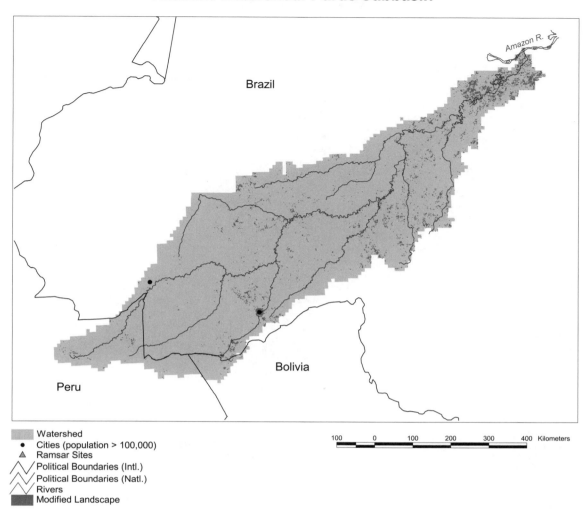

Watershed
● Cities (population > 100,000)
▲ Ramsar Sites
⋀ Political Boundaries (Intl.)
⋀ Political Boundaries (Natl.)
⋀ Rivers
▬ Modified Landscape

100   0   100   200   300   400   Kilometers

Basin area:	371,042 km²	Forest:	91%
Population density:	1 person per km²	Cropland:	4%
Urban growth rate:	-	Cropland irrigated:	0%
Large cities:	2	Developed:	< 1%
Total fish species:	-	Shrub:	0%
Fish endemics:	-	Grassland:	4%
Threatened fish species:	0	Barren:	0%
Endemic bird areas:	2	Loss of original forest:	7%
Ramsar sites:	0	Deforestation rate:	2%
Protected areas:	3%	Eroded area:	1%
Wetlands:	7%	Large dams:	0
Arid:	5%	Planned major dams:	-

Land Cover Within 5 km of Major Rivers

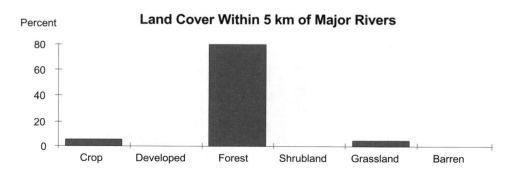

Percent

© 1998 World Resources Institute

Amazon Watershed: Marañón Subbasin

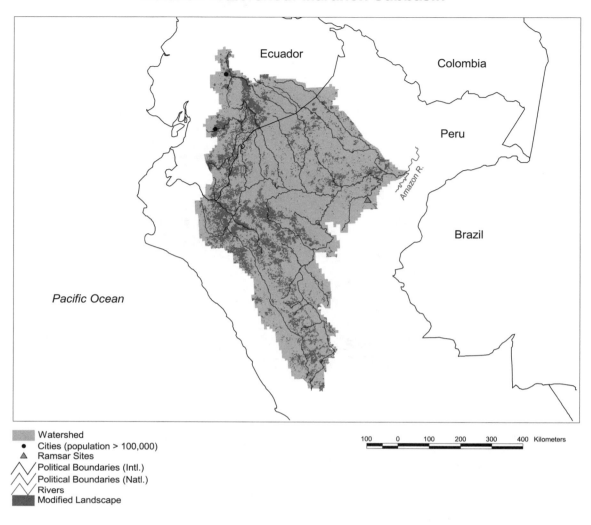

Watershed
● Cities (population > 100,000)
▲ Ramsar Sites
Political Boundaries (Intl.)
Political Boundaries (Natl.)
Rivers
Modified Landscape

100 0 100 200 300 400 Kilometers

Basin area:	382,877 km²	Forest:	61%
Population density:	13 people per km²	Cropland:	19%
Urban growth rate:	-	Cropland irrigated:	1%
Large cities:	2	Developed:	1%
Total fish species:	-	Shrub:	5%
Fish endemics:	-	Grassland:	13%
Threatened fish species:	0	Barren:	0%
Endemic bird areas:	12	Loss of original forest:	17%
Ramsar sites:	1	Deforestation rate:	7%
Protected areas:	3%	Eroded area:	7%
Wetlands:	21%	Large dams:	0
Arid:	11%	Planned major dams:	1

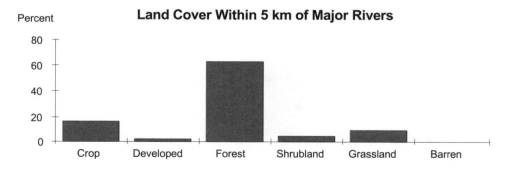

Land Cover Within 5 km of Major Rivers

Percent

Crop   Developed   Forest   Shrubland   Grassland   Barren

2 - 150

© 1998 World Resources Institute

Amazon Watershed: Tapajos Subbasin

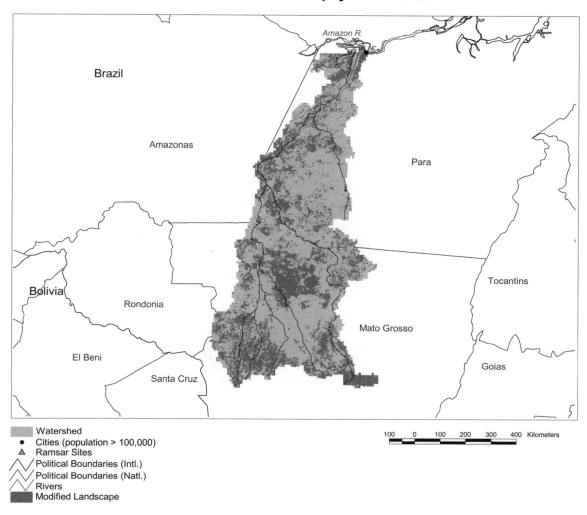

Watershed
● Cities (population > 100,000)
▲ Ramsar Sites
〰 Political Boundaries (Intl.)
〰 Political Boundaries (Natl.)
〰 Rivers
▨ Modified Landscape

100 0 100 200 300 400 Kilometers

Basin area:	486,792 km²	Forest:	57%
Population density:	2 people per km²	Cropland:	35%
Urban growth rate:	-	Cropland irrigated:	0%
Large cities:	1	Developed:	0%
Total fish species:	-	Shrub:	1%
Fish endemics:	-	Grassland:	6%
Threatened fish species:	0	Barren:	0%
Endemic bird areas:	1	Loss of original forest:	19%
Ramsar sites:	0	Deforestation rate:	7%
Protected areas:	1%	Eroded area:	0%
Wetlands:	2%	Large dams:	0
Arid:	0%	Planned major dams:	-

Land Cover Within 5 km of Major Rivers

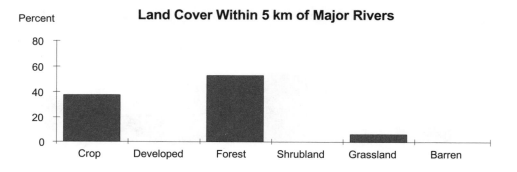

© 1998 World Resources Institute

Amazon Watershed: Ucayali Subbasin

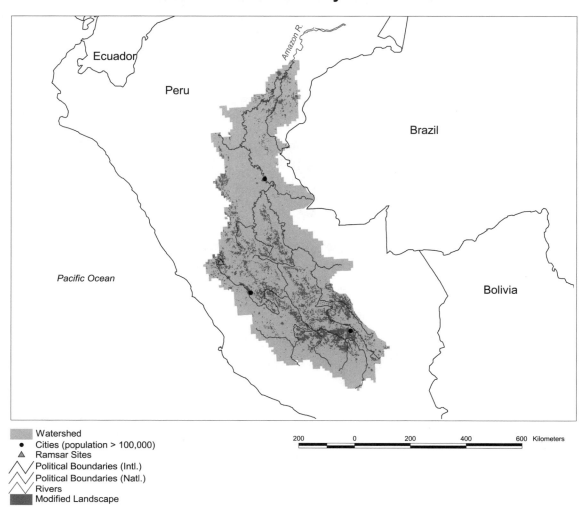

Watershed
● Cities (population > 100,000)
▲ Ramsar Sites
〜 Political Boundaries (Intl.)
〜 Political Boundaries (Natl.)
〜 Rivers
▬ Modified Landscape

Basin area:	352,388 km²	
Population density:	13 people per km²	
Urban growth rate:	-	
Large cities:	3	
Total fish species:	-	
Fish endemics:	-	
Threatened fish species:	0	
Endemic bird areas:	7	
Ramsar sites:	1	
Protected areas:	1%	
Wetlands:	6%	
Arid:	2%	

Forest:	55%
Cropland:	13%
Cropland irrigated:	2%
Developed:	1%
Shrub:	8%
Grassland:	23%
Barren:	0%
Loss of original forest:	10%
Deforestation rate:	5%
Eroded area:	5%
Large dams:	1
Planned major dams:	-

Land Cover Within 5 km of Major Rivers

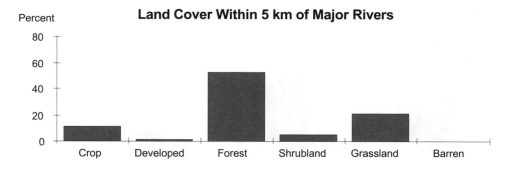

© 1998 World Resources Institute

Amazon Watershed: Xingu Subbasin

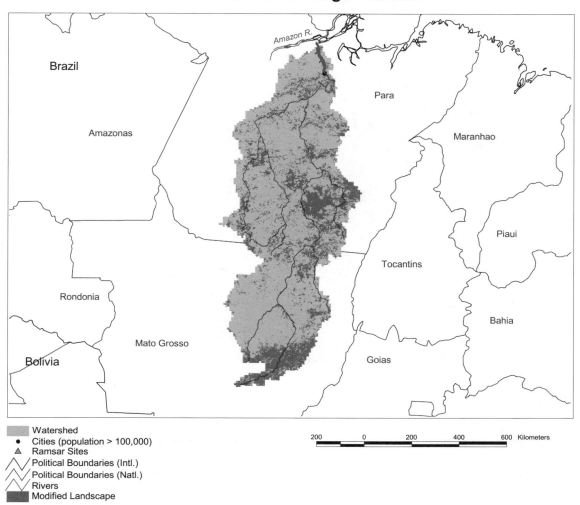

Watershed
● Cities (population > 100,000)
▲ Ramsar Sites
Political Boundaries (Intl.)
Political Boundaries (Natl.)
Rivers
Modified Landscape

Basin area:	520,292 km²	Forest:	70%
Population density:	3 people per km²	Cropland:	25%
Urban growth rate:	-	Cropland irrigated:	0%
Large cities:	1	Developed:	< 1%
Total fish species:	83	Shrub:	0%
Fish endemics:	-	Grassland:	4%
Threatened fish species:	0	Barren:	0%
Endemic bird areas:	1	Loss of original forest:	17%
Ramsar sites:	0	Deforestation rate:	7%
Protected areas:	0%	Eroded area:	0%
Wetlands:	4%	Large dams:	0
Arid:	0%	Planned major dams:	-

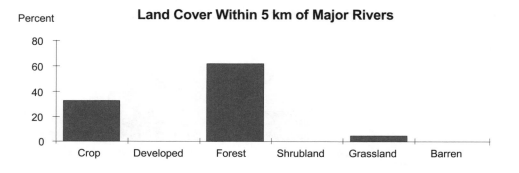

Land Cover Within 5 km of Major Rivers

© 1998 World Resources Institute

Chubut Watershed

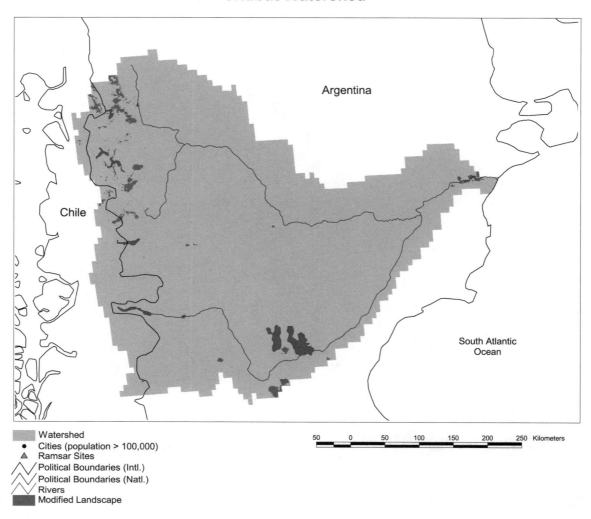

Watershed
- Cities (population > 100,000)
▲ Ramsar Sites
/\/ Political Boundaries (Intl.)
/\/ Political Boundaries (Natl.)
/\/ Rivers
Modified Landscape

50   0   50   100   150   200   250   Kilometers

Basin area:	182,631 km²	Forest:	25%
Population density:	2 people per km²	Cropland:	1%
Urban growth rate:	-	Cropland irrigated:	0%
Large cities:	0	Developed:	1%
Total fish species:	-	Shrub:	0%
Fish endemics:	-	Grassland:	67%
Threatened fish species:	0	Barren:	5%
Endemic bird areas:	1	Loss of original forest:	28%
Ramsar sites:	0	Deforestation rate:	-
Protected areas:	3%	Eroded area:	0%
Wetlands:	0%	Large dams:	2
Arid:	61%	Planned major dams:	-

Land Cover Within 5 km of Major Rivers

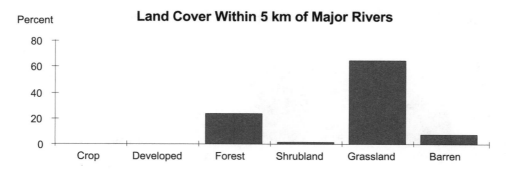

Percent

2 - 154

© 1998 World Resources Institute

Magdalena Watershed

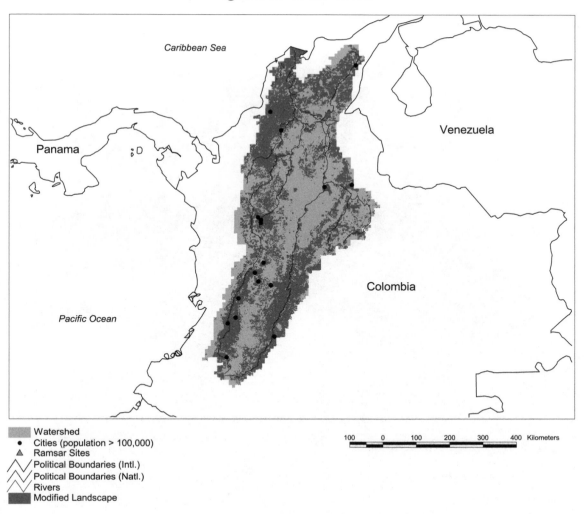

Watershed			
● Cities (population > 100,000)			
▲ Ramsar Sites			
Political Boundaries (Intl.)			
Political Boundaries (Natl.)			
Rivers			
Modified Landscape			

Basin area:	263,858 km²	Forest:	37%
Population density:	79 people per km²	Cropland:	39%
Urban growth rate:	2.6%	Cropland irrigated:	1%
Large cities:	17	Developed:	10%
Total fish species:	149	Shrub:	4%
Fish endemics:	-	Grassland:	9%
Threatened fish species:	0	Barren:	0%
Endemic bird areas:	9	Loss of original forest:	88%
Ramsar sites:	0	Deforestation rate:	26%
Protected areas:	4%	Eroded area:	10%
Wetlands:	0%	Large dams:	5
Arid:	7%	Planned major dams:	-

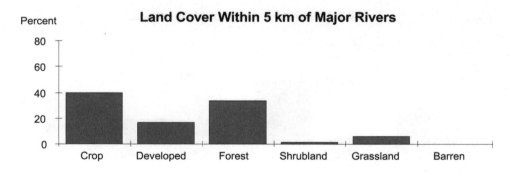

Land Cover Within 5 km of Major Rivers

© 1998 World Resources Institute

Orinoco Watershed

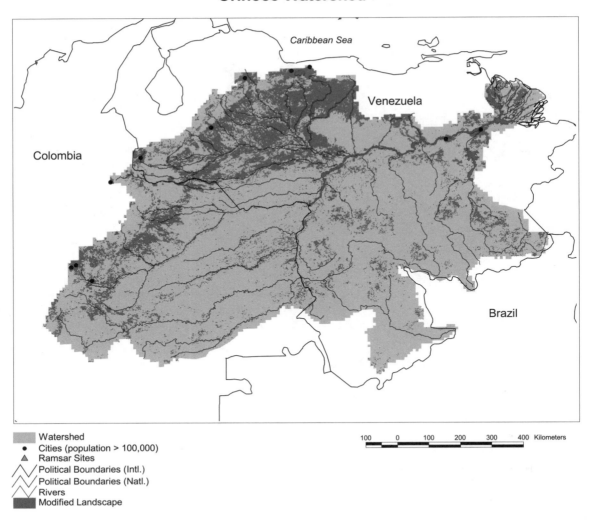

Caribbean Sea

Colombia

Venezuela

Brazil

Watershed
● Cities (population > 100,000)
▲ Ramsar Sites
◇ Political Boundaries (Intl.)
◇ Political Boundaries (Natl.)
◇ Rivers
■ Modified Landscape

100   0   100   200   300   400 Kilometers

Basin area:	953,598 km²		Forest:	50%
Population density:	13 people per km²		Cropland:	19%
Urban growth rate:	2.9%		Cropland irrigated:	0%
Large cities:	12		Developed:	3%
Total fish species:	318		Shrub:	1%
Fish endemics:	88		Grassland:	26%
Threatened fish species:	0		Barren:	0%
Endemic bird areas:	9		Loss of original forest:	23%
Ramsar sites:	0		Deforestation rate:	12%
Protected areas:	24%		Eroded area:	2%
Wetlands:	15%		Large dams:	10
Arid:	9%		Planned major dams:	2

Land Cover Within 5 km of Major Rivers

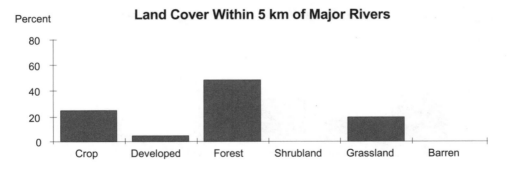

Percent

Crop Developed Forest Shrubland Grassland Barren

© 1998 World Resources Institute

Paraná Watershed

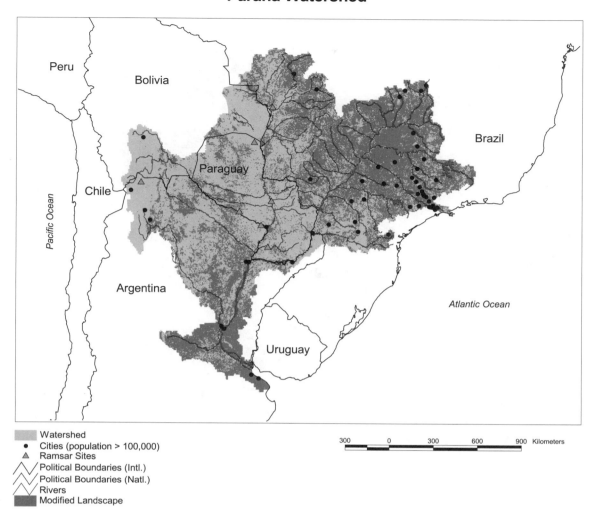

Watershed	
●	Cities (population > 100,000)
▲	Ramsar Sites
ＮＶ	Political Boundaries (Intl.)
ＮＶ	Political Boundaries (Natl.)
ＮＶ	Rivers
▓	Modified Landscape

300   0   300   600   900 Kilometers

Basin area:	2,582,672 km²	Forest:	12%
Population density:	23 people per km²	Cropland:	45%
Urban growth rate:	2.0%	Cropland irrigated:	0%
Large cities:	54	Developed:	4%
Total fish species:	355 (intr: 32)	Shrub:	3%
Fish endemics:	-	Grassland:	36%
Threatened fish species:	0	Barren:	0%
Endemic bird areas:	6	Loss of original forest:	71%
Ramsar sites:	7	Deforestation rate:	18%
Protected areas:	3%	Eroded area:	4%
Wetlands:	11%	Large dams:	29
Arid:	10%	Planned major dams:	4

Land Cover Within 5 km of Major Rivers

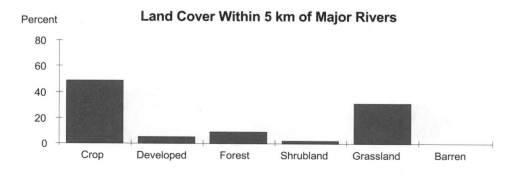

© 1998 World Resources Institute

Paraná Watershed: Paraguay Subbasin

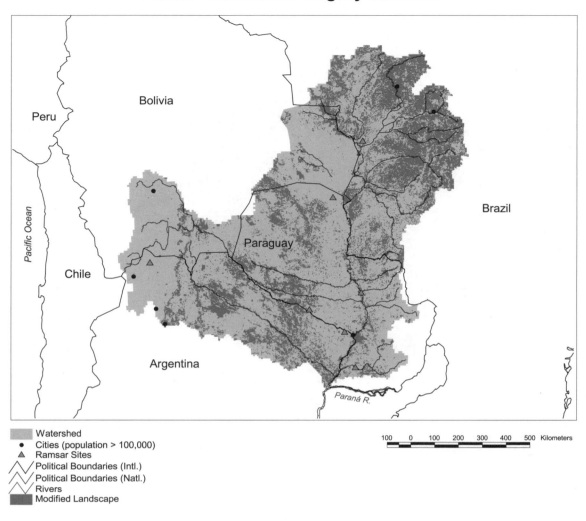

Watershed
● Cities (population > 100,000)
▲ Ramsar Sites
Political Boundaries (Intl.)
Political Boundaries (Natl.)
Rivers
Modified Landscape

100 0 100 200 300 400 500 Kilometers

Basin area:	1,168,540 km²	Forest:	18%
Population density:	7 people per km²	Cropland:	28%
Urban growth rate:	2.2%	Cropland irrigated:	0%
Large cities:	7	Developed:	1%
Total fish species:	254	Shrub:	5%
Fish endemics:	85	Grassland:	47%
Threatened fish species:	0	Barren:	0%
Endemic bird areas:	4	Loss of original forest:	35%
Ramsar sites:	7	Deforestation rate:	16%
Protected areas:	5%	Eroded area:	3%
Wetlands:	19%	Large dams:	0
Arid:	22%	Planned major dams:	-

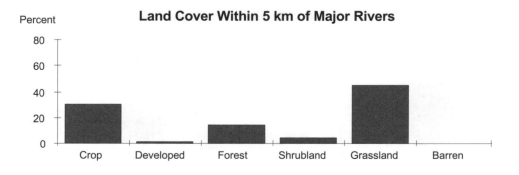

Land Cover Within 5 km of Major Rivers

Percent

2 - 158

© 1998 World Resources Institute

Parnaiba Watershed

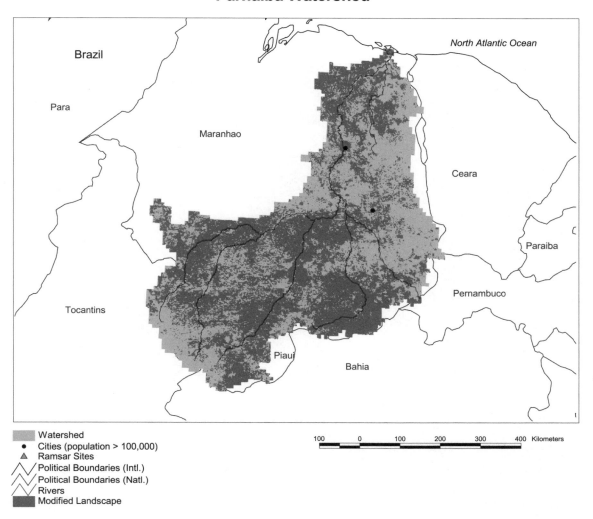

Watershed
● Cities (population > 100,000)
▲ Ramsar Sites
ⵥ Political Boundaries (Intl.)
ⵥ Political Boundaries (Natl.)
ⵥ Rivers
■ Modified Landscape

100	0	100	200	300	400 Kilometers

Basin area:	322,823 km²		Forest:	5%
Population density:	10 people per km²		Cropland:	52%
Urban growth rate:	-		Cropland irrigated:	0%
Large cities:	2		Developed:	2%
Total fish species:	90		Shrub:	12%
Fish endemics:	-		Grassland:	28%
Threatened fish species:	0		Barren:	0%
Endemic bird areas:	1		Loss of original forest:	27%
Ramsar sites:	0		Deforestation rate:	14%
Protected areas:	1%		Eroded area:	1%
Wetlands:	19%		Large dams:	1
Arid:	42%		Planned major dams:	-

Land Cover Within 5 km of Major Rivers

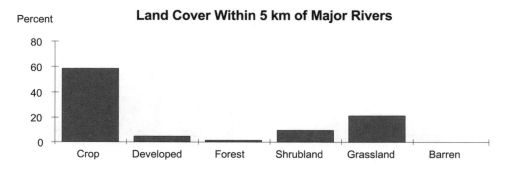

Percent

© 1998 World Resources Institute

Rio Colorado Watershed

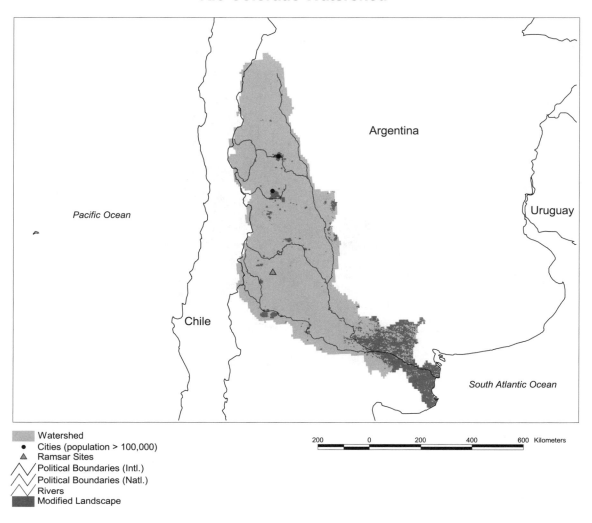

Watershed	
●	Cities (population > 100,000)
▲	Ramsar Sites
⋀	Political Boundaries (Intl.)
⋀	Political Boundaries (Natl.)
	Rivers
	Modified Landscape

200   0   200   400   600   Kilometers

Basin area:	402,956 km²	Forest:	1%
Population density:	10 people per km²	Cropland:	10%
Urban growth rate:	2.1%	Cropland irrigated:	0%
Large cities:	2	Developed:	2%
Total fish species:	-	Shrub:	27%
Fish endemics:	-	Grassland:	44%
Threatened fish species:	0	Barren:	16%
Endemic bird areas:	3	Loss of original forest:	100%
Ramsar sites:	1	Deforestation rate:	-
Protected areas:	5%	Eroded area:	0%
Wetlands:	2%	Large dams:	1
Arid:	71%	Planned major dams:	1

Land Cover Within 5 km of Major Rivers

Percent

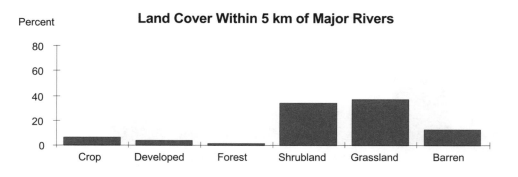

2 - 160

© 1998 World Resources Institute

São Francisco Watershed

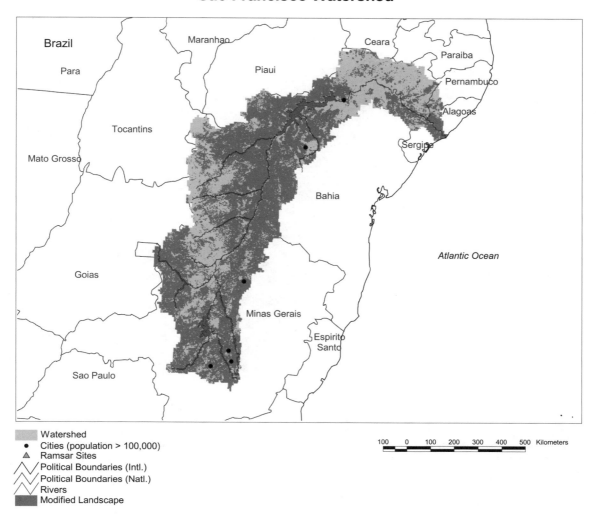

Watershed
● Cities (population > 100,000)
▲ Ramsar Sites
∿ Political Boundaries (Intl.)
∿ Political Boundaries (Natl.)
∿ Rivers
■ Modified Landscape

100 0 100 200 300 400 500 Kilometers

Basin area:	617,812 km²		Forest:	1%
Population density:	18 people per km²		Cropland:	61%
Urban growth rate:	-		Cropland irrigated:	0%
Large cities:	6		Developed:	2%
Total fish species:	-		Shrub:	14%
Fish endemics:	-		Grassland:	19%
Threatened fish species:	0		Barren:	0%
Endemic bird areas:	3		Loss of original forest:	64%
Ramsar sites:	0		Deforestation rate:	9%
Protected areas:	1%		Eroded area:	1%
Wetlands:	10%		Large dams:	6
Arid:	32%		Planned major dams:	-

Land Cover Within 5 km of Major Rivers

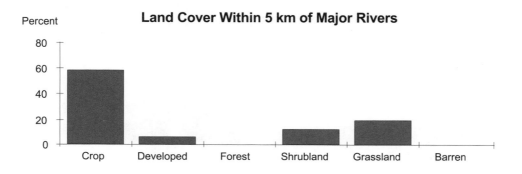

© 1998 World Resources Institute

Lakes Titicaca & Salar de Uyuni Watershed

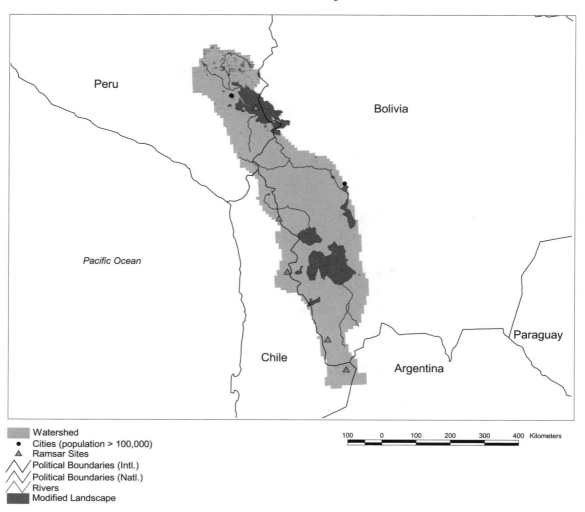

Watershed
● Cities (population > 100,000)
▲ Ramsar Sites
/\/ Political Boundaries (Intl.)
/\/ Political Boundaries (Natl.)
/\/ Rivers
■ Modified Landscape

Basin area:	193,102 km²	Forest:	0%
Population density:	11 people per km²	Cropland:	1%
Urban growth rate:	-	Cropland irrigated:	0%
Large cities:	2	Developed:	1%
Total fish species:	20	Shrub:	54%
Fish endemics:	14	Grassland:	39%
Threatened fish species:	-	Barren:	4%
Endemic bird areas:	2	Loss of original forest:	100%
Ramsar sites:	5	Deforestation rate:	-
Protected areas:	10%	Eroded area:	3%
Wetlands:	0%	Large dams:	0
Arid:	65%	Planned major dams:	-

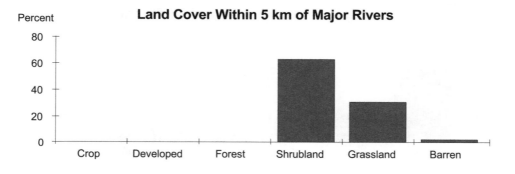

Land Cover Within 5 km of Major Rivers

© 1998 World Resources Institute

Tocantins Watershed

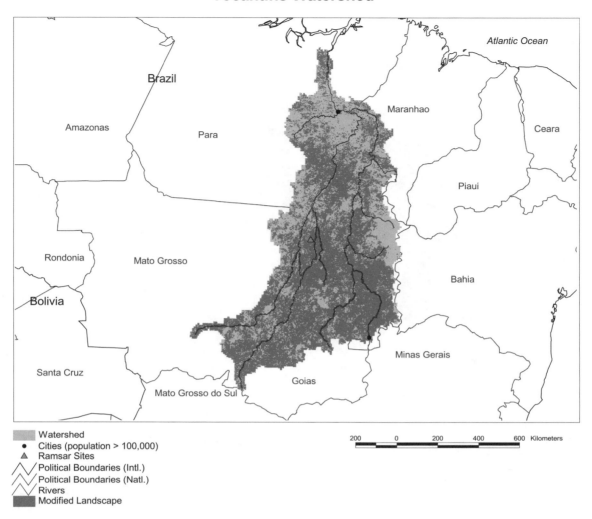

Watershed	
●	Cities (population > 100,000)
▲	Ramsar Sites
	Political Boundaries (Intl.)
	Political Boundaries (Natl.)
	Rivers
	Modified Landscape

Basin area:	764,183 km²	Forest:	9%
Population density:	6 people per km²	Cropland:	63%
Urban growth rate:	-	Cropland irrigated:	0%
Large cities:	2	Developed:	1%
Total fish species:	-	Shrub:	1%
Fish endemics:	-	Grassland:	26%
Threatened fish species:	0	Barren:	0%
Endemic bird areas:	1	Loss of original forest:	50%
Ramsar sites:	1	Deforestation rate:	10%
Protected areas:	1%	Eroded area:	2%
Wetlands:	19%	Large dams:	1
Arid:	0%	Planned major dams:	1

Land Cover Within 5 km of Major Rivers

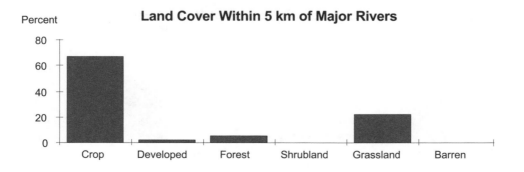

© 1998 World Resources Institute

Uruguay Watershed

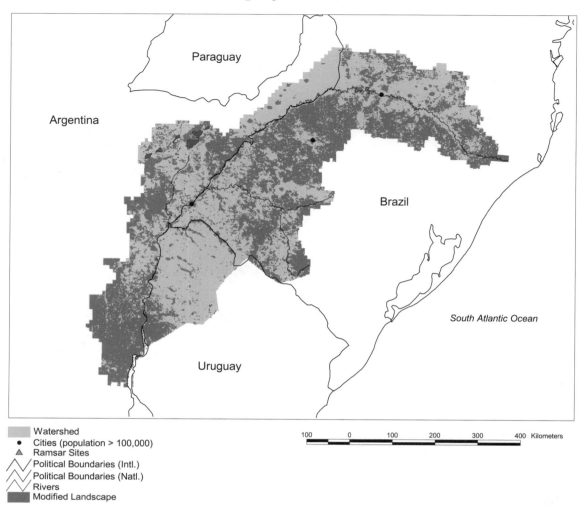

Watershed			
● Cities (population > 100,000)			
▲ Ramsar Sites			
Political Boundaries (Intl.)			
Political Boundaries (Natl.)			
Rivers			
Modified Landscape			

Basin area:	297,199 km²	Forest:	7%
Population density:	25 people per km²	Cropland:	44%
Urban growth rate:	-	Cropland irrigated:	0%
Large cities:	3	Developed:	3%
Total fish species:	160	Shrub:	0%
Fish endemics:	35	Grassland:	45%
Threatened fish species:	0	Barren:	0%
Endemic bird areas:	3	Loss of original forest:	92%
Ramsar sites:	0	Deforestation rate:	12%
Protected areas:	2%	Eroded area:	20%
Wetlands:	4%	Large dams:	2
Arid:	0%	Planned major dams:	1

Land Cover Within 5 km of Major Rivers

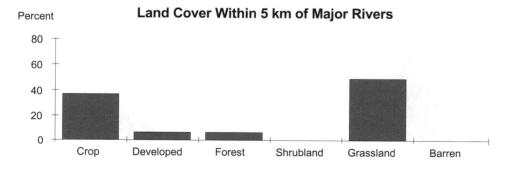

© 1998 World Resources Institute

APPENDIX
METHODOLOGY AND TECHNICAL NOTES

The watershed indicators displayed in the global maps and listed in individual basin profiles were compiled using a Geographic Information System (GIS). Summary statistics for each watershed were extracted by spatial query, overlaying the basin map on other digital datasets. The base data layer used for geographic definition of the watersheds is a 5 minute gridded dataset of major watershed basins. There are some limitations associated with the scale of this base data: watershed boundaries are coarse and some smaller basins and tributaries are not identified.

To make the statistics comparable between basins and across regions, the analysis is primarily limited to global datasets. The selection of data is also limited by the fact that, while the basic unit of this analysis is the watershed, most social and economic data, and even some data on natural resources, are collected at the national or administrative district level. Given the lack of spatially distributed data, district level data such as population counts and deforestation rates are used for some of the indicators. The potential for misrepresenting the data is greater for smaller basins, where the unit of summation is not much greater than the data unit.

The result of the geographic analysis is a database with records for 1,418 individual basins and 50 fields. The table includes fields (completed for the 145 basins selected for the analysis) that can be used to aggregate the data to primary, subbasins, and lake basins. Data were processed by region, in a Lambert Equal Area projection optimized for each region. The following is a description of core datasets and how they were used in the analysis:

Watersheds. For this analysis, a revised version of the *Major Watersheds of the World* dataset distributed on the GlobalARC CD-ROM was provided by the U.S. Army Corps of Engineers Construction Engineering Research Laboratories (CERL). The basins were digitally derived using ETOPO5, 5 minute gridded elevation data, and known locations of rivers. Because of the low resolution of the elevation data used to derive the base data layer, boundaries are coarse and an effort was made to refine the basin boundaries as follows. Basin boundaries were checked by overlaying ArcWorld 1:3 million rivers. In cases where rivers (except canals) crossed basin boundaries, the boundary was edited using a 1 kilometer Digital Elevation Model as a guide and redrawing the boundaries along identifiable ridges. In some cases, polygons were split to separate out subbasins. After editing the boundaries, all subbasins were identified and labeled for each primary basin, using several world atlases as references.

Watershed Area. Watershed area was estimated by summing the number of 1 square kilometer cells within the basin. Watersheds were modeled based on elevation data and therefore may differ from previously estimated basin areas by the United Nations in the *Register of International Rivers* (Center for Natural Resources, Energy and Transport of the Department of Economic and Social Affairs of the United Nations, Pergamon Press, Oxford, 1978). Some of these differences in basin area are due to the following factors. Water surface of rivers and lakes (e.g., Great Lakes in St. Lawrence River watershed) and areas of intermittent drainage are included in the total basin area. Drainage to tidal portions of rivers (St. Lawrence and Ob Rivers) are not included in the basin area.

Population Density. A medium resolution global dataset, *Gridded Population of the World* (National Center for Geographic Information and Analysis Global Demography Project, distributed by the Consortium for International Earth Science Information Network, 1995) was used to calculate population density. This dataset was compiled from the latest available census data, at a variety of subnational district levels, standardized to 1994. The total number of people in each basin was calculated using a 5 minute population count grid. Population density was calculated by dividing total population by land area. Data are presented as people per square kilometer.

Urban Growth Rate. The United Nations data on Urban Agglomerations (1996) was used to calculate a mean urban growth rate for major cities within each basin. The data for 432 cities was georeferenced by linking to the World Cities Population Database digital dataset. Of these cities, 213 fell within the analyzed watersheds. A mean urban growth rate for the period 1995–2000 was calculated by taking the mean of the growth rates of cities within each watershed. Urban growth rates for these 213 cities ranged from 0 to 8.77 percent, and the average growth rate was 2.14 percent. The urban population in these cities varied between 750,000 and 16,533,000. For some basins the mean urban growth rate is based on only one or two large cities, and may not accurately represent the growth rate of smaller urban areas. For several basins there were no data available.

Number of Large Cities. The World Cities Population Database (WCPD) was used to calculate the number of large cities in each watershed. The database includes population counts for some 2,700 cities. The data are derived primarily from the *United Nations Demographic Yearbook 1987*, with reference years ranging from 1960 to 1987. Data were added for approximately 120 cities lacking population

counts from the ArcAtlas: Our Earth Database. Large cities were defined as cities with greater than 100,000 people in the urban area.

Fish Species. Data on fish species, including number of endemics, diadromous, introduced, threatened, and total number of fish species were compiled by the World Conservation Monitoring Centre (WCMC) for this study. Additional total fish species numbers were added from Maurice Kottelat and Tony Whitten, *Freshwater Biodiversity in Asia with Special Reference to Fish,* World Bank Technical Paper 343, 1996; unpublished data provided by Thierry Oberdorff, Muséum National d'Histoire Naturelle, Lab. d'Ichtyologie Général et Appliquée, Paris, and Maurice Kottelat (personal communication). Data were referenced to major rivers or basins. Because there are several potential sources of error in the species richness and endemics values, these numbers should be taken as general indicators of fish diversity and not actual measures. Sources of error include: the amount of research done in a particular basin; species extinctions; and introductions of non-native species. Some rivers, for examples, have been highly sampled and most species present identified, while others, particularly in the tropics, have not yet been thoroughly studied and may contain many not-yet-identified species. Because of the correlation between basin size and species richness, basins were grouped by size into in three categories: large (more than 1,500,000 square kilometers), medium (between 400,000 and 1,499,999 square kilometers) and small (less 400,000 square kilometers). Cutoff points were obtained by selecting the highest two-thirds within each basin-size category. Basins with high fish species richness were, for large basins, those with more than 230 fish species; for medium basins, those with more than 143 species; and for small basins, those with more than 112 species. For endemic fish species, the cutoff points were basins with more than 166 species (large basins), 29 species (medium basins), and 15 species (small basins).

Threatened species refer only to those fish species that are globally threatened and are listed as such under the *1996 IUCN Red List of Threatened Animals*. Many fish species have not been assessed for threat by IUCN. Therefore the profile data for threatened fish species numbers may be underestimated.

Number of Endemic Bird Areas. This digital dataset was provided by BirdLife International. Endemic Bird Areas (EBAs) refer to areas where landbird species with restricted ranges (i.e., global breeding range of less than 50,000 square kilometers) tend to occur together. There are 218 endemic bird areas worldwide, each represented by a polygon or cluster of polygons. Some bird areas overlap. The number of endemic bird areas was calculated by counting the number of different bird areas that fall either partially or totally within each watershed. Forest ecosystems in the tropics and subtropics are better represented by the EBAs than other ecosystems such as desert and grasslands. For further information on EBAs please refer to *Endemic Bird Areas of the World: Priorities for Biodiversity Conservation,* Alison J. Stattersfield, Michael J. Crosby, Adrian J. Long, and David C. Wege, BirdLife International, Cambridge, U.K., 1998.

Number of Ramsar Sites. Ramsar sites are sites designated as wetlands of international importance according to the terms of the Convention on Wetlands of International Importance Especially as Waterfowl Habitat signed in Ramsar, Iran in 1971. Sites were geo-referenced as points by geographic coordinates included in the list. Spatial accuracy of the coordinates varies. Number of Ramsar sites includes all sites that fall within the watershed boundaries.

Percent Protected Area. Data on protected areas are from the Biodiversity Map Library, produced by WCMC. Most of the protected areas are represented by polygons, but some are represented by points only. For these latter ones, circular buffers, corresponding to the size of the protected area, were generated. Only parks designated as IUCN (The World Conservation Union) I–V management categories were

included as protected areas. These management categories include areas that are strictly protected and areas where some sustainable use of resources is allowed.

Percent Wetlands. Data on wetlands are from WCMC's Biodiversity Map Library. Percent wetlands indicates the percentage of the basin defined as wetland (bogs, marshes, lakes, seasonal, permanent, freshwater, tidal, mangroves, and lagoons). In North America the area occupied by the Great Lakes, the Great Bear Lake, the Great Slave Lake, and Lake Winnipeg are not included in the calculation of wetland area. For North America wetland polygons were not differentiated by type, instead the class field identified the proportion of the polygon—represented by a range—occupied by wetlands. To calculate wetland area polygons were converted to a 1 square kilometer grid using the minimum of the range. This method assumes that wetlands are evenly distributed across each polygon.

Percent Arid Area. The identification of arid area is based on the *World Atlas of Desertification* (UNEP, 1992) global aridity zone map, a 30 minute resolution map of 6 aridity zones. This map is based on an aridity index derived from the ratio of mean annual precipitation to the mean annual potential evapotranspiration. Percent arid area indicates the percentage of the basin that falls in an area defined as semi-arid, arid, or hyper-arid on the global aridity zone map.

Irrigated Cropland. The United States Geological Survey (USGS) Global Land Cover Characterization database with the USGS Land Use/Land Cover System Legend (modified level 2) was used to identify the extent of irrigated cropland. These data are somewhat inconsistent in identifying irrigated croplands in different regions. Irrigated agriculture is fairly well-defined for North America and Asia, but is less accurate for the rest of the world. This inconsistency is related to the lack of reference data on irrigated agriculture for some regions and to the coarse resolution of the raw data in relation to smaller irrigated areas. Data are presented as a percentage of cropland within the basin that is irrigated.

Land Cover. The USGS Global Land Cover Characterization database with the International Geosphere Biosphere Programme (IGBP) classification was used to identify the extent of different land cover types within each basin. These land cover types are described below. The land cover database was derived from Advanced Very High Resolution Radiometer (AVHRR) (1 kilometer resolution) imagery spanning April 1992 through March 1993. These are most useful for analysis of general land cover patterns at a continental or large scale, with smaller watersheds the data are less reliable. The urban areas category included with the IGBP data was not interpreted from AVHRR data, but from urban boundaries included on the Digital Chart of the World (DCW) CD-ROM. The DCW urban areas data are inconsistent and outdated for some regions, so the urban/built-up category was replaced with data from the City Lights database produced by the National Oceanic and Atmospheric Administration National Geophysical Data Center described below.

- *percent cropland* indicates the percentage of the basin classified as cropland or a crop/natural vegetation mosaic.

- *percent forest* indicates the percentage of the basin classified as evergreen needleleaf forest, evergreen broadleaf forest, deciduous needleleaf forest, deciduous broadleaf forest or mixed forest.

- *percent shrub* indicates the percentage of the basin classified as open or closed shrubland.

- *percent grassland* indicates the percentage of the basin classified as woody savannas, savannas, and grasslands.

- *percent developed area* is from the City Lights dataset, a 1 kilometer x 1 kilometer resolution map derived from nighttime

imagery from the Defense Meteorological Satellite Program (DMSP) Operational Linescan System (OLS) of the United States. The dataset contains the locations of stable lights, including frequently observed light sources such as gas flares at oil drilling sites. Time series analysis was used to exclude transient light sources such as fires and lightning. The extent of lit area may be slightly overestimated because of the sensor's resolution and factors such as reflection from water and other surface features. It is a good indicator of the spatial distribution of settlements and infrastructure, but should not be interpreted as a measure of population density (the mean settlement size required to produce enough light to be detected is much greater in developing countries than in industrialized countries because of differences in energy consumption). The City Lights data are more highly correlated with measures of economic activity and energy consumption and are therefore considered a measure of relative development within the watershed. The percent developed area is calculated by dividing the area within a watershed indicated as lit, by the total area of the watershed. Data for Africa represent simple counts of light detection, not normalized for total number of cloud-free observations. Data were not available for regions in Asia below the equator or regions above 54° N in North America.

Percent Modified. Modified landscape is a combination of the cropland and developed land cover categories. Percent modified represent the percentage of the basin given over to this type of development.

Loss of Original Forest. Current forest cover refers to closed canopy forest in existence today. Original forest cover refers to an estimate of the extent of closed canopy forest in existence 8,000 years ago, assuming current climate conditions. The Original Forest Map and Current Forest Map were produced by WCMC, 1996. Loss of original forest was calculated by dividing the difference between original and current forest cover by the extent of original forest cover within each basin. Data are presented in the profiles as percent loss of original forest.

In the global map, data are presented as percent of original forest cover remaining and extent of forest cover lost. Percent of original forest cover remaining was calculated by dividing the extent of current forest (square kilometers) by the extent of original forest cover (square kilometers) for each basin. Forest loss in square kilometers is the difference between the extent of original and current forest.

It is important to note that some areas denoted as having remaining original forest cover, particularly in Western North America, Mexico, and Scandinavia, are really covered by intensely managed fiber plantations. The management practices in these plantation can have detrimental effects on water quality and aquatic species. Therefore these data should be interpreted with caution.

Tropical Deforestation Rate. Deforestation rate is based on data from the Food and Agriculture Organization of the United Nations (FAO) on forest area for the years 1980 and 1990. The data were georeferenced by administrative district. Deforestation rate was calculated as forest area lost divided by forest area in 1980 for each district. The values were then converted to grid and the mean calculated for each basin. Data presented are not annual rates, but mean percent loss of forest for the period 1980–90.

Eroded Area. The source for eroded areas was the Global Assessment of Soil Degradation (GLASOD) developed by the International Soil Reference and Information Centre (ISRIC) for the United Nations Environment Programme (UNEP). The basic units of this digital database are based on physical geographic criteria, but attributes assigned to each unit are based on expert opinion, not empirical data. For this analysis, polygons identified as having a moderate to strong degree of erosion from water as the primary cause of soil degradation were selected. The polygons were converted to a 1 square kilometer grid using the factor field, which indicates the proportion of the polygon affected. This method assumes that the erosion is evenly distributed across each polygon. The sum of grid cell values within each basin was calculated, representing the total area in square kilometers affected by erosion. Data are presented as a percentage of the total basin where erosion is occurring.

Number of Large Dams. A large dam is defined by the industry as one higher than 15 meters or with reservoir volume greater than 1 cubic kilometer. There are almost 40,000 large dams worldwide. In the absence of a complete georeferenced global dataset of large dams, a subset of reservoir dams available in the ArcAtlas: Our Earth database (Environmental Systems Research Institute, 1997) was used for most of the basins. Dams with reservoir volume greater than 1 cubic kilometer (627) were included in the calculation of number of large dams. This number represents a small fraction (627/40,000) of large dams in existence worldwide, but is the most comprehensive global digital dataset available.

For watersheds in the United States, a complete set of 75,187 dams from the National Inventory of Dams (Army Corps of Engineers, 1995–96) was used. A subset of this database that included dams higher than 15 meters (5,055) was used to calculate the number of large dams for the North American profiles.

Major Dams. A complete digital dataset of 306 major dams was created for this project using the list of The World's Major Dams and Hydro Plants from the International Water Power and Dam Construction Handbook, 1995. Dams were georeferenced using the nearest city. A large dam is defined as those with a height greater than 150 meters; a volume greater than 15 million cubic meters; a reservoir storage capacity of at least 25 cubic kilometers; and/or a generating capacity greater than 1,000 megawatts.

Planned Major Dams. This is a small subset of major dams planned or under construction in 1994. This subset of 56 dams was selected from the list of "Dams (>15 meters) under construction" from the International Water Power and Dam Construction Handbook, 1995. Dams selected fell within one or more of the following criteria: the height of the dam was more than 150 meters, dam volume was at least 15 million cubic meters, and/or reservoir volume was at least 25 cubic kilometers. It is important to note that information on dam construction for many countries was not available.

Water Availability. Water availability per capita was calculated using average runoff and basin area for major river basins from *Water Quality of World River Basins*, Global Environment Monitoring System (GEMS), 1995. Runoff (meters/year) was multiplied by basin area (square meters) to calculate total runoff. Per capita water availability was calculated by dividing total runoff by total population.

ABOUT THE AUTHORS

CARMEN REVENGA   World Resources Institute; 1709 New York Avenue, N.W.; Washington, D.C. 20006; U.S.A.; e-mail: carmenr@wri.org

SIOBHAN MURRAY   World Resources Institute; 1709 New York Avenue, N.W.; Washington, D.C. 20006; U.S.A.; e-mail: siobhan@wri.org

JANET ABRAMOVITZ   Worldwatch Institute; 1776 Massachusetts Avenue, N.W.; Washington, D.C., 20036; U.S.A.; e-mail: jabramovitz@worldwatch.org

ALLEN HAMMOND   World Resources Institute; 1709 New York Avenue, N.W.; Washington, D.C. 20006; U.S.A.; e-mail: allen@wri.org

WORLD RESOURCES INSTITUTE

1709 New York Avenue, N.W.
Washington, D.C. 20006, U.S.A.
http://www.wri.org/wri

WRI's Board of Directors:
Maurice F. Strong
Chairman
John Firor
Vice Chairman
Manuel Arango
Frances G. Beinecke
Robert O. Blake
Derek Bok
Bert Bolin
Robert N. Burt
David T. Buzzelli
Deb Callahan
Michael R. Deland
Sylvia A. Earle
José María Figueres
Shinji Fukukawa
William M. Haney, III
Calestous Juma
Yolanda Kakabadse
Jonathan Lash
Jeffrey T. Leeds
Jane Lubchenco
C. Payne Lucas
William F. Martin
Julia Marton-Lefèvre
Matthew Nimetz
Paulo Nogueira-Neto
Ronald L. Olson
Peter H. Raven
Florence T. Robinson
Roger W. Sant
Stephan Schmidheiny
Bruce Smart
James Gustave Speth
Meg Taylor
Mostafa K. Tolba
Alvaro Umaña
Victor L. Urquidi
Pieter Winsemius

Jonathan Lash
President
J. Alan Brewster
Senior Vice President
Walter V. Reid
Vice President for Program
Donna W. Wise
Vice President for Policy Affairs
Kenton R. Miller
Vice President and Director of Program in Biological Resources
Marjorie Beane
Secretary-Treasurer

The World Resources Institute (WRI) is an independent center for policy research and technical assistance on global environmental and development issues. WRI's mission is to move human society to live in ways that protect Earth's environment and its capacity to provide for the needs and aspirations of current and future generations.

Because people are inspired by ideas, empowered by knowledge, and moved to change by greater understanding, the Institute provides—and helps other institutions provide—objective information and practical proposals for policy and institutional change that will foster environmentally sound, socially equitable development. WRI's particular concerns are with globally significant environmental problems and their interaction with economic development and social equity at all levels.

The Institute's current areas of work include economics, forests, biodiversity, climate change, energy, sustainable agriculture, resource and environmental information, trade, technology, national strategies for environmental and resource management, business liaison, and human health.

In all of its policy research and work with institutions, WRI tries to build bridges between ideas and action, meshing the insights of scientific research, economic and institutional analyses, and practical experience with the need for open and participatory decision-making.

ORDER FORM

ORDER MULTIPLE COPIES NOW AND RECEIVE A SPECIAL DISCOUNT

Single copies are available for US$30.00
Order 5-9 and receive a 10% discount or US$27.00 per copy
Order 10-49 and receive a 15% discount or US$25.50 per copy
Order 50-100 and receive a 25% discount or US$22.50 per copy
Order 100 or more and receive a 40% discount or US$ 18.00 per copy

_____ YES, please send me _____ copies of **Watersheds of the World: Ecological Value and Vulnerability** at US$ _____ each. Please add US$5 shipping and handling for orders of 50 copies or less and US$18 for orders of more than 50 copies.

PAYMENT INFORMATION (MAIL CODE WS8):

_____ Check enclosed in the amount of US$ _____ *(U.S. funds drawn on U.S. bank)*

_____ Please charge my credit card:

_____ Visa _____ MasterCard

Account Number: _____

Expiration Date: _____

Signature: _____

SHIP TO:

Name: _____

Address: _____

City, State, Zip Code: _____

Daytime Phone: _____

In a hurry? Order by phone Monday through Friday (9 a.m. to 5 p.m. EST) with a Visa or MasterCard by calling 1-800-822-0504 (continental U.S.) only or 410-516-6963.

_____ Please check here if you would like to receive a complete catalog of WRI publications.

Return this form with payment to: WRI Publications; P.O. Box 4852; Hampden Station; Baltimore, MD 21211. All orders must be prepaid. Prices subject to change without notice.